Allan Fels

A Portrait
of Power

Allan Fels

A Portrait of Power

FRED BRENCHLEY

WILEY
John Wiley & Sons Australia, Ltd

First published 2003 by
John Wiley & Sons Australia, Ltd
33 Park Road, Milton, Qld 4064

Offices also in Sydney and Melbourne
Typeset in 11.5/15 pt Berkeley LT

National Library of Australia
Cataloguing-in-Publication data:

Allan Fels: A portrait of power.

Includes index.
ISBN 1 74031 070 5.

1. Fels, Allan, 1942– . 2. Consumer affairs directors — Australia —
Biography. 3. Consumer protection — Australia.

381.34092

Cover photo © Moshe Dinor
Author photo (back cover) © Lorrie Graham
Cartoons © Ron Tandberg

The publisher wishes to thank the Fels family for allowing us to include
photographs from their private collection.

Printed in Australia by McPherson's Printing Group

10 9 8 7 6 5 4 3 2 1

CONTENTS

What do people say about Fels?

'I think he's mischievous and dangerous. I think he's done irreparable harm to the Australian economy.'
—Gerry Harvey, retailer

'Overall he's done a very good job. It's just in the later part of his 13-year [career], the balance got out of kilter.'
—Dick Warburton, Caltex chairman

'He's done an extraordinary job in promoting the interests of consumers, in making consumers and business aware of their rights and responsibilities under the Act, and in vigorously enforcing the Act against all those in business who don't believe in the fundamental principle of vigorous, lawful competition. I'll be doing exactly the same. Hopefully I can do a job at least as good as Allan Fels.'
—Graeme Samuel

'the Evil Genius of competition policy … you'd have to say that, after Paul Keating, Fels is the most influential and effective economic rationalist of our times.'
—Ross Gittins, economics editor of *The Sydney Morning Herald*

For Elizabeth

PREFACE

Leaving Parliament House one afternoon in late 1999 I was hailed down from behind by a striding Allan Fels. 'Can you give me a lift back to my office?' he asked. There were some mumbled words about a 'lost car' which I never quite picked up on.

Chatting on the drive to his office Fels asked if I would be interested in writing a history of the Australian Competition and Consumer Commission. 'Find a tame academic', was my immediate response. Nevertheless, we agreed to talk about it over dinner one night.

I had known Allan since a stint on the National Consumer Affairs Advisory Council in the early 1990s, and enjoyed his enthusiasm. We had also met up in Europe a few times, when Allan had attended meetings of the OECD in Paris which I had covered as European correspondent for *The Australian Financial Review*.

A check of libraries revealed several university texts on competition policy and theory, but no history of the ACCC. Later, I booked a dinner appointment in the full expectation of enjoying a meal with Allan but also of turning down his idea that I should write a history. As we entered the restaurant the head waiter took my name and began glancing down his booking list. His eyes shot over my shoulder to my guest.

'Ah, Professor Fels, your table is this way', he said, sweeping us down the restaurant to 'Allan's' table — booked in my name. 'You must eat here often', I remarked to Allan as we sat down. 'Never been here before', he replied.

Having spent the mid-1990s working in Europe, I had missed Allan's transformation to media star. The book started to form in my mind. Not a history and not a biography, but a story of how competition policy was changing Australia with the aid of a previously obscure, slightly eccentric academic who, in the process, had achieved head waiter recognition status.

If this book can explain that head waiter's reaction, it will have achieved its aim.

Many people helped in this project. Some of them would best appreciate thanks by not being named. 'Thank you' also to Helen Ritson, Anne Wykes, Kay O'Leary, Alexis Yeadon, Elizabeth O'Callaghan, Lee Ridley, Max Suich, the late John Iremonger, Russell Miller, Ron Bannerman, Bob Baxt, David Cousins, Ross Jones, Alan Ducret, Sitesh Bhojani, Rod Shogren, Hank Spier, Brian Cassidy, Lin Enright, Tom Connors, David Smith, Geoff Eva, Allan Asher, Maurice Haddad, Brian Johns, David Lieberman, Gary Banks, Stephen King, Geoff Allen, Mitch Hooke, Mike Potter, Michael Delaney, David Chalke, David Hawker, Robert Bain, Maureen Brunt, Peter Crowley, Peter Costello, Daryl Williams, Joe Hockey, George Brandis, Robert Maidment, John Martin, Bob McMullan, Michael Duffy, Dudley Jackson, John Schubert, Dick Warburton, Graeme Samuel, Louise Sylvan, Barney Cooney and John Edwards.

Also thanks to Nan Lundy for those many cups of tea.

Allan Fels, his wife Isabel and daughters Isabella and Teresa were very tolerant of my journalistic intrusions.

Fred Brenchley
June 2003

CHAPTER 1

SOCIETY'S A-LIST

In June 2002 *The Sydney Morning Herald* published a guide to the selection of Sydney's society A-list. The old society establishment of the Packers, Fairfaxes, MacArthur-Onslows and the like had been swept aside by the brash and beautiful A-list of invitees, an American idea. So who were the new crowd?

'The way it works is simple', reported the *Herald*'s Daphne Guinness. 'If the Australian Competition and Consumer Commission Chairman, Professor Allan Fels, is not already on the list, he is now. "He'd like to attend the Archibalds? Fabulous. We'd love to have him, what's his address?" says the Art Gallery of New South Wales' PR, Jan Batten. He gets his pix in the social pages. He is noticed by A-list compilers. The rest follows. Easy as that.'

Two remarkable points emerge here. First, the head of a Canberra regulatory agency was being promoted in the Sydney social pages. Second, he lived in Melbourne.

More was to follow. Four months later *The Australian Financial Review* surveyed Australia's power elite, and they concluded that Allan Fels was the third most powerful person in the nation, behind Prime Minister John Howard and Treasurer Peter Costello. Fels had risen from fifth to third spot in a year, and was seen as more powerful than the Opposition Leader Simon Crean, Reserve Bank Governor Ian MacFarlane or media magnates Kerry Packer and Rupert Murdoch.

How had this happened? The head of a federal competition agency would normally be rightfully seen behind his Canberra desk wearing a cardigan. Yet here he was on the society A-list and being judged the third most powerful person in the country — a media star who had outshone his political masters.

Something very odd had taken place in Australia's society. Among tabloid columnists 'the Felsta's' views were sought on everything from cricket to food. The public recognition factor was extraordinarily high. 'Watch those petrol prices, Felsy', people would call in the street. Fels had become a phenomenon. One federal minister even likened Fels to Robin Hood for his consumer advocacy.

At the same time, sections of business openly reviled him. One leading businessman whose company was under investigation by the Australian Competition and Consumer Commission — the 'A Triple C' as it is commonly known — likened him to a member of Nazi Germany.

Media coverage reflected these widely varying opinions of Fels. A Murdoch newspaper business columnist called him a 'fraud'. But Ross Gittins, *The Sydney Morning Herald*'s economics writer, sees Fels as the most influential person in Australia's recent economic history, whose only crime was to 'bite the big boys'.

Like him or loathe him, there is no doubt that Allan Fels became an emblem of contemporary Australia: a powerful regulator whose skills with the media in exposing business rorts and sticking up for consumers filled a definite void. He is also a man whose integrity has never been in question. Indeed, during a long battle with one industry over deregulating prices, a private detective hired to dig up dirt on Fels came back empty-handed. Apparently it was a fruitless task.

By 2002 Fels had achieved unique status for an academic-turned-regulator — he had become a brand name. 'Fels' represented no-holds-barred enforcement of competition: a regulator with real bite.

Whatever the brickbats of business and vested interests, there was no wilting. Not that there wasn't a touch of overzealousness on occasions, even mistakes. Despite that, the 'punters' still gave him credit: at least he was 'having a go'. His regulatory brand had found a niche in the contemporary Australian psyche.

In days gone by some of the 'old school' of mandarins had become widely known. Chifley's 'seven dwarfs', men such as John Crawford, Henry Bland, Richard Randall, HC 'Nugget' Coombs and Roland Wilson — small in stature perhaps but powerful intellects — were postwar identities. 'Nugget' Coombs was named Australian of the Century in the Bicentennial year. Then in the '60s and '70s came secretaries of departments Arthur Tange, Fred Wheeler, Alan Westerman and John Bunting, who dominated their political era. These days no secretary of a government department is known outside Canberra, with the recent exception of Max 'The Axe' Moore-Wilton.

Still, no regulator or public servant in Australia's history has done a 'Fels' — aggressively enforcing the laws on business behaviour and becoming in the process one of the most powerful figures in the nation, with an entrée to the society set.

Fels achieved this using something mandarins normally eschew — the media. His media passion became almost as legendary as Fels himself. Prime Minister Keating called him a 'media nymphomaniac'. His successor, John Howard, said more diplomatically that 'Fels has a view on everything'. He is possibly the only public servant in Australia's history to have kept the Prime Minister waiting in the Cabinet room while he gave a press conference outside.

Fels' media profile became a source of much envy and humour around Parliament House, and politicians were painfully aware that it gave him more power than them. 'He had a media reputation which a politician would kill for', joked Peter Costello at one of Fels' farewell functions. 'In fact it was always said that if you ever appeared at a function with Allan Fels, get ready to come off second-best.' Calling off the consumer watchdog was politically impossible.

Business was completely outfoxed as well. Fels used what he came to call the 'full five channel blast' of media exposure to highlight issues. Business leaders had no answer to this open style of relations, other than the traditional backdoor lobbying of Canberra to fix Fels.

Part of the secret of his success was that Fels did not use the media for self-promotion — which is all too often the rationale for politicians. Media was simply a tool in the competition regulator's armoury. Fels harnessed the media to his cause. His idea was to couple the strong enforcement powers of the ACCC with media exposure to make the regulator a force to be reckoned with. Media became a weapon in the war for a new culture of competition, in a society where decades of protectionism and insulation had bred laziness and monopoly among business, unions and the professions.

Media coverage gave Fels' ACCC the image of being a powerful player in the market. The competition regulator had long held many of the enforcement powers, but had been seen as a marginalised player. In a blaze of publicity Fels took on cartels, winning landmark cases. Publicity also became a means of shaming. He took on the politicians, forcing the arrogant New South Wales Olympics minister Michael Knight to fix the Olympics ticketing fiasco. He took on big business, variously skewering the oil companies, the banks and Telstra. Even the hallowed royal colleges of medicine were not exempt from his competitive blowtorch. The unions did not escape either, as the Maritime Union of Australia found in the 1998 waterfront dispute.

In all of this, Fels had a subtext — competition works. The drip, drip effect of that constant message was something his opponents never quite understood. Fels was actually conducting his media campaign on two fronts — enforcing the ACCC's competition powers, but also simultaneously selling the benefits of competition. Opponents were just unable to match this combination of enforcement and evangelism.

Fels broke the mould of quiet, ineffectual regulators, the ones who had worked harmlessly behind their desks for decades. A 1986 book by two academics, Peter Grabosky and John Braithwaite, shows the extent of this break. *Of Manners Gentle* was their summary of a survey of the enforcement strategies of 111 federal and state agencies. In their introduction, the two academics said:

> Not only is this [gentle manner] reflected in the attitudes of the regulators, it also characterizes their policies and regulatory outcomes such as prosecutions, licence suspensions, plant shutdowns, injunctions, or the informal use of adverse publicity. Litigation or any kind of adversarial encounter with industry is commonly undertaken only as a last resort.

In 1985, under new chairman Bob McComas the Trade Practices Commission (TPC) had even publicly adopted a 'soft approach' to enforcement. The Commission had just lost two major cases against freight express and concrete firms. 'Consultation rather than going to court is a new role which is looking forward, not backwards', a TPC spokesman was quoted in *The Australian Financial Review*.

It is not as if Australian regulatory agencies lack powers, then or now. Many are vested with statutory powers of entry, search, seizure and investigation, such as the ACCC and its predecessor, the Trade Practices Commission. But before Fels such powers were rarely used. 'When it comes to big business that is being regulated, the propensity to non-adversarial regulation is especially pronounced', Grabosky and Braithwaite reported.

Such timidity opens regulatory agencies to 'capture' by the very industries they are supposed to regulate. The ACCC later came across a classic example of regulatory capture in its review of the anti-competitive practices of the royal medical colleges. The West Australian Government overrode its own Health Department to urge reforms of the royal college system.

For Grabosky and Braithwaite, the conduct of Australian regulatory agencies was marked by platitudinous appeals to industry to act responsibly, token enforcement, keeping the lid on problems which could blow up into scandals, and passing the buck to other agencies in the labyrinth of Australian federalism.

This is an eerily prescient description of the HIH case, Australia's biggest corporate collapse, almost 20 years later. The Australian Prudential Regulatory Agency (APRA), whose job it was to regulate the big insurer before its $5.3 billion collapse, allowed the company to continue despite its near-terminal state and repeated warnings from whistleblowers. 'For all the influence and impact which APRA had on the operations or activities of HIH, or the ultimate outcome of those activities, APRA may as well not have been there', concluded Wayne Martin QC, counsel assisting the HIH Royal Commission.

APRA's sister regulator, the Australian Securities and Investments Commission (ASIC), escaped with a mild slap on the wrist and promptly passed the buck. ASIC rejected suggestions it should have acted earlier in the HIH case, saying this was the job of APRA.

Ironically, both agencies had been created in 1997 in response to the Wallis inquiry into Australia's financial system, which recommended transferring consumer regulation of financial services from Fels' ACCC to the new ASIC.

Falling asleep at the wheel was never a charge laid at Fels' door during his 12-year term in office. Quite the reverse. The main business accusation against him was overenthusiasm both in pursuing cases and in using the media.

Between 1991 and late 2002 the Commission instituted proceedings in 271 cases. Of these, 170 were decided by a court while 101 were settled between the parties. (The Commission won 94 per cent of the court cases. Most actions were for breaches of the main anti-competitive sections of the *Trade Practices Act*, or consumer protection. Fels pumped out media releases on all his big court wins. The vetting of mergers, or setting conditions on them, the ACCC's other major work area, is not included in these figures.)

The sheer volume of prosecutions muscled the ACCC into business consciousness. If you peruse the 271 cases, almost every industry sector is represented: the banks, insurance companies, transport, petrol, the media and the professions.

The firms involved are the blue-ribbon companies of Australian business, too, including Colonial Mutual, Telstra, Master Builders Association, TNT, NRMA, Ampol, Woolworths, Chubb Security, Channel 10, Unilever, Kmart, Sony Music and NAB.

Fels' view was always that if Parliament had passed the *Trade Practices Act* it should be enforced 'without fear or favour'. In that view he found an unusual ally when he was appointed chairman in 1991. Allan Asher, who was to become the deputy chairman under Fels, reworked the Commission's entire enforcement strategy to give it a harder edge. The two formed a working double act — Asher as Mr Inside, riding shotgun on the Commission's enforcement committee, Fels as Mr Outside, pushing the publicity.

In the end, however, his media profile, the very thing which made him so powerful, led to his departure from the ACCC becoming something of a personal disappointment. On his reappointment in 2000, the Howard Government quietly cut the usual five-year term to three years eight months, with the implication that his time would be up then. Cabinet's fear was that Fels was becoming too powerful.

Business opponents have rejoiced in the end of the Fels era. But Fels may have the last laugh. In the lead-up to the Dawson inquiry into the *Trade Practices Act* (called by the government at the behest of business opponents) and throughout the inquiry, he pushed hard for a series of new powers for the ACCC, using his well-honed media skills. Though he was unsuccessful with some, Dawson did recommend a Fels idea that business executives should face jail terms for serious or hard-core cartel behaviour. Only fines apply at present. Fines, of course, hurt, but the prospect of a jail term really concentrates the mind! Every executive facing this in the future will remember — and likely curse — Allan Fels.

⁀

In society terms, Fels does not present as a typical member of the A-set. Expensive clothes are not part of his make-up. Indeed, Fels is one of life's messers — his suit often appears rumpled. (The suit might look even worse if he selected it himself. Fortunately his wife, Isabel, does that for him.)

There are two Allan Felses, the formal competition regulator that the world sees, and the informal person that the public caught glimpses of only towards the end of his era, as he loosened up somewhat with homely appearances on the ABC's *Australian Story* and the Nine Network's *Burke's Backyard*.

In his ACCC chairman role, Fels' public image has been a combination of the stern protector of consumer interests and the slightly eccentric professor. Both are accurate.

Fels has an unmistakable aura of power. It seems completely unaffected, stemming from the quiet confidence of his operation of the ACCC. He is also blessed with both optimism and a calm temperament. Isabel marvels at his style of dealing with life's problems. 'In 33 years of marriage I have never seen Allan in a tantrum, never', she says. 'It is an amazing thing.'

Isabel is not the only one who ponders over Fels' remarkably even temperament. It has also fascinated work colleagues. Anger, shouting or bad language are just not part of his make-up. Colleagues who have differences with him report that exchanges will be direct, and that he never bears a grudge.

To opponents, however, he can appear formidable. The bushy eyebrows can furrow into veritable verandahs and the hooded hazel eyes can appear menacing. Fels' voice, too, is raspy and authoritative in personal conversations. Surprisingly though, it assumes a reedy, almost singsong character in public speaking, perhaps displaying an internal nervousness despite the outward self-confidence. Fels also has a habit of shuffling his feet in a dance-like way when, in professorial fashion, he launches into a lecture on the finer points of competition policy.

He is a 'big picture' person, leaving a trail of paperwork in his wake from home to office, much to the despair of Isabel and ACCC assistants. The paperwork is littered with his indecipherable scrawl.

ACCC staff often huddle with each other trying to work it out. 'I don't know what goes on in his mind', Isabel says as she fusses over him.

Then there are his occasional eccentricities. Fels has 'lost' a car. He once turned up for a portrait sitting wearing three ties. Academic friends recall him wearing an overcoat on a boiling day in Melbourne; he had dressed in the dark not wanting to wake his wife Isabel and had put on different suit trousers and jacket. Rather than doffing his jacket on a hot day, Fels had put on a topcoat so that he would not look conspicuous in the clashing trousers and jacket.

Money appears to hold little interest for him. Although the Felses live in a trendy, architect-designed home in Prahran, an inner-Melbourne suburb, Isabel's mother had helped them financially to buy the old house before demolishing to build their ideal residence.

Fels may be a publicity hound, and he does have an ego. But it is an ego that is kept well in check by a wry sense of humour and personal modesty. In public, Fels' sense of humour is not always evident. Yet he likes to swap email jokes with his younger daughter, Teresa, and loves collecting puns. Fels would scribble a joke on a piece of paper and pass it around a meeting of ACCC commissioners, much to the consternation of staff, who could not see what the commissioners were laughing about.

Fels' energetic leadership generated an amazing esprit de corps at the ACCC. The high-profile cartel busters basked in media comparisons to Elliot Ness and the Untouchables, even posing for photographs in gangbuster style. 'He gave staff a sense of mission, and you knew that Canberra was backing you to the hilt' says one former ACCC investigator. 'He insisted investigators responsible for cases be in settlement meetings, and he backed your judgement against the high-powered corporate lawyers sitting across the table. He was there with you. It was an extraordinary feeling.'

Fels may have won genuine loyalty from staff, but he had no close friends at the ACCC. 'Nobody gets close to Allan', says one of Australia's senior trade practice lawyers. A small business lobbyist also says there are never any special favours in dealings with Fels.

'What you get is fully paid up membership of a debate on what needs to be done.' For Fels, the bitter ending of his soulmate relationship with union leader Bill Kelty was a painful lesson about mixing friendship and competition regulation. Kelty and the union movement gave Fels a leg up into regulatory life, offering him a career path at a point when his academic career appeared to have stalled. However, Fels nurtures a few very close friends outside the ACCC.

Allan and Isabel ran very independent lives during Fels' years at the ACCC. His weekly absences in Canberra and interstate, not to mention overseas, conferences, left Isabel to look after the home and family finances, and bear more of the responsibility for their elder daughter Isabella, who suffers from schizophrenia. Still, he is an attentive husband and father, ringing daily, and sometimes pulling himself from meetings to help Isabella.

Isabel has long come to terms with Allan's work, even his carrying a pager while walking along the beach on their holidays. 'You know, you can never relax because there's always something, a delivery of office papers, newspapers everywhere, four or five briefcases with different documents all over the place upstairs', she says with a sigh. 'Everything's upside down because he has too many things to do.'

Despite Allan's work schedule, the Felses tried to keep weekends separate for walks, books, the cinema and church. Fels' idea of a top weekend would also include watching Carlton win and getting his airmail copy of *The Economist* from the local newsagent on Saturday. They have an active social life, too. Isabel runs an open house for Allan's work colleagues and a parade of visiting international competition regulators.

Religion is another of the unseen sides to Fels. He was raised in a strongly Catholic home and educated by Jesuits, with their emphasis on discipline, social justice and missionary work. 'He is unquestionably, a genuine Jesuit intellectual', wrote John Little after an interview with Fels for *Together* magazine. 'The most trivial subject is afforded reasoned analysis, even something as nebulous as good fortune.' Fels says that though he was inspired as a youngster by the story of Christ, the spiritual side of Christianity never moved him quite so much as the practical. He does go to church regularly with Isabel, who is a more conscientious Catholic. But when Isabel is away visiting her family in Spain he will more than likely stay at home of a Sunday.

His Catholic upbringing, however, has left Fels with a strong appreciation of the ethical, social justice side of Christianity. Fels sets quite a store on the examples set by the life of Christ. When a local corner shopkeeper was threatened by the opening of a large supermarket, the ACCC chairman offered him advice, unfortunately unsuccessful. At church functions, Fels has been seen giving advice to elderly people in dealing with worrying paperwork. 'He hates the idea of there being special interests who gain at the cost of the community', Professor Owen Hughes, who worked with Fels at the Department of Management at Monash, told *Together*.

While religion is important in Fels' life, he is careful about its relevance to the ACCC. 'There are not many specific messages in the Bible about opposing mergers or issuing press releases', he says. Reading a biography on John D Rockefeller, whose incredible oil empire building was the impetus for US antitrust laws, taught Fels a lesson in the mid-1990s. Rockefeller was deeply religious, believing he was on a mission from God to make money. 'This gave me a strong warning that you should be careful about invoking religious beliefs as justification for public actions', says Fels. Impishly, though, in an interview for the *Catholic Weekly* he talked of the implications of his religious side by citing the example of Jesus throwing the money-changers out of the temple. This must have caused nightmares around the banks.

A personal motivation for Fels is his firm belief in the *Trade Practices Act* and that competition is a public good, something worth fighting for. Advising the corner storekeeper is good as far as it goes, but the chairmanship of the ACCC enabled him to address consumer welfare and monopoly behaviour on a broad scale. He loved the job and his evangelist role.

Fels does not get hung up about the stings of critics, preferring to shrug his shoulders and move on. One of Fels' unusual characteristics is his ability for blunt self-analysis. If this makes him appear somewhat passionless, it also renders him less vulnerable to critics, who are often infuriated that he doesn't seem to get upset by their remarks.

Everyone needs a crutch in life, however, and for Fels it is an almost boyish delight in the accolades of others. Fellow commissioners relate how Fels would report back on every snippet of praise for the ACCC's work from its political masters. That trait may also help explain the media 'affair'.

His ease with the media puzzles even Fels, who sees it as one of the complications of his otherwise quiet personality. There is nothing in Fels' family background to explain it, and he showed no acting flair in school. Cast as a guard in a university Shakespearean play he spent the entire time worrying that his stockings would fall down.

In his initial regulatory career in Victoria his role was to make the minister look good. That changed at the Prices Surveillance Authority in 1989, when the Hawke Government specifically requested him to lift the profile of the prices watchdog. 'I went for it, and gradually got used to it', he says. So how does he explain the streak of showmanship in his personality? 'I think I like attention.'

~

The mistake of so many of Fels' critics has been to underestimate him and also the forces that swept him to the position of third most powerful person in Australia.

In Fels' early years in the job this may have been understandable. Fels hailed from academia via the Prices Surveillance Authority, derided by most as just a sop to the unions to keep them on side for the Hawke Government's accord. And Fels' somewhat crumpled, craggy appearance, matched by a slightly defensive public image, did not immediately mark him out as a mover and shaker in the Canberra power pen.

Although Fels had been a devotee of prices regulation to combat inflation he grew to realise — along with many others — that competition can be more effective for market discipline. He didn't just jump ship; he became an ardent salesman of the consumer benefits of competition.

Fels' competition and consumer proselytising through the 1990s coincided with a period of profound change in Australia's economy and society. The wave of economic reforms of the Hawke, Keating and Howard governments may have shifted the Australian economy up a gear but it also unsettled people.

Within a few years, many formerly government-run agencies and utility service providers were converted to private enterprises or scaled back. The rollback of tariff protection, floating of the dollar and deregulation of industrial relations exposed Australia to the full force of global markets for the first time.

The reforms set off tremors in many different directions. Anxious Australians looked back on what they saw as a more secure past. Australia witnessed the rise of right wing forces in the form of Pauline Hanson's One Nation Party, which made stunning wins in a Queensland state election in a backlash against change and Asian migrants. The 'bush' became prime territory for One Nation as banks and other services disappeared. Unions shed members at an alarming rate, and John Howard's coalition of Liberals and Nationals promptly tacked to the right.

Amidst all this change Fels was one of the few constants, sticking up for consumers and taking on big business. No other government regulator took up such a position on the 'front line'. Nor did many politicians.

The increasing corporate greed and ineptitude apparent from the mid-1990s created a longing for greater government regulation. The stream of executives walking away from companies with multi-million-dollar payouts after short stints became obscene. The collapse of HIH, One.Tel and Ansett in Australia, and WorldCom and Enron in the US, fuelled widespread public cynicism that corporate leaders had their snouts in the trough, and nobody appeared willing to take responsibility or exercise some discipline.

'Trust', or lack of it, became an issue that hung in the air. And not just in Australia. World Economic Forum surveys showed an alarming drop in public trust of governments and business in 47 other countries. National armed forces, particularly in their anti-terrorist roles, were the most trusted, followed by non-governmental environmental and social advocacy groups, the UN and churches.

In this vacuum, the professorial Allan Fels assumed a significance beyond that of a mere competition regulator. He stood up to politicians like New South Wales Minister Michael Knight over Olympic ticketing and raided petrol companies over alleged price fixing, and people cheered. His stature among the public rose the more business attacked him. Somebody was 'having a go'. Fels may have seen himself as just a competition regulator enforcing the *Trade Practices Act*. But he was also fulfilling the desire of Australians to be able to place more confidence and trust in their civil society.

When Fels proposed jail terms for business executives found guilty of hard-core collusion, in 2002, a staggering 87 per cent of people surveyed by Roy Morgan Research agreed with him. Only 6 per cent disagreed, with the remaining 7 per cent having no opinion on the issue.

Australia Scan, which monitors cultural change by annual audits of 2000 adult Australians, offers a unique insight into the Australian mind after an era of rapid economic reform. Australians now want more regulation as well as better policing of business.

This was a huge shift in public opinion in less than a decade. In 1996, for instance, only 11 per cent of Australians thought more regulation of business was necessary. Some 28 per cent felt there should be no change, or even less regulation, and the remaining 63 per cent thought the answer was better policing of business activity. By 2003 the bulk of people, 62 per cent, still felt the answer was better policing. But the balance between those who wanted more regulation and less regulation has reversed. Now 20 per cent want more regulation, and only 6 per cent less or no change.

David Chalke of Quantum Market Research, which runs Australia Scan, says these figures reflect the love of Australians for big government. Quantum operates these scans in North America and China. 'The belief in big government in Australia is way ahead of that in America and as strong as in China', he says.

Australia Scan reveals another factor contributing to the public support behind Fels' consumer activism. The ideological period of the Keating era in the early 1990s, when Australia embraced 'visionary' economic reforms, has been followed by a backlash. The emphasis now is not on 'vision' but 'finding solutions and getting results'. 'Everytime [Fels] connects with a target, say on misleading advertising, the public applaud and he is a winner', says Chalke. 'This is the age of results.'

Fels' consistency through a long period of change and his status as a professional regulator — one of a dying breed — gave him an appeal beyond that of a mere Canberra public servant. Even by 1995, four years into his competition supremo role, commentator VJ Carroll noted that Fels was an exception in that he refused to be a captive of the industries he was supposed to watch. Unlike many contemporary public servants who see the public service as a stepping stone to other careers, Carroll saw Fels as the direct successor to those notable early postwar mandarins. 'Fels is committed to making competition and deregulation work just as the earlier generation of public servants were committed to making a managed, fully-employed economy work', he said. 'The common factor is public service as a vocation.'

It was this kind of integrity that struck a chord with a public anxious for reassurance in the age of economic rationalism. When the Howard Government was faced with 'selling' its GST, Howard and Costello took a back seat as the image-makers 'borrowed' Allan Fels and his obvious credibility with the public.

⌐

Has Allan Fels' ACCC helped lift Australia's economic performance? That, after all, is the idea. The specific aim of the *Trade Practices*

Act is to 'enhance the welfare of Australians through the promotion of competition and fair trading and provision for consumer protection'. And economic growth is the single biggest contributor to enhanced welfare.

It is a difficult question to answer, not least because the concepts of 'competition' and 'competition policy' are hard to pin down. Economists and courts have many different readings on the meaning of 'competition'. Is competition just an economic concept, or does it also have a social policy dimension, such as provision of services in country areas?

As SG Corones points out in his book *Competition Law in Australia*, economists use the word 'competition' in two different senses. One is to refer to the market structure of a perfect competition model, where there are many sellers. The other is to refer to the rivalry in a market where firms strive against each other. Competition in this second sense is a process, rather than a situation, as the Trade Practices Tribunal has noted.

That process can be tough. 'Competition, by its very nature, is deliberate and ruthless', Justices Mason and Wilson noted in the landmark 1989 Queensland Wire Industries case. 'Competitors jockey for sales, the more effective competitors injuring the less effective by taking sales away. Competitors almost always try to "injure" each other in this way … These injuries are the inevitable consequence of the competition Section 46 is designed to foster.'

Section 46 is crucial; it controls abuses of market power which eliminate or damage competitors. The judges had put their finger on an issue that would plague trade practice for decades, and become a major political issue in the wake of the High Court's decision on the Boral case in early 2003. After the court ruled that aggressive pricing was not in itself illegitimate, and that deep pockets did not necessarily constitute market power, Fels' ACCC worried that it no longer had the power to protect viable small businesses. The issue raised the question of what Section 46 should be about — protecting competition but not individual competitors, or protecting small business against big business.

'Competition policy' is equally difficult. For many years it was mainly just the former Trade Practices Commission vetting mergers and ensuring as fair a market as possible. Then, in the mid-1990s after the Hilmer report, new strands were added. The National Competition Council was created and given the task of overseeing payments to the states to remove anti-competitive barriers in their laws. The idea was to achieve an open domestic market for goods and services.

In the Hilmer shake-up the Trade Practices Commission was renamed the Australian Competition and Consumer Commission and also given the task of looking at the competitiveness of government business enterprises and the professions, while ensuring access for competitors to major bottleneck facilities such as gas pipelines, rail tracks and electricity grids.

Competition policy is also the broad term often used to describe the micro-reforms of the 1980s and 1990s, when Australia cut tariffs, deregulated its labour and financial markets, and floated the dollar. Australia's recent solid growth and higher than usual productivity is widely attributed to this process, along with the nation's rapid take-up of information technology.

Unfortunately, the narrow definition of competition policy — the actions of the ACCC — is not directly measurable in terms of economic growth. But the broader context shows that Australia has been a real winner from competition policy and micro-reforms. Gary Banks, chairman of the Productivity Commission, says Australia's multifactor productivity in the market sector — which measures the contribution of labour, buildings and machinery to national output — increased by 1.5 per cent a year in the 1990s. This was double the growth of the previous 15 years. Put another way, as Banks said, the growth that would have taken 13 years had been achieved in just six.

Australians benefited from this golden age of growth. Gross domestic product per person grew by 2.5 per cent a year, compared to

1.5 per cent through the previous two decades. Income per household rose some $7000, says Banks. The price of telecommunications, electricity, rail freight and port charges all fell.

Competition policy reached right into the bowels of the Australian economy. The so-called non-traded goods sectors such as the professions, services and government agencies, which had been largely immune from competition, suddenly found they were in a new world.

Fels and the ACCC also contributed to the cultural change in Australian business that accompanied the economic micro-reforms. The 'old' economy was shackled by tariffs and marked by protected domestic monopolies, some even sanctioned by government. New business investment and innovation, two of the drivers of growth, were discouraged in this climate. The micro-reform process changed this. Australian companies began to realise that if they didn't lift their game, imports could kill them. And if they tried to counter using restrictive deals with competitors, then Allan Fels and the ACCC would come down on them. This two-way squeeze driving greater efficiency helped the attitudinal change towards a new competitive culture. Allan Fels' high profile left no doubt that the ACCC 'untouchables', as they were nicknamed, were on the beat.

Dick Warburton, then chairman of David Jones and Caltex, and an outspoken critic of Fels, was one of the panellists in the survey by *The Australian Financial Review* that identified Fels as the third most powerful Australian. Warburton's view of Fels' influence, as outlined in the *AFR* survey, ran like this:

> He has built up enormous power over the last number of years in so many different fields. It is not just the media exposure; he gets himself involved in some way, somewhere, in some form, in every facet of business life. He is in the forefront of many of our minds when we make decisions as to what we do.

Whatever else might be said about Fels, he has clearly focused the collective mind of Australian business on competition policy. And the public mind as well. He has sunk so deeply into the Australian psyche that, for example, in early 2003, a Brisbane radio morning show was running a comedy spoof on *Star Wars* featuring a character called 'Lord Fels', the competition warrior who took an obscure nation and made it the envy of the solar system.

If changing a culture turns out to be his only achievement, it will be a significant one.

~

For aficionados of political theatre, 16 April 2003 was not to be missed. Treasurer Peter Costello called a news conference in the 'blue room' adjoining the Cabinet suite in Parliament House to release two big reports — the findings of the Royal Commission into the $5.3 billion HIH insurance collapse and of the Dawson inquiry into the future of the ACCC.

Preceding Costello, staffers carried in a table and set it out next to the lectern. Costello wanted to have a full set of the reports to refer to as he was quizzed by the media. This was not an occasion for mistakes.

It was a very delicate task. HIH's collapse had left thousands of policyholders stranded, and cost its shareholders millions. Hadn't Costello himself created the Australian Prudential Regulatory Authority, the watchdog that saw HIH disintegrate in front of it without raising any alarm? And Costello's other new corporate regulator, the Australian Securities and Investments Commission, had not covered itself in glory over HIH either. Newspapers on the very morning of Costello's media release had even suggested the Royal Commissioner had not been asked to look at the role of the government in the collapse. Political mines littered the HIH landscape.

Costello is a polished performer. His legal training and university-honed debating skills make him the most formidable minister in parliament. The 'blue room' show was up to par: he rattled off decisions to refer possible prosecution of the leading HIH players to relevant authorities; to consider using a special prosecutor; to sack the board of APRA while creating a new commission; and impressed on the media that the Royal Commission had indeed been asked to look at the role of government and had pointed to the activism of then minister Joe Hockey in raising HIH with APRA.

APRA's future received special attention. Agreeing with the Royal Commission, Costello wanted the prudential regulator to be more sceptical, questioning and aggressive in performance of its duties. APRA, as the Royal Commission found, had not itself caused the collapse of HIH, but it had failed to pick up on any of the many warning signals. Had it acted earlier the collapse would have come sooner, possibly saving many policy holders from financial hardship.

Sceptical, aggressive and tough — Costello's desired formula for APRA — sounds exactly like the upfront regulatory style of Fels and his ACCC. And indeed, the new APRA would get a style of leadership similar to the ACCC.

When Costello turned to the Dawson report on the future of the ACCC, it was a different story. The government had accepted the major findings — collective bargaining by small business, further investigation of jail sentences for hard-core cartel behaviour, and streamlining of the merger test to allow parties to go straight to the Trade Practices Tribunal.

It took a journalist to raise what Costello had not mentioned — the effective 'gag' on Fels proposed by Dawson in the form of a new media code of conduct for the ACCC. Costello, of course, did not use the word 'gag', but agreed that a media code of conduct was 'fair enough'. Enforcement, he said, was best taken in the courts, not the newspapers. Sometimes proceedings could be overstated. It was an obvious criticism of Fels' publicity style.

'I think it is always very important that regulators are careful with the evidence', Costello said in answer to the question of whether the proposed media code would end Fels' using public shaming against unscrupulous operators. 'At the end of the day shaming a company doesn't achieve a fine or a conviction. A fine or conviction under our law can only be done in a court.'

The contrast could hardly be more stark. The government wanted the failed regulator APRA to be more upfront and aggressive while the effective ACCC needed to be restrained.

Of course the two regulators have different beats. As a prudential regulator APRA has to be careful not to spook financial markets. The ACCC, however, deals with consumer interests and is required by its legislation to go public. The government's dilemma was exquisite: how to kick one watchdog that had failed to bark, while muzzling another that, in the eyes of some, barked too much. Moreover, it wanted to perform this contortion at a time when both it and many regulators believed Fels' barking-dog style was the vogue.

In the wake of the big corporate collapses, the Australian Securities and Investments Commission seemed to be taking a leaf out of Fels' regulatory manual with high-profile court convictions of businessman John Elliot for insolvent trading and society stockbroker Rene Rivkin for insider trading. The Therapeutic Goods Administration took a very hard line with Pan Pharmaceuticals, ordering the withdrawal of hundreds of products.

'Maybe some of the other regulators are learning that being aggressive is not as dangerous as you might think', says Fels. The most startling compliment to the Fels style, however, emerged from the Cole Royal Commission, which recommended an Australian Building and Construction Commission modelled on the ACCC to clean up the industry. 'The building industry would benefit from more ACCC type activity', noted Tony Abbott, the Employment and Workplace Relations Minister.

So, the irony of Costello's message was that the ACCC was being pulled back just as Fels' style was catching on among other regulators. While he was careful to praise Fels, Costello was signalling that the Fels era was over. Fels, he said, had come to embody competition laws in Australia, he had taken competition law to consumers and made it 'live'. Costello went on:

> But institutions move on and they evolve and we thought
> it was time to look at it and we have and, rather than

> being a young regulator, this is going to be a middle-aged
> regulator shortly. We have got to look at how it is going
> to, in its next phase, operate.

Fels had been too outspoken and had offended too many powerful
interests who had lobbied against him in Canberra's corridors of
power. His talent for publicity had gone against the grain of the
traditional secrecy about government affairs. Fels had bypassed
politicians to talk direct to the public, putting political noses out of
joint. Quite simply, Fels had become too powerful.

Costello was intimating that the ACCC after Allan Fels would be
a different animal. Australia might never again see his like.

CHAPTER 2

THE SLOW REVOLUTION

Australia came late — and with considerable reluctance — to competition, and certainly to Allan Fels' vigorous style of enforcing it. Although a competitive culture pervades the modern-day economy, forty years ago it was decidedly different. The postwar boom arose in a business structure dominated by monopolies in key areas and riddled with price fixing and other cosy anti-competitive agreements. Ron Bannerman, the initial Commissioner of Trade Practices and the first to fully document these restrictions, later described them as an 'astonishing web covering a very great deal of Australian industry'.

How different it might have been. In 1906, five years after Federation, the new Commonwealth Parliament passed the *Australian Industries Preservation Act*. Taking its cue from the US Sherman Act, introduced to curb the power of the railway trusts and the 'robber barons' who had scandalised America in the late 19th century, the Australian Act sought to prohibit attempts to monopolise trade between the states.

But this early bid to introduce a competitive culture failed. Its constitutional basis was called into doubt. As well, the High Court rejected a case brought against some collieries and shipping companies for price fixing. Prices had not been raised to an unreasonable level, declared the court, finding that coal producers were not 'trustees for consumers'.

Although amended several times, the *Australian Industries Preservation Act* withered on the statute books. Given the ethos of the early Federation period this is perhaps not surprising. Federation Australia had embraced state paternalism and so-called New Protection. Historian Manning Clark said the idea of New Protection was simple: manufacturers who paid their workers a 'fair and reasonable wage' would receive tariff protection against imports.

Protection coupled with an industrial arbitration system with its revolutionary minimum wage was the domestic bulwark of the Federation settlement, which also introduced the White Australia policy to quarantine against hordes of cheap Asian labour and the Empire policy to ward off any other sort of invasion. Obviously an Australian industry protected from foreign competition would not be burdened with domestic competition either: this was the emerging Australian 'club'. It was part of early Australia's search for security and the 'fair go', insulating the new nation from outside forces.

New Protection and state socialism may have seemed to offer a South Sea nirvana, but as the century progressed Australia slipped down the economic performance ladder. The resources boom had made Australia one of the wealthiest countries in the world at the turn of the century. But the combination of highly regulated product, capital and labour markets proved costly in terms of competitiveness. Australia lost traction. From a ranking of third in terms of per capita income at the end of World War II, Australia slipped to fifteenth by the late 1980s. Gradually, the cost of high tariff protection and restrictive trade practices became too obvious to be ignored. New companies that could not gain entry to the webs of trade associations that controlled prices and regulated industries began to complain. So did state governments angry with bid-rigging for tenders.

The anger might have gone nowhere. The lazy business culture with its high tariff walls still enjoyed bipartisan political support. A 1963 comment from the Chamber of Manufacturers of Australia reflected the prevailing climate: 'It is obvious and needs no apology', said the Chamber pompously, 'that the primary origin and object of [restrictive trade] agreements must be the benefit the industry expects thereby for itself. Benefits to others, however great, come second, although in the ultimate what benefits industry is an addition to the national interest'.

No Australian business lobby group would be caught dead urging such naked self-interest today. Indeed, the Australian Industry Group, as the Chamber of Manufacturers is now known, regards competition policy as 'an essential part of Australia's growth strategy', albeit a policy that must be enforced 'fairly and responsibly'.

Garfield Barwick, Liberal Attorney-General in Menzies' Cabinet in the early 1960s, set himself the task of injecting some freedom into the Australian market. Barwick was the child of a working-class and small business family. He had spent a good part of his brilliant career at the bar defending the big cartels and monopolies. But David Marr, Barwick's biographer, says Barwick's own ideas of a freer marketplace survived 30 years of service 'with some of the most ruthless exponents of market-rigging in the country'. Barwick, says Marr, believed free enterprise was at heart not just an economic arrangement but also a moral force. 'It was a Methodist vision of the little man testing himself and getting ahead', says Marr. 'Success was a mark of virtue but the test must be fair: the marketplace was the scene of the contest, and the marketplace must be free.'

Barwick certainly brought a vision of a different Australia. 'One of the most important effects of restrictive trade practices is that they tend to remove or suppress incentive — the incentive to be more efficient, to be more enterprising, to be more resourceful and to introduce innovations', he said. 'This is a socio-economic effect; it affects our whole outlook ... it does so in a manner that is most undesirable in a developing economy.' Barwick, of course, was writing at a time when cartels fixed the price of just about everything.

Evidence from a Tariff Board inquiry in 1963, later reported by Professor Maureen Brunt, glaringly illustrated the frustration of firms trying to compete against trade associations and the widespread acceptance of price fixing. A Mr Coke, the representative of a ball bearing distribution company trying to break into the market by lowering its prices, told the inquiry his accounts department received so many complaints that his list prices were changed to agree with competitors. 'We found that our invoices were being corrected by a number of companies, and we were actually being paid more than we had charged certain customers', he said. Customers were so used to the fixed price they were actually changing cheaper invoices!

By the mid-1960s two characteristics defined Australia's business structure — monopoly and trade associations. Professor Maureen Brunt and Peter Karmel in their 1962 book *The Structure of the Australian Economy* found that in manufacturing, mining, finance and retailing 'the great part of activity takes place in monopolistic or oligopolistic markets'. Australia stood out in terms of actual single-firm monopolies. Whereas these were virtually nonexistent in Britain and the US, according to Karmel and Brunt, Australia had no less than 14, including those in steel, refined sugar, glass, aluminium, copper, newsprint, heavy paper and paper board.

High concentration was also evident across the industries of chemicals and primary metals, motor vehicles, transportation equipment, rubber goods, fuels, lubricants, light and power. Across these stretched the web of price fixing agreements, retail price maintenance (where manufacturers insist their product be sold at a set price), distribution agreements that locked out competitors, and tender rigging. State governments puzzled when 'competing' tender bids came in identical, down to the pennies. Western Australia reported 46 identical tenders for goods as varied as cement, electrical cables, strings, tyres and toilet rolls.

This was the natural way of Australian business. The economy may have prospered in the early postwar years, but it remained hamstrung by thousands of trade associations that tightly controlled prices, supply and membership — many with penalties for members who did not toe the line. The associations, of course, strongly believed what they were doing was right and proper. Karmel and Brunt report the following exchange at a West Australian Royal Commission on restrictive trade practices:

> *Question:* Can you indicate why you are not in favour of government control and yet are in favour of private control in regard to price fixation?
>
> *Witness:* Yes, because firstly we stand primarily for free enterprise and the voluntary conducting of our affairs without being bound by a statute.

In 1961 Barwick persuaded Menzies, apparently without Cabinet approval, to include in the Governor-General's speech opening parliament the first indication of federal concern about competition since the ill-fated 1906 legislation. 'The development of tendencies to monopoly and restrictive practices in commerce and industry has engaged the attention of the government, which will give consideration to legislation to protect and strengthen free enterprise against such a development', said the Governor-General.

'Consideration' was certainly an apt description. It took five years for there to be any action. Barwick's only real constitutional base was the corporations power which enabled the Commonwealth to regulate trade between the states — the very power queried by the High Court when the 1906 legislation was tested. Cabinet and business were opposed to any new measures, while the Labor Opposition taunted the inaction.

Barwick went on the offensive. He gave speeches around the country, outlining his intention to create a register of anti-competitive practices, borrowed from a British idea. As evidence of the need for change, Barwick cited the example of a trade association which prohibited the entry of a migrant until he had been a naturalised citizen for 10 years. He also produced documentation of 32 cartels which had been revealed in court cases and royal commissions.

As well as the secret register, which would then permit the government to challenge the more egregious cartels, Barwick proposed an outright ban on collusive marketing and tendering, price-cutting to ruin competitors and misuse of market power. His reforms would also include the professions, thus sweeping doctors, lawyers and the trades into a new competitive world.

Opposition mounted. By mid-1965 a subcommittee of Cabinet was listening to the cries of business lobby groups. In September Menzies addressed the annual dinner of the Chamber of Manufacturers at Sydney's Australia Hotel. Cabinet, he said, had heard from industry the 'most balanced, sensible and impressive idea on this matter [restrictive trade practices legislation] that I have ever heard'. Menzies told the assembled businessmen that the advice 'had been so helpful, and that it may well determine the future course of action'.

Barwick had been dumped, said his biographer, David Marr. By this time, of course, Barwick had already moved on to a seat on the High Court. His successor, Billy Snedden, introduced the *Trade Practices Act 1965*, which Barwick contemptuously dismissed, according to Marr, as 'milk and water'. About the only item that remained from the original concept was the register. Business lobbyists had persuaded Cabinet — not that it needed much persuading — to drop the outright bans on anti-competitive conduct, except for collusive tendering and monopolisation. Even anti-competitive conduct was permissible if registered. Professions were to remain exempt. There was no mention of merger laws.

It would not be the last time that business and political interests combined to block free market reforms. Adam Smith's much-quoted dictum that 'people of the same trade seldom meet together even for merriement and diversion, but the conversation ends in a conspiracy against the public, or on some contrivance to raise prices' resonated deeply two centuries down the track in Australia.

Nevertheless, the Snedden Act was a start. Ron Bannerman, a bantam of a man but an intellectual force to be reckoned with, was plucked out of the Attorney-General's Department to be the first Commissioner of Trade Practices. Bannerman's job was to open the register, negotiate what changes he could in restrictive agreements, and refer the worst to the new Trade Practices Tribunal, run by a judge. The Commissioner could challenge agreements before the Tribunal, which would then decide if they were in the public interest.

Opening a small office in Canberra's City Mutual building, Bannerman was swamped. A staggering 10 841 agreements were registered in the first year. Bannerman reported they stretched across all known — and some unknown — variations, including price fixing, distribution clubs (usually linked to price fixing and used to impose trade boycotts), collusive tendering, collusive bidding, standardisation of production that possibly impeded innovation (supposedly to enhance efficiency), and production agreements.

Bannerman's initial reports to parliament revealed how the Australian economy was hobbled. There were 1307 national trade associations. Many trade association agreements, he reported, contained provisions for members' books to be inspected to ensure compliance with price lists. Distribution agreements typically included resale price maintenance, which initially was not unlawful. Distributors agreed not to stock or sell products competing with their suppliers. In turn, the suppliers agreed not to appoint another agent or distributor within defined areas. Wool was then a major Australian export, yet an informal agreement between wool buyers restricted bidding at auctions. It was a secure, clubby atmosphere. The only losers, of course, were consumers, who had no idea of these private deals.

Bannerman played his new role very cleverly. The idea of a secret register under the new Commissioner was something of a con to get the trade associations to at least 'fess up. They could then continue unless challenged. But Bannerman used his annual report to parliament to reveal a great amount of detail, and to highlight weaknesses in the new law. The media picked up on the issue. It was an early variation of the media card played so effectively by Fels. But Bannerman needed the cover of parliament to disclose anti-competitive agreements. Such were the times.

The climate in which Bannerman operated was hostile. Now living in retirement in Canberra, Bannerman describes it as one of 'fear and non-understanding, hostility and hurt'. Business, he says, felt virtuous about its trade practices.

But as the scope of restrictive practices revealed in Bannerman's annual reports sunk in, and the new Commissioner tackled specific cases involving frozen vegetables and books, the climate began to change. Competition — and particularly resale price maintenance — was starting to become a political issue.

One reason for this was the intrusion of the flamboyant Australian Council of Trade Unions (ACTU) leader Bob Hawke into the debate. The new-style ACTU had gone into partnership with Bourke's department store in Melbourne. The idea was that trade unionists would receive discounts at Bourke's. But discount shopping was anathema to the prevailing retail culture. Resale price maintenance was still lawful, enabling manufacturers to set minimum prices. Hawke launched a high-profile campaign, using Dunlop as an example. Dunlop, supplier of tennis shoes and balls as well as a range of rubber goods, felt the union heat, and rapidly caved in. Resale price maintenance was clearly indefensible, and big business was embarrassed at being caught out. Didn't they claim they believed in competition?

By the early 1970s the mood was even changing within the Coalition Government, now led by the hapless William McMahon. With the trade unions and the Labor Opposition under Gough Whitlam stealing a march on popular opposition to resale price maintenance, McMahon rushed through legislation in late 1971 banning it outright. This was aided by a High Court decision upholding the corporations powers as the basis for the 1965 Act. Somewhat inconveniently, however, the court decision forced the reconstitution of the *Trade Practices Act*.

Also foreshadowed by the McMahon legislation was a new Monopolies Commission, again along British lines. But the McMahon Government lost the 1972 election before the commission could be introduced, and the incoming Attorney-General, Lionel Murphy, had radical new ideas. Murphy, one of the nation's most activist AGs, entered office with sweeping plans for new economic law across monopolies, trade practices, companies and securities. He derided the Barwick competition law as 'one of the most ineffectual pieces of legislation ever passed by this Parliament'.

Not for him secret registers or a restrained British approach. Murphy lifted ideas straight out of the tougher US Sherman and Clayton antitrust laws. For the first time Australia would have fused competition and consumer protection laws, enforced by a strong commission backed by court processes and steep fines of up to $250 000. Contemporary commentators were in awe. 'In due course the *Trade Practices Act 1974* may come to be described as the most important piece of business legislation of this century, at least as far as its impact upon business decision-making is concerned', wrote Maureen Brunt and Professor Bob Baxt in *The Australian Economic Review*. Brunt was a pioneer of the study of trade practices in Australia, while Baxt went on to become the third chairman of the Trade Practices Commission.

If Barwick's legislation had been seen to leave Australia still somewhat lagging, Murphy's now put it well in front of comparable nations. Since 1974 governments on both sides have tinkered with it, particularly on merger law, but Australia's current competition law remains basically the Murphy model. The core of the Act is Parts IV and V. Part IV prohibits anti-competitive practices such as price fixing, primary boycotts, misuse of market power, exclusive dealing, third line forcing (where a supplier can force acceptance of the products of other suppliers), and resale price maintenance. Part V, which governs consumer protection, prohibits such things as misleading advertising, and also deals with defective goods and product safety.

Murphy may have borrowed from the US model, but he also introduced what Baxt and Brunt described as an 'Austerican' approach. Anti-competitive conduct is generally prohibited by the Act. The more blatant resale price maintenance, naked price fixing and monopolisation are banned outright. However, other market power activities, including anti-competitive pricing, exclusive dealing and mergers, are able to be authorised — provided the new Trade Practices Commission found the detriment was outweighed by public benefit.

The Trade Practices Tribunal was retained to allow Commission decisions to be appealed. This dualism of prohibition and authorisation subject to public benefit reflected the reality of Australia's small market. It created a balance between banned and permissible market power which distinguished the Australian legislation. Activities judged as causing 'substantial lessening of competition' are banned, but can be authorised if there is a countervailing public benefit.

Lionel Murphy was clearly delighted with his new baby. One of the first cases the new Commission began investigating concerned Sharp, which was advertising that its microwave ovens complied with certain Australian standards. The Commission believed they did not, and was about to launch proceedings. Murphy, wanting fast action, grabbed the case and used his Attorney-General's Department to prosecute. The first case of the new era thus became initially *Lionel Keith Murphy v. Sharp*. The electrical goods producer was eventually fined $100 000, a huge sum in those days.

Ron Bannerman now found himself the first chairman of the Trade Practices Commission (TPC), with formidable powers to prohibit anti-competitive behaviour. But his first action annoyed Murphy. Bannerman promised all businesses interim authorisation for their anti-competitive practices (provided they were not of the type banned outright in the new Act) if lodged by February 1975. The new TPC was suddenly hit with 29 000 anti-competitive business deals guaranteed blanket authorisation pending investigation.

'Murphy didn't like it', Bannerman now confides. 'He knew about it after it happened. I never made a practice of telling people what was going to happen.' Murphy may have regarded this as against the spirit of his tough new law, but in retrospect it turned out to be a smart move by Bannerman. Australian industry bared its soul. The TPC gained an invaluable document base. 'There we had laid out for us the whole basis for future investigation across Australia', says Bannerman.

The TPC had only just started work on the cases it regarded as the most important — the tied petrol and hotel systems, the Media Council's control of advertising and the building societies' practice of forcing borrowers to use particular insurers — when the Whitlam Government was trundled out of office.

The incoming Fraser Government put the TPC under the new portfolio of Business and Consumer Affairs, headed by ministerial neophyte John Howard, and also commissioned a new inquiry into the Murphy Act. Many feared it would not survive. But the inquiry, led by TB Swanson, deputy chairman of Imperial Chemical Industries of Australia and New Zealand, broadly endorsed it.

The question was, would the Fraser Government accept Swanson's report? There were still pressures from business for a return to the quiet life. Swanson, however, had recommended something that really appealed to a conservative government — extending the *Trade Practices Act* to cover unions. Businesses could not engage in collective boycotts under the TPA, why should unions be allowed to? Secondary boycotts had been one of the most powerful instruments in the unions' armoury. A business facing industrial action from its own union over, say, a pay rise, could then also find its mail cut off by postal workers. But how to stop them?

Before responding to Swanson, Howard chewed over ideas with Tony Hartnell, deputy secretary of his new department, and Paul McClintock, his senior private secretary. (Hartnell would later become chairman of the Australian Securities Commission, and McClintock, after a new career in private enterprise, would run the Cabinet Policy Unit during Howard's future prime ministership.) 'We decided on the amendments over a bottle of scotch one night in my office', Howard told his biographer David Barnett. A Cabinet battle ensued as Tony Street, the Industrial Relations Minister, opposed the idea. But Fraser backed Howard. Sections 45D and 45E, created over the bottle of scotch, were set to become a touchstone of Australian political support for competition policy.

Bannerman, however, was not keen about the new secondary boycott provisions, believing enforcement of them would take the new TPC into dangerous political territory. His solution was to take 45D action only when real competition issues arose, leaving companies to take private legal action using the *Trade Practices Act* if they were caught by secondary boycotts. Some did, but others steered clear of taking action, knowing it would bring down the wrath of the union movement. 'They were terrified', says Bannerman.

The secondary boycott provisions then became something of a litmus test for political interference in the TPC and later the Australian Competition and Consumer Commission (ACCC). Coalition governments would nudge the commissions to take action, while Labor governments played it down, with Keating in the early 1990s handing much of the responsibility for it back to softer industrial courts. The Fraser Government itself took on a couple of actions against unions when Bannerman refused. (Departmental staff crawling over sheep transport subject to union boycotts later discovered that some of the sheep in question were owned by Fraser and his fellow grazier Tony Street.)

The wash-up of the Swanson inquiry produced another time bomb for the TPC. At the last moment, and with no warning, Howard introduced amendments to water down the merger provision in the original Murphy Act. The Act had prohibited mergers that 'substantially lessened competition'. Swanson had urged retention of the substantial lessening test, but with a threshold that would limit it to big mergers. Howard at first seemed to favour no merger law at all, arguing that mergers promoted efficient companies. Then, at the last minute, he proposed a new test that would permit all mergers that did not result in 'dominance'. The Howard merger test would catch only proposed monopolies, or near-monopolies.

Where had the new weaker merger test come from? It seemed a compromise between having no test at all and appeasing business supporters facing hostile takeovers. South Australian and Western Australian brewers had reportedly lobbied Fraser for some merger test to prevent any takeover by Victoria's aggressive Carlton and United Breweries.

Howard was only a junior minister at this stage. 'I would suspect that this came to him as a direction from on high', says Bannerman.

Yet Malcolm Fraser said later, when complaining to a Commission staffer about the power of News Limited, that he was never fully aware of the potential effect of the change and had 'left it all to Howard'. Whatever its origin, the dominance test was pushed through by the Fraser Government.

The weaker merger test was to cut a swathe through Australian media and retailing in the late 1980s. Howard also removed the power of the government of the day to override the merger decisions of the TPC. The Whitlam Government had already used this power several times.

Bannerman now had the task of cutting the new agency's teeth. He was not helped by Fraser's razor gang. The cost cuts were deep. In one year the TPC's legal budget was slashed to just $43 000. Bannerman, however, was determined that the TPC would survive whatever the cost cuts. He transferred his personally modest style to the agency. Reportedly he volunteered for a pay cut — probably the first civil servant ever to do so. Hank Spier, who began his long career at the TPC under Bannerman and later rose to become the agency's chief executive officer, says many a TPC officer tells stories of sliding down in their Commonwealth white car while passing Bannerman walking to the airport bus.

Inside the new TPC, Bannerman struggled to control the new band of commissioners. One, VG Venturini, proved more than a handful, and the Fraser Government eventually had to reconstitute the TPC to get rid of him, reappointing only those commissioners it wanted to retain. (This is the usual technique governments use to get rid of troublesome people appointed for set terms.) Venturini later privately published a book about the TPC, *Malpractice*, not only alleging incompetence in pursuing zinc cartels but also making outrageous claims of Nixonesque connivance between top public servants 'and those born to rule'.

Despite the teething problems, Ron Bannerman led the TPC and its predecessor for 17 years, becoming as Hank Spier says, Australia's first 'Mr Antitrust'. He retired in 1984. There were some big wins, such as prising open the club of the stock exchange. In a glucose case the TPC had its first win under the new market powers provisions, obtaining the first penalty under this section. But there were also some big losses. A case launched in Bannerman's day but decided under his successor, Bob McComas, was a major setback. The TPC had alleged anti-competitive activity in the freight forwarding industry. The courts threw it out, with costs awarded against the Commission. It was a severe blow, and eventually the government had to pay the bill. McComas decided not to appeal, despite strong internal pressure to do so.

McComas, a corporate lawyer with a tobacco industry background, aroused deep scepticism among consumers. Ironically, he fought moves by the Hawke Government to remove consumer protection to a new agency within the Attorney-General's Department. McComas reportedly threatened to resign over the issue. In the event, the TPC lost only product safety, which it got back some years later. Despite initial consumer misgivings, the McComas years — 1984 to 1987 — saw the first national study of consumer issues, as well as action on both misleading labels and misleading advertising.

Commission staff still chuckle at one incident of the McComas era. In his early days as Commissioner, McComas felt he should deal more with real consumers. So, during one lunchtime the Commission's consumer hotline was put through to his office. Chatting to one complainant, McComas invited him over to the office. Five minutes after the man arrived, McComas was seen fleeing from his office with the complainant in pursuit, swinging punches. Staff called police to escort the man away. McComas never took live complaints again.

It was in mergers, however, that the McComas years will be remembered, and perhaps not favourably. The 1980s was the era of corporate excess. It saw a wave of mergers, with a new market wrinkle to finance them, junk bonds. Three big mergers of the late 1980s — the acquisition of The Herald & Weekly Times Ltd by Rupert Murdoch's News Limited, Coles/Myer and Ansett/East West — are now held up as deals the ACCC would not allow today but which got through under the 'dominance' test. (The ACCC now operates under a revived 'substantial lessening of competition' test.) When Coles bid for Myer, McComas went to see Woolworths and asked them to publicly oppose it. Woolworths declined, and the deal went through.

News Limited's bid for H&WT as Treasurer Paul Keating was rewriting the media landscape with his new cross-ownership rules brought Murdoch back to the Trade Practices Commission's door. Bannerman had knocked back Murdoch's earlier bid to acquire H&WT, earning the publisher's ire. This time Murdoch played his cards more cleverly. Owning a property just outside Canberra, Murdoch took to just dropping into the TPC's new offices in Canberra's Belconnen to argue his case. He turned up one day direct from his nearby property wearing moleskins. A staff member, thinking he was some cocky who had just wandered in off the street, told him to 'b____r off'. The TPC management felt they could deal with Murdoch. The merger was approved, but the TPC's hopes that it had created a new media entrant, Northern Star, by divestiture of some of the old Murdoch newspapers, failed when Northern Star fell foul of the new cross-media ownership rules after buying a TV channel and had to sell off the newspapers. The newspapers later collapsed.

McComas' successor in 1998, Professor Bob Baxt, felt the newspaper sell-offs may have been a sham, and ordered an inquiry. This did not find any conduct in breach of the *Trade Practices Act*. The Murdoch acquisition and subsequent sell-offs meant that News Limited controlled 59 per cent of Monday–Saturday newspaper circulation in Australian capital cities, and 60 per cent of Sunday circulation. Many in the ACCC believe the 1987 TPC could have done more to lessen this.

After the public stoush with McComas over merger decisions, Baxt, a trade practices academic and legal practitioner, proved a handful for the Labor government. Internally, Baxt instituted significant changes, introducing the first priorities and directions statement in 1988, a practice continued to this day. He also created the TPC Consultative Group, bringing together business and consumer groups to discuss trade practice issues. Though some big mergers were flagged through, the TPC stopped the Arnotts/Nabisco deal. Baxt was angered by Bob McComas for representing Arnotts in this case only a short time after leaving the TPC. Around the TPC Baxt acquired the nickname 'No Deal Baxt'.

The Baxt TPC tackled some big competition law enforcement cases, including Carlton and United Breweries' on misuse of power in relation to beer prices and Paterson Chaney on price fixing in automotive parts. But the landmark case of the era — *Queensland Wire v. BHP* — was a private action. The case, now cited in all trade practices textbooks, significantly expanded the misuse of market power provision contained in Section 46 of the *Trade Practices Act*. BHP had refused to supply the y-bar used in country fencing to Queensland Wire, which took the refusal all the way to the High Court. The court found that BHP had taken advantage of its market power in refusing to supply the y-bar. By broadening the interpretation of 'take advantage', the High Court introduced a new sting into Section 46. But the 'misuse of market power' section remained bedevilled by legal interpretation of whether it was the 'purpose' or the 'effect' of the action that should constitute misuse. That debate would find echoes in the 2002–03 review of the Act.

Baxt's TPC also undertook the first 'unconscionable conduct' case for consumer protection. The 1997 Swanson inquiry had recommended the *Trade Practices Act* deal with harsh or unconscionable conduct, which usually involves one party misusing superior bargaining power. Initially this was limited to consumer transactions. The provisions were later extended by the Howard Government to protect small business. In the first case, National Australia Bank was caught engaging in unconscionable conduct over obtaining and enforcing personal guarantees, the first of four such cases for the bank.

Unconscionable conduct was to become a big issue for consumers and small business, particularly in franchising. In one franchising case in 2000, a court found that Simply No Knead Franchising had not just been unreasonable, but 'bullying and thuggish'.

Baxt did not enjoy good relations with his political masters. His public campaign for more resources and wider trade practices powers, and his early drive into micro-economic issues in the waterfront, the airlines and the professions, annoyed the then Attorney-General Michael Duffy. At one stage, when the TPC was pressing for minor changes that would enable it to operate while the chairman was abroad, Duffy's office shot back a refusal accompanied by the comment, 'not as long as Baxt is chairman'.

Baxt's criticisms of the Labor Government over resources for the TPC hit a real nerve. He says that, after his term as chairman, when fines were quadrupled to $10 million, Duffy said to him: 'You weren't going to get this one, you were too critical of us. You kept speaking out against us. We waited until you went and then we increased the penalties'. There were also numerous clashes with Labor ministers over the competition regulator's reach. The issue arose again of removing consumer affairs from the TPC's purview. 'They just wanted to weaken the Commission', says Baxt.

Two ministers warned the TPC not to put their noses into consumer credit, communications and trans-Tasman shipping.

Political interference in the fledgling agency was not new. During the Fraser Government, the Nationals virtually ordered Wal Fife, then business and consumer affairs minister, to stop a TPC court case involving the banana industry. He did. Another Fraser minister, John Moore, told the TPC to delay its investigation of the opening up of the Stock Exchange. The eventual deregulation was forced by a writ of mandamus from the Merchant Bankers' Association.

Until the mid-1980s, ministers had to consent to all consumer protection cases. This had great potential for lobbying, with the TPC often mystified as to why some actions did not go ahead. Perhaps the most consistent political pressure came over newsagents and the deregulation of their industry. Allan Fels has commented that if he ever gets around to writing a book about power in Australia, newsagents will top the list, ahead of newspaper publishers.

Baxt could see the writing on the wall. As his term expired he made it known he would not be seeking reappointment, also preferring to live in Melbourne. His departure, however, raised an issue that successive governments have failed to address: conflict of interest. Baxt formally proposed that outgoing commissioners be barred from private sector work in their area for at least a year. It was ignored, and this issue remains a continuing blot on Australian public life, and not just in relation to the competition regulator. Baxt returned to legal work in Melbourne, but declined any direct relations with his former Trade Practices Commission for a year.

The Baxt, McComas and Bannerman eras had consolidated the 1974 *Trade Practices Act*. But the Commission itself remained a marginalised agency in the Canberra bureaucracy. That was about to change, however, as the arrival of both Allan Fels and micro-reforms of the Australian economy in the 1990s ushered in a new era of competition policy.

CHAPTER 3

FISHY

B lame it on persecution. In the middle of the 19th century small groups of German Catholics facing religious persecution in Prussia began migrating to the free settler colony of South Australia.

According to Fels family legend their forebears were part of an entire village that upped stakes from Hohenfriedeberg, Silesia, in modern-day Poland just near its borders with the Czech Republic and Germany.

The South Australian Register of Monday 18 August 1856 reported the arrival in Adelaide of the barque *August* from Hamburg, carrying 231 adults and 33 children as its only cargo. The voyage from Hamburg had taken more than three months. Among the passengers were Franz Felz, his wife Henrietta, daughter Mathilde, and sons Joseph, Francis and Paul. They settled around Sevenhill, north of Adelaide. Only three years earlier other German Catholics fleeing persecution and loss of property because of their Catholicism had blessed a small chapel at Sevenhill, now the St Aloysius Catholic Church.

Franz was a cook and confectioner by trade, but in Sevenhill he started a tannery. Henrietta, meanwhile, ran a small wine shop, catering for the bullockies and carters carrying copper from Burra to

Port Wakefield. The family quickly adopted the anglicised version of their name, Fels.

Their four children sparked leafy family trees. One offshoot bore 19 children in two marriages. A Fels family reunion in Bairnsdale, Victoria, in the mid-1990s saw some 350 people swapping details of their relationships. When Allan and his wife Isabel booked into the local motel, announcing their name, the receptionist asked, 'Everyone here's Fels, which Fels are you?'

Around 1889 Allan's grandfather, Ernest Fels, son of Francis Fels, left Sevenhill for the West Australian gold rush. In the event, he found a job with the posts and telegraphs, rising to become Superintendent of Mails in Western Australia. His fourth child, Herbert James Fels, Allan's father, later joined some of his brothers on a farm, but was forced off in the 1929 Depression.

Back in Perth, Herbert met and married Muriel Slattery, a young woman born in Australia of Irish descent. Allan jokes to friends that he has the best qualities of both the Irish and the Germans, rather than combining, as some of them suggest, the worst qualities of both.

There must have been little joking when Allan Herbert Miller Fels was born on 7 February 1942 during some of the darkest days of World War II. The US fleet had been bombed at Pearl Harbour only two months earlier and Singapore fell the same month young Fels arrived. Herbert, by now a physical training instructor with the Air Force, was posted to Darwin.

Fearing Japanese invasion, Muriel took Allan and his older brother Robert inland, like many mothers on both the exposed west and east coasts of Australia.

After the war the reunited Fels family settled into a suburban brick house right on the Stirling Highway in the beachside suburb of Cottesloe. Muriel's family had established a soap manufacturing business, Westralian Soaps, making brands called Peak, Zoak and Zoff that claimed to be especially suitable for West Australian waters — a claim that might very well attract the attention of a modern-day consumer regulator. Herbert joined his brother-in-law Stan in the business, rising to company secretary and later running the business when Stan died in the 1960s. Shareholders later sold out to Johnson Wax. Allan remembers accompanying his father to the factory in North Fremantle to see how the soap was made, as a child.

The Fels family, as Allan recalls, was 'middle, middle class'. Herbert, as an employee but not a shareholder in the soap business, was entitled to a company car. In 1953 Muriel won the lottery and the three thousand pound prize enabled her to buy her own car. A two-car family was unusual in those days, but Fels remembers the family's situation was still 'fairly tight' compared to today's standards. Herbert was often on the road, ensuring the company's soaps were stocked in stores. Friday night was usually spent around the radio, listening to the variety show sponsored by Westralian Soaps. Holidays were very modest, just driving down to Bunbury for a few days sometimes. Fels did not visit the eastern states until he finished school.

With Cottesloe beach nearby, however, childhood in Perth in the 1950s had that hazy dreamtime quality so well evoked in Robert Drewe's novel *The Shark Net*. Cottesloe beach beckoned most summer days.

Young Allan was enrolled at St Louis School, Claremont, where the Jesuit teachers pursued a rigorous program to ensure the mental, spiritual and physical development of their charges into 'complete persons'. Religion was a powerful force on the young Fels. Regular Sunday Mass with the family, weekly church sessions to gain special indulgences, prayers before every class at school, courses in religious instruction from the Jesuits and Catholic boys club retreats all added to 'a religious atmosphere being there all the time'.

Muriel taught piano at Loreto Convent across the road from the Felses' home and Allan had half-hour piano lessons every day from his mother, finishing school with a distinction in music. However, he never played again. 'I had too many music exams, and when I finished the last I lost all my enthusiasm for playing the piano', he says.

At school 'Felsy' or 'fishy Fels' as he was called, was popular in all the sports teams and usually finished in the top quarter of the class when it came to studies. Schoolmate Bill Quin remembers him as also having a 'bit of the devil' in him, smoking down behind the shed like most kids of that era. John Farrer, another classmate, says however that Fels was never one of the school tearaways, unlike himself and some other boys who ran away from school or got caught stealing bullets from the local rifle range. 'The difference is that we were boarders, while Fishy lived at home.' Fels' home life, with its emphasis on religion and achievement, had put him on a different path than his boarder schoolmates.

One episode, however, tested the patience of the Jesuit teachers. Fels' entire class was caught smoking on a day-trip to Yanchep — some of the boys had got their hands on many packets of cigarettes. Fels recalls smoking about two packets, making himself sick. The teachers lined up the whole class, giving each of the boys 'six of the best' on the backside. Fels never smoked again, and just as well. Throughout his life he has suffered from mild asthma.

Farrer says Fels' later intellectual achievements were not foreshadowed in his school years. The outstanding memory of his school chums remains Fels' cricketing prowess. 'You would never have predicted he would become the most famous guy in the class', he says. 'Fishy was not in the debating team. He was always more reticent.' Farrer, nevertheless, does believe 'Fishy' matured scholastically earlier than his classmates, and was grabbed by economics while his mates were busy fooling around with girls.

Why 'Fishy'? 'What rhymes with Fels when you are 10 years old?' responds Farrer. 'He is always "Fishy" to us when he comes to our get-togethers.'

Cricket was young Allan's early passion. There is a black-and-white photograph of him during that era showing a young boy proudly holding up a cricket bat almost as big as himself. On his eighth birthday he was given Don Bradman's autobiography. 'I finished that real quick', he says. Cricket then became an obsession. He learned all the statistics of test games from 1878, spending countless hours in the Bradman-like practice of hitting a ball against a wall at home. Fels would play out against the wall all the great innings from the record books.

Developing the ability to bowl leg spin, top spin, outswingers and wrong-uns, he was a star in St Louis' cricket team. In one under-10s match he bowled out the entire opposition team for 23 runs!

A cricketing career looked so promising that his father had him coached by a Sheffield Shield player, Charlie Puckett, to improve his batting. It worked, with young Allan regularly hitting 50 to 70 runs. However, although he continued playing through university, Fels had a very ungainly, back foot spin bowling technique. The balancing feat involved was possible for a child, but as he got older and heavier he could not maintain the accuracy. Indeed, he had trouble as a child. Bill Quin well remembers Fels' incredible but erratic bowling action. So erratic was it that he sometimes failed to land the ball on the pitch! 'But when he did it was unplayable', says Quin. Although the door of a professional cricketer's life closed, the game remained a lifelong love, and opened many doors for Fels. He played in university teams in Perth, the US and Cambridge, only giving up when he returned to Australia in the early 1970s. 'There were too many young bowlers hitting your head', he says.

Allan's wife Isabel believes cricket has had an 'amazing' impact on Allan's development and his mind. 'I have never understood cricket at all', says Isabel, who grew up in Spain. 'But I have this idea that Allan was very influenced by cricket. He says it is a very subtle game.'

Fels' other early dream was to become a writer. Aged 11, 'A. Fels' published his first article. It was an account of Australia's historic 1882 cricket victory over England, which created the modern-day series of 'Ashes' test matches. In *The Eagle*, the school magazine, Fels weaved a short but colourful account of 'a great test match', recording that the excitement was so great that one spectator gnawed pieces of wood from his umbrella, while another died under the strain.

In another article in *The Eagle* towards the end of his school life, Fels devoted two pages to analysing Shakespeare's Hamlet, a character he describes as 'one of the greatest creations of literature'. His conclusion showed Fels was rapidly developing an insightful mind, while perhaps needing some help with sentence construction:

'In painting him Shakespeare probed far beneath the surface of appearances into the abysses of his own heart and soul, dissecting his own mind and thought, contemplating the mystery of human personality, depicting, some critics believe, himself troubled by and dubious of the world; yet, for all that, a man of great intellect and character', he wrote. Fels attended writers' meetings where budding authors would stand up and read their work.

Young Fels was somewhat sceptical on spiritual matters — a disbeliever, as he prefers to call it. But he was taken by the teachings on the life of Christ and the social beliefs of Catholicism. This was the initial stirring of what was to blossom into a social conscience and a yearning for a career in public service. The combination of the Catholic emphasis on helping the poor and public service were formative influences on Fels' later career. *The Catholic Weekly* in 2001 claimed Catholicism could take much of the credit for tempering Fels' belief in free markets with strong social welfare safeguards. 'Avenging angel who puts people and justice first', it headlined an interview with Fels.

The iconoclastic, visionary economist Colin Clark was much in vogue in Catholic circles in Fels' school era. An expert in national accounts, Clark's conversion to Catholicism saw him advocating intensive settlement on the land, the creation of regional cities, higher food production, lower tariffs and strong restrictive trade practices laws to combat inefficient industries. Clark heavily influenced BA Santamaria's Movement, with its policies of high migrant intakes, encouragement of big families and decentralisation. The Jesuits at St Louis gave their charges a big dose of Clark's pro-Catholic social policies via his book *Australia's Hopes and Fears*, published in 1958.

It was the sort of social vision that stimulated 'maybe I'll be a public servant' thinking in the young Fels' mind as he finished school. A business career had no attraction. Despite visits to the soap factory with his father he had no interest in it. Indeed, in those days he did not see business as a service to the public. 'Now I can see it's a real service, and actually a very concrete one, making goods and services. But in those days I didn't think of business in those terms. I always thought of "service to the public" as the government doing things.'

There was never any question that he was going to university. Both parents were keen, and his mother was always encouraging Allan and his brother Robert to be ambitious. Muriel's ambition for her sons was one of the driving forces in young Allan's life.

As a reward for his matriculation — with distinctions in Latin, maths and music — Fels' parents took him on holiday to the eastern states. This was a major adventure for the 16-year-old. Not only did he want to see the test cricket in Sydney and Melbourne, he wanted to explore the possibilities for a writing career.

In Melbourne the young 'writer' audaciously telephoned Vance Palmer, the famous poet, playwright, novelist and short-story writer, regarded as the foremost man of letters of his day. Palmer, who tried to set down 'Australian rhythms' in his writing, must have been somewhat taken aback. But he invited Fels over for a chat with himself and his wife, Nettie, also an important literary figure. The three discussed literature for several hours.

In Melbourne also Allan indulged his other obsession — cricket. He spent five of the six days of his holiday at the cricket test against England.

Returning to Perth, Fels enrolled in arts/law at the University of Western Australia. Another passion quickly developed — student politics. Studies almost took a back seat as Allan dived head first into the students' Societies Council (the council of various student groups such as drama, literary and all faculty clubs), the Newman Society for Catholic studies, the Arts Union, and then the Guild of Undergraduates. As well, he co-edited *The Westerly*, a literary magazine.

'I just loved it', says Allan. 'It was terrific education, meeting a lot of people. I liked all the machinations involved in running committees and winning elections.'

Daryl Williams, now Attorney-General in the Howard Cabinet, was a year behind Allan at the University of Western Australia, and remembers the young student politician. 'His desk just became one mounting pyramid of paper', Williams recalls. 'It got higher and higher, and was something to admire for its engineering. I don't know what sort of system he used, if any. I don't know whether he did anything more than deal with the pieces of paper on the top.' It was the start of paper piles that followed Allan Fels throughout life.

There were also signs that the student Fels was starting to think about competition policy, or at least the sporting side of it. Allan and Daryl Williams played squash together. Williams recalls Fels telling him that he liked to play with someone who was better than him, someone who was about the same, and someone who was not as good as him. This was the way he refined and improved his game. 'He kindly pointed out to me that I was in the third category', says Williams. 'Even as an undergraduate he was refining competition policy.'

Fels had taken arts/law in first year because he had an author's career in the back of his mind. That dream now started to fade, and he realised he was 'no budding Conan Doyle'. He began to focus instead on subjects which would be useful for a life in public service. He changed to economics/law — both relevant to public policy — although he believed lawyers had a limited approach to issues. 'Even then I knew enough to know how narrow the legal approach was', he says.

Surprisingly, the economics department resisted the law/economics approach, limiting Fels' credits for law subjects. Fels drifted along, taking two years of public administration as a minor in his economics degree. The difficulty of gaining credits just prolonged Fels' university course, which he did not mind at all as it gave him more time for student politics. This came before studies, with Fels spending at least four days a week on student politics. He became president of the Societies Council as well as the Guild of Undergraduates.

As president of the Guild he was following in the footsteps of HC 'Nugget' Coombs, Bob Hawke and John Stone. Contemporaries on the Council included Fred Chaney, the late Robert Holmes à Court, and his wife-to-be, Janet. Daryl Williams and Kim Beazley would follow. At the University of WA, the Guild was a powerful body, representing not just students, as in most universities, but also running all student facilities such as the union, refectory and some of the sports grounds.

The Guild took Fels into national student politics, where he mixed it with the late Peter Wilenski and Michael Kirby, now a High Court judge, at meetings of the National Union of Australian University Students. Fels' era in student politics coincided with the backlash against communist and left wing domination of the unions, with their emphasis on foreign affairs and politics. Students were no exception. Fels recalls that the brilliant Wilenski, who was later a key adviser to Gough Whitlam and a noted public servant, had a clever line to get the students into political activity. Australian students, Fels recalls Wilenski arguing, should express solidarity with students in Africa and Latin America who were then mounting independence movements against colonial era regimes. 'If they chose to get into politics in their country we should not be holier than thou in our attitude', Wilenski argued to stir the Australian students. His argument worked with Fels, who was weaned off his former belief that student politics was solely about student welfare.

The usual reward for holding high office in student politics was a trip to an international student conference in an exotic venue. Fels was unlucky. In his year, the conference was held in Australia. Perhaps in compensation, Fels took himself on student trips through much of Asia, including India, Pakistan, Nepal and Sri Lanka in early 1964. The next year he visited Indonesia, Singapore, Malaysia, Thailand, Hong Kong, Taiwan and Japan. These tours imbued Fels with a new interest in development economics. He went on to do his minor in development economics, majoring in public administration.

The Guild also took Fels into some unusual confrontations with the powers-that-be. The university's vice-chancellor, Sir Stanley

Prescott, wanted to cut back on some of the Guild's powers, particularly its control of one of the halls of residence, Currie Hall. The students lobbied to no effect. Then they heard that 'Nugget' Coombs, one of the university's most illustrious graduates, was coming to receive an honorary doctorate at a graduation ceremony. Coombs, a former Guild president himself, ranks as Australia's most respected civil servant. In his long career he was personal adviser to seven prime ministers, with enormous influence on Australian economics, arts and indigenous policies.

At that time, Coombs was head of the recently created Reserve Bank of Australia. Fels, again showing a touch of telephone audacity, got through to him in his Sydney office. Just ringing the eastern states was a big deal in those days, much less being a student and getting through to the Reserve Bank governor. He laid it on Coombs. The Guild had enjoyed the dual functions of student representation and operating student facilities since Coombs' days, and now there was a threat to remove some of these powers. The Guild was worried about its future. Would Coombs put in a word?

Coombs did. With the entire university assembled for the graduation, Coombs fondly recalled his own days on the campus. And it was not just the formal education. His experience as Guild president, he said, had stood him in good stead for his future life in public service and banking. He was a strong believer, he went on to say, in the autonomy of the student body. 'The vice chancellor just sat there', recalls Fels. 'This really finished the debate.' It was an early lesson for Fels in the power of behind-the-scenes lobbying.

University politics was to return to ironically bite Fels later in his career. In Fels' university days, student union membership was compulsory. Fels himself had been influenced by the work of the American economist Mancur Olson, whose book's title *The Logic of Collective Action* announced its central tenet. In recent times, however, the shift has been towards voluntary membership. As chairman of the Australian Competition and Consumer Commission, Fels was faced with an application from James Cook University to, effectively, allow compulsory unionism. Fels initially rejected the request on the grounds that a competition regulator just had to come down against compulsory membership. The university pressed its case, arguing that students would pay the fee one way or another, either to the student union or through a university fee that would be passed on to the union. Fels agonised, and finally approved the university's enrolment system.

Another student episode brought Fels into contact with Paul Hasluck, then Minister for Territories in the Menzies Government, but also the author of *The Government and the People 1942–1945*, a history of Australia in World War II. *The Westerly* magazine, of which Fels was co-editor, was angered by a report that its government funding had been cut, while funds for *Meanjin*, another literary magazine, had been maintained. The decision had apparently been made on the basis that *The Westerly* received university funding while *Meanjin* did not. Fels knew Hasluck's son Nicholas (now an author) through university and used this avenue to approach the minister. Hasluck's own literary background made him interested, and he promised to look into it. Unfortunately, the impatient young Fels fired off an editorial in *The Westerly*, attacking the funding cut. Hasluck was quite angry. 'Look, you've got me investigating this thing and here I read this big attack on me and the government', he told a suitably chastened Fels. In the end, the funding cut was not restored, but *The Westerly* continued.

This was not Fels' only contact with Hasluck or senior Liberals. A chance incident opened up prospects of a career in Liberal politics. On campus Fels was gaining quite a reputation as a student organiser. Obviously impressed by this, a mature age law student approached him with the following message: 'Look, I'm president of the Nedlands Branch of the Liberal Party, but I have to give it up. There's a meeting in a few days, and the position will become vacant. I haven't told a lot of people. Why don't you come along, and if you're interested stand for the presidency?'

Fels was intrigued. His parents were Liberal supporters, and he had picked up a strong dose of anti-Labor DLP-style politics from the Jesuits. So there was some conditioning the Liberal way. But at university it had been the era of nonpartisanship. Now a party political opportunity loomed. Nedlands was probably the most powerful Liberal branch in Western Australia, a blue-ribbon conservative territory. Paul Hasluck was the federal member and Sir Charles Court, later to become premier, the state member.

Fels did not live in the area. By now his parents had moved to Mosman Park and Fels still lived at home. Residential address, however, did not matter. What did matter was that Fels was not a member of the Liberal Party, a prerequisite for party office. Fels solved that by joining up the day before the Nedlands meeting. The next evening at the meeting his friend resigned, proposing Fels as his replacement. The new Liberal Party student member was duly elected president of the Nedlands branch, aged 21. There were no other candidates for the post.

Amazingly, the energetic student was shortly afterwards also elected as secretary of the Liberals' Curtin federal division, where Hasluck was the Member of the House of Representatives. This gave him membership of the party's state council. Fels found himself spending three nights a week on party affairs. 'It was an education in how political parties work.' Fels spent a good deal of time explaining to friends that he was not in the Young Liberal Club (best known for its cocktail parties) but in the 'real thing'.

As Fels' final university exams approached in 1965 he faced a dilemma. What would he do in life? His moonlighting in Liberal Party affairs seemed to open the prospect that party endorsement for a seat might come his way. A political career beckoned. But his daytime studies inclined him either to a career in the public service or to further education.

In 1965, his final year, Fels had at last picked up his studies and eased up somewhat on student politics. He gained first-class honours in economics, with a pass in law. Honours in economics qualified him for a position with the Federal Treasury, so Canberra also beckoned. But higher education and a doctorate were also attractive.

Politics, public service or a higher education? Which road to take in life? The lure of politics was already starting to fade. As 1965 turned to 1966, Australians were increasingly divided by the war in Vietnam, and the heat was on inside the governing Liberals to shore up support for the war and Australia's military commitment. The West Australian Liberals were top-heavy with Vietnam supporters. By this time Hasluck was Minister for External Affairs, while WA Senator Shane Paltridge was Defence Minister. Fels, by now reading *The New York Times* and taking an active interest in foreign reports about the war, thought their understanding of Vietnam was shallow.

Vietnam aside, Fels was becoming disillusioned with the strictures of party membership. While the nonpartisanship of student politics offered freedom of expression, party members had to toe the line, or else. 'I could see that politics slightly dulled the soul, going to party meetings several nights a week and being very careful not to express too many opinions.' A further disillusionment was the emerging factionalism of the West Australian Liberals, with one faction being quite reactionary. This was later to become the Crichton-Brown set, which created enormous tensions in the party. 'I did wonder what life would be like if I hung around with them.'

As the attraction of a political career dimmed, Fels' enthusiasm grew for doing a doctorate and getting a chance to see more of the world. A streak of independence from the religious rigours of his childhood was also pointing to another world beyond Perth, reinforced by his interest in development economics. His Indian trip had led Fels to the belief that higher populations for India and China would be economically harmful: opposition to contraception should not blind one to the real world. The Catholic view that birth control was immoral should not lead to the conclusion that population growth was good. Fels drew this distinction in a talk to the Newman Society. The priests did not like it.

Fels applied for a Rhodes scholarship to Oxford, but was beaten by Daryl Williams. 'He didn't wilt after that because he won a scholarship to Duke University', says Williams. Not only was a Duke scholarship on offer, but also assistance to study in the US through the University of Western Australia's Hackett Scholarship and a Fulbright Travel Award to boot.

Fels had applied to Harvard and Chicago as well and been accepted by both, but they had no scholarships available. That narrowed it down to Duke. After a trip through South-East Asia, Fels arrived at the 'Harvard of the South', in Durham, North Carolina in February 1966. It was certainly a change. Fels' scholarship was in economics, with a planned thesis for his doctorate on the econometrics of Australia's arbitration system. Fels found the coursework a real grind.

'They worked me very hard', he recalls. 'We did huge amounts of reading, fairly intense examination. A bit like a snake swallowing the horse, you digest this huge amount of reading. You are exposed to huge bodies of literature in economics intensively. Then it takes you about 10 years to digest it all.'

The economics was mostly macro, with heavy emphasis on the Chicago school of money supply and free market advocates. Even development economics was taught as a market problem. Fels did no law, and his earlier university interest in public administration was not to reappear for some years. He let the dose of Milton Friedman free markets wash over him. 'It did not sink in and have a really powerful effect on my thinking', he says. 'I was a bit sceptical about it. But I sort of learnt it — you had to pass exams.'

Another blast came from the big student anti-war movement. Fels attended the fiery American Student Union meeting at the University of Illinois at Urbana as an Australian delegate. He increasingly felt the war was a mistake, but he did not become a radical. Any radicalism in Fels was reserved for future competition policy. 'I never demonstrated against the war. It was just an intellectual opposition. Meantime back to the books.'

But not only to the books. A chance meeting was to change his life. Because of the different Australian university year, Fels had arrived in February in the middle of Duke's academic year. The other new foreign economics student, who was from Peru, shared the same problem, and they decided to initially share a room in Duke's International House. Through this link Fels fell into Duke's South American and Spanish set.

At a party one night he met Maria-Isabel Cid, whose vivacity, sparkling eyes and fashionably bobbed hairstyle clearly charmed Fels right off the economics pages. Maria-Isabel was the daughter of a Madrid lawyer, who in the Spanish system was half judge and half private practitioner. She was two years older than Fels, and one of seven children.

Isabel, as she was known, had been encouraged by her parents to be educated and independent — somewhat of a rarity for women in conservative Catholic Spain in the Franco era. She had majored in both literature and languages, and studied the evolution of Latin into the Romantic languages such as Spanish and French, at Madrid University, and had taught Spanish in Paris before accepting a tutor's post at Duke for a year.

It was interest at first sight. Allan and Isabel spent a lot of time together as they mixed in Duke's large international student set. With a shared Catholic background, the two clicked. Although Fels was sceptical on the spiritual side, he and Isabel attended Mass together. Isabel had been a student at Sacred Heart, the so-called sister school of the Jesuits, and as a Spaniard she knew all about the Jesuit founder St Ignatius. Fels enjoyed the atmosphere of the strong theological school at Duke, finding the American priests thought-provoking. He began to read more widely around the subject. The writings of Dietrich Bonhoeffer, the German Lutheran killed by the Nazis, struck a chord. Bonhoeffer argued for a 'religionless Christianity' that would preserve Christian values without adhering to ideas about a supernatural god.

Time, however, started to impinge on the budding romance. Isabel had only a year's teaching at Duke, which was drawing to a close, and then planned a trip through South America with a female student friend. Fels and a male colleague followed down the South American trail, meeting up with the girls in Chile and Peru, where Fels, unfortunately, suffered one of his worst bouts of asthma. The group visited the famous Incan hill city of Machu Pichu where the altitude can also take the breath away.

Fels was obviously feeling light-headed even when he came back to sea level. The two corresponded when Isabel returned to Spain. Then, in the northern summer of 1968, Fels followed her to Spain, spending three months, as he says, in 'ardent pursuit'. Australian male friends were puzzled. This wasn't the bookish student activist they knew. Female friends, however, thought it quite romantic.

Isabel's parents could have been excused if they also wondered about what was going on. Here was a complete stranger who for three months spent almost every day at their house, sometimes taking Isabel out for supper, although there was a strict 10.30 pm curfew. Fels even followed the Cids to their holiday home in Galicia in north-western Spain, where the family originally came from.

The Cid family, however, was very accepting and friendly towards the Australian interloper. On his part, Fels, on an early merger mission of his own, was on his best behaviour: Isabel recalls her family quizzing her on whether her Australian suitor was always so polite. In his effort to impress, one night Fels hosted a dinner at an expensive Madrid 19th century restaurant, Botin on Plaza Mayor. 'Doing my best to appear to be a visiting Australian millionaire, I grandiosely suggested dinner at Botin', he later joked. 'The restaurant bill was in pesetas, so I didn't worry that night about all the zeros. Three days later, after bread and water rations, my budget was again in the black.'

The proposal occurred on a visit to Portugal, but there is some disagreement on who proposed. Fels thinks he might have. Isabel, however, believes she did the proposing. The two felt very romantic towards each other, says Isabel, and she remembers saying to Fels, 'You are going back to America, what is going on? I really want to know what is going on because I am not going to be left like this, putting up with uncertainty. I said that. So in the end he realised. He was afraid of proposing, I think.' Diplomatically, Fels cannot recall.

Allan and Isabel were married in Madrid, with Fels' parents flying over for the event.

Just prior to the wedding, Fels had been trying to organise his post-Duke career. Cambridge beckoned. The Cambridge School, as it was known, had been for decades the most famous economics department in the world, although it was starting to lose its lustre to US universities, including the Chicago free-marketers. After the war the Cambridge School's leaders included economists such as JM Keynes, Joan Robinson and Nicholas Kaldor, and neo-classical economics was overturned in favour of the Keynesian demand-management macro growth theory.

Visiting Cambridge on his way to Spain to woo Isabel, Fels arranged a meeting with Professor WD Reddaway, the famous economist who then headed Cambridge's Economics Department, to talk about a research assistant's job. The meeting was to be brief, as Reddaway had a lunch appointment at the other side of the campus. He asked Fels a virtually unanswerable question at the heart of the student's unfinished Duke thesis on econometrics and arbitration. It dealt with the difficulty of distinguishing wage rates and actual earnings. Fels sat there open-mouthed.

'I've got to go', said Reddaway. 'Walk with me.' Going down the steps and across campus the two fell to talking about cricket as they passed a cricket ground. Fels was able to give Reddaway a dazzling and scholarly display, not only of cricket history, but of those statistics that cricket tragics recite. He was instantly offered the job.

CHAPTER 4

FELTY TOWERS

C ambridge changed Fels' life. It set him on a course that would eventually make him Australia's 'prices technocrat' in the early 1990s. His Cambridge-inspired knowledge of pricing policy would provide the springboard for a new career in competition, propelled by Fels' unique relationship with Australia's trade union movement at a time when Labor was in government in Canberra.

At first, however, Cambridge was somewhat of a let-down. Fels had visited Cambridge before his marriage to Isabel in Madrid in April 1969 to arrange accommodation. He leased a flat in an unpleasant area around Cambridge, now gentrified. When Isabel arrived a few weeks later, she was horrified at the uncomfortable, tiny rooms. Fortunately, she had also arranged a job at Cambridge, tutoring in Spanish, and was able to use this to obtain better accommodation from the university. These flats were supposedly available for only a year, but the Felses found a solution to keep their accommodation. 'By virtually having a baby every year or so we were able to stay in,' says Fels, grinning. Isabella was born in June 1971, and Teresa followed in July 1972.

Fels' new research job turned out to be as boring as the first flat. Britain's Labour government had dreamed up the idea of a Selective Employment Tax. The Chancellor needed extra revenue and, with personal, company and sales taxes already high, the Cambridge economist Nicholas Kaldor devised this new tax, on the number of employees in service sector firms, in lightning-quick time. Levied only on service firms, it was quickly dubbed 'the silliest ever tax'. (Ted Heath's Conservative Government would later combine the Selective Employment Tax and sales tax into a Value Added Tax, similar to what Australia did by collapsing the wholesale sales tax and some other taxes into the GST.) Fels' job was to go around interviewing companies on the application of this Selective Employment Tax. Though boring, it gave him a first-class grounding in the application of a goods and services tax, handy training for his later oversight of the Australian GST.

If his first job was humdrum, life in Cambridge compensated. The new flat obtained by Isabel was in Causewayside on the Cam River only a few minutes walk to the Department of Applied Economics, where Fels was working. The pretty Grantchester walk was nearby. Fels was enchanted by the medieval campus, and awed by the big economic names in the Department — Joan Robinson, Nicholas Kaldor, James Meade and WB Reddaway — and by those who visited, including JK Galbraith and Joseph Stiglitz, later to win the Nobel Prize.

Fels quickly settled into the cricket set, becoming somewhat of a star. Fellow researcher at the time, Dudley Jackson (later professor of economics at Wollongong University), recalls an incident when the department was playing King's College. The economists needed 105 to beat King's, but their 'star batsmen' were all out for only about a dozen runs. Fels, although forced to use a runner because of a hamstring muscle injury, chalked up 92 runs to win the match. 'He knocked their bowling all over the place', says Jackson. 'It went all around Cambridge that this injured Australian was a good cricketer.'

Cricket pervaded Fels' life to such an extent that he was even laid up with another cricketing muscle injury when Isabel woke him at 3 am to announce the second child was due. 'She got me out of bed, made me a cup of tea and helped me hop into the taxi that she called', he recalls. 'When we arrived at the hospital they mistook me for the patient.'

In 1970, out of the blue, Fels got what later transpired to be his big break. The British Government decided to review the future of the National Board for Prices and Incomes, known as the PIB. Professor HA 'Bert' Turner, Cambridge's Professor of Industrial Relations and a member of the Department of Applied Economics where Fels was working, was also a part-time member of the PIB, and suggested that it undertake an independent study of what it had achieved in its five years. The PIB readily agreed, and commissioned Turner to do it, who promptly roped in a delighted Fels as his assistant. Then the PIB had a sudden change of heart. How could Turner be on the board and do an 'independent' study? Turner suggested Fels take over. 'Who the hell is Fels?' asked the PIB. 'So I stepped forward, and said, "Well, I'm an Australian therefore I'm independent" ', said Fels. 'I was also an expert on wages policy because I'd been writing this terrific thesis at Duke University, as yet incomplete but really an emerging masterpiece', he jokes in his self-deprecating style.

The 28-year-old researcher got the job, spending the next 18 months 'killing himself' writing a report that later became a book. It also converted into his doctoral thesis at Duke. Fels regards the book, *The British Prices and Incomes Board*, as his best academic work, and it is dedicated to Maria-Isabel. Fels was true to his independent review pledge, handing the PIB a few bricks as well as bouquets.

The project gave Fels an early lesson that controversy does not necessarily wound careers. His mentor, Bert Turner, was an unusually entrepreneurial academic, an original thinker who could cut through problems and size up the detailed research around him in reportable, big picture terms. He also thought ahead to answers for likely criticism of his research works, and then enjoyed the controversy. 'Better to be abused than ignored', was one of his sayings. The very title of one of the books he co-authored with Fels' friend Dudley Jackson — *Do Trade Unions Cause Inflation?* — showed Turner's provocative style.

Fels' ACCC style owes a lot to Turner, particularly his habit of dispassionately analysing the pros and cons of actions, including his own, and asking his people to think through responses to likely criticisms.

The charismatic Turner later roped Fels into an African project in 1978, helping Zambia establish a prices and incomes policy. This research was conducted in a building with some of the most fetid air Fels ever encountered, and it took him two days to find out why. The Zambian authorities had confiscated a lot of illegally caught fish, leaving the 'evidence' to putrefy in a rear yard.

Turner was quite inspirational for the young Fels in at least two ways. First was his habit of offering people around him an interesting idea, and then leaving them to develop it. 'It was up to you to research it, test it, develop it', says Fels. Another was his approach to publicity. While other Cambridge dons were reluctant to rush into print, Turner was quick to pen an article on his latest ideas for *The Times*, *New Statesman* or *New Society*.

Aubrey Jones, the chairman of the Prices and Incomes Board, was also notable for his media-handling skill. Jones, independently wealthy with a colourful career in the military, business and politics, had what even Fels thought was a media obsession. After convincing the PIB to undertake studies and issue challenging reports, Jones would issue the press release, becoming a national figure on television and in newspapers stirring up business and unions. Did Fels learn any lessons from him in this regard? 'Oh, I might've learnt one or two', he responds with a shy grin.

The major lesson for Fels from the PIB, however, was that prices and incomes policies appeared to be THE answer to inflation. Keynesian demand management was then the accepted economic doctrine, and Keynes taught that the postwar goal of full employment would inevitably induce inflation. The message then prevalent — until superseded by Chicago-style control of money supply and its accompanying supply-side micro-economics — was that prices and incomes policies in which employers and unions were restrained could knock the edges off inflation growth.

This was the economic 'religion' that drove Fels for almost 20 years. At the back of his mind was the realisation that competitive labour and product markets could also lower inflation in full employment markets. But these were long-term forces. Regulated prices and incomes accords could make changes here and now.

Fels left the PIB exercise as somewhat of an expert on pricing regulation. Duke also awarded him his doctorate on the subject, after he switched his thesis from wages. The expertise may have been in place, but how to promote this into a career? Fels saw that his future at Cambridge was limited. Even aspiring to be an assistant lecturer was ambitious, because every one of these was a world beater. 'They have excess talent at Cambridge on a massive scale', he says. An application to lecture at the London School of Economics failed when Fels talked his way out of the job by misunderstanding what they wanted. A bid to teach at the University of WA, his old alma mater, also failed. 'The areas I wanted jobs in people didn't want me, and some of them knew me too well', he says with a smile.

Then, in September 1972, Melbourne University offered him a lecturer's job. Owing to an administrative mix-up Fels arrived in Melbourne a week late, and on the very day he was due to start lecturing. Spurning an offer to have the class taken for him, Fels made it to the 5 pm lecture, although he had not studied the subject, Australia's arbitration system, for a few years and was also exhausted by the flight from London. He ran out of material after 35 minutes, and the students burst into applause. 'The only time I've ever been clapped in an undergraduate lecture', he jokes.

Fels was nervous about a return to Australia: it was a big move for his new family. But he wanted to pursue his academic interest in prices and incomes policies, and could see no job in the UK. He toyed with the idea of joining the British public service, but it was too problematic. 'I was reconciled to returning', he says.

Isabel was also challenged by Australia. She had had a good impression of a sunny, delightful country from a very brief visit for Fels' father's funeral in Perth. But living in Melbourne was something different altogether. 'The first two years were hell', she says. There was no Spanish community, and Isabel could not drive. Accustomed to the independence of inner-city life, her problems were compounded when the Felses moved out to the suburbs. Allan thought they had better start building a property asset, with a garden for the children. He had attended a few auctions, but with limited funds was forced out to Glen Waverley, 20 km from the city. It was a mistake. As soon as finances permitted they moved to Clayton, near Monash University, where Fels had accepted a post as senior lecturer shortly after the return to Australia.

The first few years back in Australia were tough ones for the Fels family. Isabel struggled to cope with the new environment, and Fels could not see a career path ahead. 'We felt a bit trapped', says Fels. In 1978 he seriously considered applying for a chair in political economy at the University of Aston, near Birmingham. Visiting his old Cambridge friend Dudley Jackson, now at Aston, the two spent a weekend writing up the application for Fels, who stood a real chance for the job. Later, with Isabel, they decided to have a drive around Birmingham to see what their likely new home would be like. Isabel looked at the city and within half an hour told Fels 'never'.

The Felses were also worried about their oldest daughter, Isabella, who had started to show disturbing signs in kindergarten. Isabella appeared very withdrawn and would cling to her teachers, never making friends. The Fels spent a lot of time reading to her, trying to stimulate her mind. It was not until much later, after a traumatic adolescence, that Isabella would be diagnosed as suffering from schizophrenia.

Fels stayed at Monash as senior lecturer in economics until 1984. Still feeling somewhat trapped, he threw himself into an extra job as part-time regulator. The Whitlam Labor Government had just been elected, and was casting around for members of its new Prices Justification Tribunal. The Australian Council of Trade Unions, influential with any Labor government, nominated Fels. It was the start of an association that would see the ACTU push the young academic for various posts.

While there is no doubting the ACTU push, the impetus for it came from Fels himself, who had obviously learned something about self-promotion and media from his British mentors Bert Turner and Aubrey Jones. BHP was pressing for a price rise, and the Whitlam Government prior to the PJT had established an inquiry into the matter under Justice John Moore. Fels' experience with the British PIB gave him a unique insight into the issues any inquiry should examine, including BHP's cost of capital and ways to make the 'big Australian' more efficient. As the inquiry was starting, Fels dropped into the Melbourne office of *The Australian Financial Review* to suggest an article on what the inquiry should examine, based on his experience at the PIB. The sharp-minded journalist Trevor Sykes, now the author of the paper's popular Pierpont column, accepted but told Fels he would have to submit it immediately. Sykes offered Fels a desk and typewriter. The two-page piece in the paper attracted the attention of the ACTU, which was considering making a submission to the steel price inquiry, and their research advocate Rob Jolly sought out Fels for some advice.

Later, Jolly asked Fels to speak at an ACTU seminar at Brighton on pricing policy. Fels gave a lift back to town to another young ACTU research officer, Bill Kelty, and the two struck a rapport. Fels saw the ACTU as trying to be serious and sensible about pricing. 'They didn't want to be taken in by business', he says. 'They were prepared to be reasonable and they wanted someone who knew about it to give them some lead.'

Fels obliged. The leg up to the Prices Justification Tribunal courtesy of the ACTU nomination was Fels' first breakthrough into a regulatory role. Fels was a part-time member, appointed as an independent academic expert. The chairman was Justice LH Williams from the arbitration commission. 'He saw price control as just arbitration', says Fels. 'If someone asks for nine they might deserve six.' The PJT was run in a legal mode, with Williams and some of his members forming a bench to hear submissions. 'We looked down from the bench on these QCs, including Murray Gleeson and Daryl

Dawson', Fels delights in recalling. Gleeson is now Chief Justice of the High Court, while Sir Daryl Dawson, previously on the High Court, recently conducted a review into Fels' ACCC.

With inflation in the Whitlam years soaring into the mid-teens, companies began piling price-rise bids into the PJT. Inflation was rising so fast that companies even asked the PJT for extra price increases for delayed decisions. Fels gained significant business contacts. Kelty came back into his life, as an ACTU representative opposing altogether another BHP price-rise application. Under the welter of applications, the PJT switched from an arbitration style to one of cost-plus price increase decisions. There was no attempt to measure productivity gains. While it was written off by many economists, Fels believes the PJT had a 'hell of an effect' for a short time. 'No-one ever dared to fight us because the unions would've taken them on and Bob Hawke would have denounced them', he says.

Competition policy was not an issue for the PJT, but it was already starting to intrude into Fels' vision. Maureen Brunt, professor of economics at Monash and to become the unsung heroine of Australian competition reform, proposed to Fels that they jointly run a new course in competition and regulation. The idea was to look at the tensions between market regulation by competition and direct regulation of businesses by pricing authorities. Writing her PhD at Harvard on industrial organisation, Brunt later collaborated with Peter Karmel on the path-breaking book *The Structure of the Australian Economy*, revealing the types of restriction that helped drive both the Barwick and Murphy reforms in the 1960s and 1970s. 'Just about every restrictive practice known to man is used in Australia', was one of her more biting lines.

Brunt was one of the first academics to take an active interest in the emerging issue of competition policy. As one admirer says, 'Maureen has been a mover, many have been shaken'. Fels was attracted by Brunt's suggestion of a joint course on competition and regulation. 'I'd never thought much about the link between the two', says Fels. 'I said, "Sure, you do 12 lectures on the *Trade Practices Act* and I'll do 12 on how to regulate prices". She said, "No, no, we have to integrate it". This was a very good idea. I hadn't really picked up how far-sighted it was.'

The course compelled Fels to think hard about the possible connection between prices and competition policy, a connection that would come to the fore in the micro-reform era of the '90s. With Brunt teaching about cartels and Fels about pricing, the issue arose in the courses of whether the PJT was causing collusion. 'Oil companies, for example, were not allowed to collude', says Fels. 'What they did is go to the PJT and get approval for the same price. So do competition law and regulation complement each other or conflict?'

The competition-regulation course was part of Fels' gradual conversion to a belief in the primacy of competition policy. 'He was certainly challenged by the subject matter he had to deal with', says Brunt. Cambridge Keynesians, as mentioned earlier, had left Fels with a firm belief in prices and incomes policies as the antidote to inflation. The Brunt courses led him to think of ways to turn competition issues into pricing. He still believed in wages policies to halt inflation, but price controls, the other side of any incomes accord, could harm investment necessary for economic growth. So 'smart regulators', given the impossible task of exercising price control to balance union support for wage control, could use their powers to lower prices by looking at competition within industries. Fels would later use this to great effect when he savaged book and CD prices.

By the late '70s Fels was moving a lot more in ACTU circles. The link with Kelty had blossomed into a solid family friendship. The two lunched regularly — in later years weekly — at one of the many cheap eateries near Melbourne's Trades Hall. The friendship became so close that later, at the ACCC, staff would refer to their building as 'Felty Towers'.

Rob Jolly had gone into state politics, becoming treasurer in John Cain's Labor Government. Petrol pricing had become a big political issue. The Liberal Government, facing increasing internal upheaval, had promised to control prices, forcing Cain to do likewise. Jolly and

Kelty pushed Fels for the new job of Victorian Prices Commissioner. When Cain was elected in 1982 Fels got the nod.

Through the 1980s Fels was the epitome of 'have regulation, will travel'. He popped up as the chairman of the Egg Industry Prices Panel, and was called in as an independent arbitrator on prices paid to chicken processors, and winegrape and tomato growers. As well, he advised on solicitors' remuneration, and later chaired Victoria's shop trading hours panel. (The eggs job led to a string of Fels puns about 'egg-ceedingly egg-regious' prices, and so on, culminating in 'un oeuf is un oeuf'. Fels could hold his own with tabloid newspaper sub-editors when it came to puns.)

Fels learned a lot about media presentation from the savvy John Cain, who managed to always keep petrol prices on the boil in the media. Fels watched Cain riding one petrol price crisis after another, and the public supported him. 'He just knew how to hurt all these companies', says Fels. 'I learnt a hell of a lot from Cain.'

Cain had an ability to shock the media owners as well. He once took the Fairfax directors aback by telling them over lunch that he wasn't much concerned what their prized *Age* newspaper reported. Cain said that by orchestrating his daily press release at the right time for television he could be assured of greater reach to Victorian living rooms on evening news bulletins than the morning *Age* could offer.

Fels also learnt a great deal about the ability of successful politicians to distil complex subjects down a popular pitch for the media. Cain had asked Fels to do a long study on petrol pricing. But Cain's staff could not get the premier to look at it. Fels boiled it down to a twenty-page summary. Still the premier didn't look at it. A two-page summary suffered the same fate. Finally Fels and Cain's press secretary knocked up a media release, and got the Premier to read out the first few sentences. 'Then he just went out and spoke with the press really brilliantly', says Fels. 'Little of what he said was in my report, but he just knew how to play it. It was a fantastic education in how to play symbolic politics. Cain used lines such as "Every Victorian is concerned about petrol prices … my government will act to protect the public against any rip-offs … we're determined to act … I put the oil companies on notice … any wrong actions and my government will take action".' Newspaper headlines shouted: 'Cain Acts on Petrol'. Cain of course was just jawboning.

Petrol was to play a big role in Fels' next pricing appointment, as a part-time member of the Hawke Government's newly created Prices Surveillance Authority between 1984 and 1989. The Fraser Government had abolished the old PJT in 1981. Kelty, by this time assistant ACTU secretary, had been working on an accord idea before Hawke came to power. A prices authority was seen as a necessary trade-off for wage restraint. Fels urged Kelty to ensure that the PSA had as wide a brief as possible, including prices set by government agencies. Treasury wanted the PSA constrained to only a few sectors.

Later, when Hawke was elected Prime Minister and Treasurer Keating was establishing the new PSA, Kelty told him: 'Keating's agreed with you being chairman'. Then Kelty went away on holiday to Fiji. Keating rang Fels and told him: 'I'm offering you a part-time membership. I'm sorry, something's gone wrong'. The Kelty plan had indeed gone astray. The head of the new PSA was Hylda Rolfe, an economist who apart from a long regulatory career also spent two terms as Mayor of Woollahra in Sydney. Keating told Fels that the Business Council of Australia had vetoed him as chairman. However, by this time Fels had good contacts among 'big business' and learned that this was not correct. Apparently there had been a complex series of 'blackballs'. Kelty had blackballed the Treasury candidate, nominating Fels instead. Treasury then blackballed Fels, who had not made himself popular with Treasury with his advocacy that the PSA should have a wider brief over prices.

Michael Little, who was the self-confessed 'big business' representative on the PSA between 1985 and 1987, recalls that he and Fels were 'sparring partners' on petrol pricing. Little, then chairman of Unilever and a director of several large companies including Rothmans and Castlemaine Tooheys, says Fels urged speed when it came to petrol price cuts that the PSA approved, but was a little slow on price rises. Little took him to task a few times, but the exchanges were in good humour. Little recalls Fels as being dedicated to competition. Now living in retirement near Noosa, Little has watched Fels' career with interest. Fels, he believes, is the one talent who has lasted the distance in the last 20 years. While the politicians and business leaders of the 1980s have come and gone, Fels has stayed around, 'keeping a beady eye on their goings on'. That beady eye would anger Little's successors in the Business Council of Australia in the late 1990s.

By the late 1980s the ACTU was angry at what it saw as the PSA's tardiness in price restraint to match the wage restraint in the accord. In 1989 it lobbied the Labor Government to have Rolfe 'unappointed' as chairman and Fels appointed. Given the influence of the ACTU over the accord, it happened. Rolfe told the press on her departure that her one regret was not spending enough time convincing the public the Authority was doing a good job. Rolfe might not have appreciated that it was the ACTU, not the public, she had to convince.

Fels walked into the PSA chairmanship with some clear views about what needed to be done, and some riding orders from government. These boiled down to high visibility, demonstrated concern at high prices, and a need to avoid doing economic harm. Fels would later describe this as knowing how to play the game. The basic aim, of course, was to make companies take notice of the PSA and not regard it as just a union pay-off for the accord. It fitted neatly with Fels' emerging view that competition could be used to stir up industries on prices.

Clearly this was a job for a media 'identity', and Fels had to become one. In 1991 Andrew Casey reported in *Workplace*, the ACTU magazine, about Fels' unlikely conversion from academic to media talent:

> At the time [he] took over, we had a chat about how the Authority could raise its image. Privately, being a bit of a media smarty-pants, I thought: God help anybody trying to turn Allan Fels into what radio and television call 'good

talent' … Two years later, Allan Fels has his photo in the
paper almost every week, pumping petrol and talking
about oil prices, or there he is on radio or television,
questioning record prices, cinema tickets or the price of
a funeral.

Casey reported that Fels did a media course. 'I was told to wear a red
tie on television', Fels told him, leading up to one of his jokes. 'But I
soon discovered that no-one else wore a red tie, and a few journalists
have told me since that power dressing is now out. So I bought a
blue tie.'

It was more than blue ties, however, that began to attract media
attention. Fels was indefatigable, posing in supermarkets checking
prices, visiting record stores to do the same, launching pricing
inquiries into everything that moved, and some things that did
not, like funerals. 'The cool and calculating man who counts your
cents', reported *The Age*. 'Authority to lift lid on funeral prices',
punned another newspaper. *The Age* sprung on Fels a quote from
the Committee for Economic Development that the PSA was
nothing more than a public relations ploy to encourage union wage
restraint. This, replied Fels, turning the question, meant the job
was not an easy one. Privately Fels was inclined to the CEDA view,
increasingly believing that price controls were being superseded
by competition policy.

Other sections of the media were not so impressed. Fels blocked
the big cinema distributors' attempts to change their pricing structure
to exhibitors. He argued the change would hurt small exhibitors.
Fels also secured approval for studies into the prices of books and
CDs from the minister assisting the Treasurer, Nick Bolkus. Both
books and CDs would ricochet around politics through the 1990s —
it was a classic example of Fels trying to use competition to lower
prices rather than price control. Books resurfaced again in 2001 when
the ACCC tried unsuccessfully to end restrictions on cheaper parallel
imports. Fels had stirred up a hornets' nest.

Fels' jousting with the oil companies continued. With the first Gulf War looming, Fels found himself on television a lot explaining why petrol prices were rising so rapidly. The PSA had shifted its petrol pricing base off domestic costs onto international prices. Unfortunately, it shifted to international pricing just before the Gulf War, which saw oil prices skyrocket. In five days, as the Hawke Government was negotiating another round of the accord with the ACTU, petrol rose five cents a litre. Fels was in Sydney meeting with service station owners on this very issue when he took a call from Treasurer Keating. A breathless Keating — he was on his exercise bike at home — told Fels: 'We just can't have these petrol price rises. They're going to blow the accord. Could we freeze them?' Fels replied: 'You've got the power to freeze them for 21 days'.

It was just on three minutes to ten. The arrangement with the petrol companies under the new pricing formula was that they would notify proposed price rises early in the morning, and the PSA would tell them at 10 am if they were approved or not. Fels told Keating he would have to get off the telephone urgently if he was to stop the rises that day. When Fels delayed the price rises the oil companies were furious. They had abided by the formula, and now prices were blocked. Later that day Keating brought in a formal 21-day freeze.

If the late 1970s had been a flat period for Fels, the advent of Labor governments in Canberra and Melbourne, coupled with his now strong contact with the ACTU, meant things had changed fast. He had gained a reputation for independent, academic advice, and was now regularly sought out for agency appointments, speeches at conferences and chapters in books. Some of the titles of his speeches and contributed chapters of that period give a flavour of the work: 'The Political Economy of Regulation', 'Prices Policy and the Firm', 'Economics and the Process of Law Reform'.

The tension between academic independence and political affiliations was clearly on his mind. In one speech in 1987 he outlined the balancing act of the social scientist appointed to a statutory agency. The issue of whether the social scientist was a servant of the public or the political party did not even arise. 'The social scientist appointed to a statutory body is a servant of the public and his or her task is, on professional matters, to state fearlessly the best technical advice that there is', he said. 'In addition, party political considerations, the likely acceptability of decisions to politicians, and other such complications are normally irrelevant in policy-making. This does not mean, however, that the social scientist can necessarily proceed to make decisions based exclusively on his or her view of what is best. The policies of the statutory authority may be governed in some measure by legislative aims or criteria with which the social scientist may partly disagree, but he or she must accept and abide by them for purposes of decision-making.'

Clearly independence has limits, a reality Fels would later experience.

Fels' academic career also blossomed. In 1985 he was appointed Chair of Administration at Monash, beating other contenders in the final ballot by a single vote. Dr Fels became Professor Fels. He proved an extremely active professor, renaming an existing course a 'Masters in Business Administration', introducing fees and increasing the number of international students.

'I had this idea to set up a public sector research institute, but I called it public sector management to sound more innocent', he says. 'Then, making considerable use of ACTU contacts, I persuaded Labor to fund a very big research school on public sector policy issues. Crean, Kelty, later even Martin Ferguson, helped me get the money and get it renewed. Quite good research occurred.' The grant of $625 000 a year ran for six years. Fels' Public Sector Management Institute was fortunate to tap Labor support during its cerebral period. Labor saw the grant as offsetting government aid for private business schools.

Fels' long interest in public administration culminated in 2003 in his appointment as the first dean of the new Australia and New Zealand School of Government, designed to develop future generations of public sector leaders.

It had been a long struggle for Fels to carve out a twin career as academic and regulator before moving full time into prices and then competition regulation. While the extra income helped, he spent many hours in the early years driving between the two jobs and home.

If the career side of Fels' life was heading up by the late 1980s, the home front deteriorated as daughter Isabella's illness became much more acute in her teenage years. This is the traditional pattern of schizophrenia, although in Isabella's case it was not diagnosed as such until she was in her mid-twenties. Various medical opinions kept fobbing off the Felses with phrases such as 'developmental arrest'.

This was little help. Sibling rivalry was strong, as everything the younger Teresa touched seemed to turn up trumps, while Isabella's school life seemed continually to fall apart. Although she performed well academically, Isabella's behaviour was erratic, and she formed obsessions about fellow pupils. The Felses moved Isabella to a new school, and for one year even engaged a private tutor for her to study at home. Later they tried a boarding school, but problems continued.

'It was hell, absolute hell', recalls Isabel. 'For Allan it was really bad because he found the stress of living with Isabella very, very hard.' At times Allan and Isabel had to front storekeepers to try to correct bizarre purchases by Isabella. Fels wore a cap on one such occasion to disguise his identity. He did not want the shopkeeper to think he was being approached by the chairman of the consumer and pricing agency.

Isabel herself had adjusted to life in Australia. She had started teaching Spanish at Monash, near the Felses' home at Clayton. This gave her a renewed sense of independence, which was aided further by an annual trip to her family in Spain. Later, thanks to some financial assistance from Isabel's mother, the Felses bought an old house in inner Prahran, knocked it down and built Isabel's dream house, influenced by the work of Mexican architect Luis Barragon. The house, with interior courtyards and polished concrete floors, offers only a walled appearance to the street. 'I told our architect I would like a house where you can really withdraw from the world and just live in peace with courtyards, not with gardens, near the city', Isabel says. 'I really wanted something that was very private, just a place where we could relax and where you could have a certain atmosphere that reflected your own world.'

Fels' career rise lifted Isabel's spirits as well, although his long work absences thrust greater responsibility onto her for Isabella. Isabel, however, could see the family benefits of her husband's blossoming career and dedicated herself to making the home front work for him.

The Felses are still disappointed at the years of therapeutic psychiatric treatment Isabella received with no recognition she suffered schizophrenia. Many times they told doctors of a family history of schizophrenia — two of Isabel's sisters have children with the disease — but it went unheeded. Only when Isabella was 25 was it finally diagnosed. 'More could be done (at the GP level) to ensure that there is early identification of its likely future onset', Fels wrote in a paper for the *Medical Journal*, arguing that early treatment can lead to better outcomes. Isabella takes medication to relieve her psychotic symptoms, but even so she requires occasional hospitalisation.

The Felses kept knowledge of Isabella's schizophrenia to a tight circle of friends for many years. In 2002 they decided to reveal it during a profile of Fels on the ABC's *Australian Story* program. Isabella appeared on the show, and subsequently was buoyed by the support and recognition from viewers. While revelation of the illness could have damaged her, in fact it gave her more confidence. Isabella had taken up writing for *Big Issue* magazine under the pseudonym of Lisa Fenton. Following *Australian Story* she began writing under her own name.

CHAPTER 5

'OUR FRIENDSHIP IS ENDED'

The combination of Allan Fels and the 1990s sparked the Big Bang of competition in Australia. Before Fels and his brand of activism, the Trade Practices Commission was a second-tier government regulator. A decade into Fels and the new Australian Competition and Consumer Commission created in 1995 was so powerful, so omnipresent, that a growing legion of critics cried that it was out of control. The Howard Government, facing an election in 2001, appointed not one, but three separate inquiries — Dawson, Wilkinson and Uhrig — with briefs to look at either the ACCC powers or reforming its structures. The latter, of course, was a euphemism for corralling Allan Fels.

No single factor caused this 1990s explosion of competition policy. Certainly a tightening of the merger law, coupled with new powers enabling the TPC to negotiate court-enforceable undertakings in its dealing with business, particularly in mergers, were crucial. A dramatic lifting of fines to $10 million also played no small part. Then the 1993 Hilmer inquiry resulted in an extension of competition policy across almost all the economy, including the professions and government agencies, while also extending the Commission into utility regulation. The 1998 waterfront dispute also sent a powerful message to unions that the competition regulator at last was serious about secondary boycotts.

Finally, a new activism energised the Fels-led TPC, with major cases — and wins — accompanied by huge fines. Freight express companies and their executives were hit with fines and costs of more than $14 million, while mixed concrete companies and their executives paid $20 million, in two separate cartel busts. An early case against freight express forwarders in the Bannerman era had failed. Fels moved to lift the consumer protection side, taking action against a number of life insurance companies. In one case AMP refunded some $50 million to consumers over misleading policies. In others, Colonial Mutual and Norwich Union paid refunds after the TPC took action on their misleading selling of insurance to indigenes. Mercantile Mutual was also caught on misleading insurance policies. Separately, Telstra refunded $45 million in telephone wire repairs.

In 1991 the TPC could see Fels coming as their new boss. 'Baxt to basics in one Fels swoop' one staffer quipped. Bob Baxt was not seeking reappointment, and it was no secret that the powerful ACTU wanted Fels, then chairman of the Prices Surveillance Authority, to also run the TPC. In this high summer of Hawke's accord with the trade unions, the ACTU and Treasurer Paul Keating were seen as running Australia, even though Bob Hawke was actually prime minister.

Fels was the obvious candidate. Under his direction the PSA was already straying into many areas of consumer protection and competition policy. The PSA inquiry into the books and CD industries was a classic example of the PSA's 'mission creep' under Fels, edging into TPC territory.

Michael Duffy, the Attorney-General, at least injected some formality into the appointment by advertising the job and asking a panel of senior public servants to vet any applicants. The panel recommended Fels, and Duffy took the name to Cabinet. It went through. Duffy requested Fels not do a Baxt and publicly attack the government.

Fels immediately saw the sense in merging the PSA and TPC. Under Baxt and Fels the two agencies were showing signs of overlap, if not rivalry. The petrol pricing issue had flared again, and to Fels' and the PSA's surprise, the TPC issued a report which appeared to favour so-called rack pricing, which would have reduced opportunities for price discounts. Without much consultation, the PSA, controlled by the Treasurer, engineered its own inquiry into petrol pricing.

This was an example of regulatory rivalry Fels used as ammunition in a meeting about the merger with Treasurer John Kerin (Keating had headed for the backbench to pursue his challenge to Hawke) and Duffy, who as Attorney-General controlled the TPC. The two ministers asked Fels to prepare a paper for Cabinet. The stumbling block of any merger, however, was the obvious issue of whether Treasury or the Attorney-General's Department would control the new agency. In power-conscious Canberra turf warfare is always a major issue.

Treasury, the key player on the economy, was ambivalent on the future of the two agencies. On one hand it was suspicious of Fels and the PSA, even though it came under Treasury's aegis. Treasury regarded the PSA as something of a smoke-and-mirrors outfit, a political gesture to keep the unions at bay. On the other hand, if it was merged with the TPC into a more powerful outfit, Treasury wanted to control it. Under Attorney-General's supervision all its life, the TPC had never received much support from Treasury (nor from Attorney-General's for that matter).

Unfortunately for Fels the 'iron law' of bureaucracy applied: if the two agencies could not agree the proposal was doomed. In the end, sheer nagging won the day — Kelty was always in Keating's ear urging a merger. By the time of his prime ministership, Keating was tired of the argument and agreed to it.

Meanwhile, in 1991 Fels had agreed to be joint chairman of the TPC and PSA. Business was alarmed that Fels might use confidential information given to the PSA for trade practice cases in his capacity at the TPC. Some uncomfortable pressures quickly came to bear. TNT launched legal action after it was issued with investigatory notices, alleging Fels' two hats were in conflict. When the court indicated that conflict of interest might be a problem, the notices were withdrawn. Fels could see the looming problem, and in late 1992 gave away the PSA, with David Cousins becoming its new chairman. Cousins was one of Maureen Brunt's many students, who now dot the regulatory, corporate and legal world around competition policy.

By now Fels could firmly see that competition policy, not pricing, was where the action was. He told the *Financial Review* in his final months as PSA chairman: 'Excessive prices occur only in industries characterised by a lack of competition. Competition is the best regulator of prices'. For Fels, this marked the end of his long march from Cambridge waving the price regulation banner as the means to curb inflation. Interestingly, he had had a prophecy of this from Ron Bannerman, the first TPC commissioner. Back in 1974, wearing his new PJT hat, Fels had spoken at an Economics Society function in Canberra, and Bannerman had pinned him down on whether it would be a real tribunal, or just a board. After the meeting, Bannerman told him: 'At the moment the PJT is glamorous, high profile, with everyone knowing about it. But in the long run it's the *Trade Practices Act* that will be more important'.

Seventeen years later, as he took up the chairmanship of the TPC, Fels began to realise just how perceptive Bannerman's words had been. A few days after arriving, a Commission staff paper landed on his desk asking whether he wanted to make a submission to the new Cooney inquiry into merger law.

An inquiry into merger law might sound innocuous enough, but mergers were — and still are — a cornerstone of big business concern about competition regulation. Mergers, of course, can be good for an economy, sharpening up managers and product development, while also benefiting consumers and shareholders. But they can be damaging if they create monopolies that can control prices. A loose 'dominance' test means that the competition regulator can really only stop mergers that result in a monopoly. A tighter test, one that stops mergers resulting in a 'substantial lessening of competition', obviously gives the regulator more power to say 'no', and makes potential merger partners think twice.

Mergers are hence very much the cutting edge of competition policy. The choice between a 'dominance' and a 'substantial lessening of competition' test dictates not only how the competition regulator will view a merger but also impinges on industry structures and whether governments should deliberately encourage 'national champions' in the small Australian economy — large-scale corporates that some see as necessary for effective global competition. This issue would loom larger later in the decade.

Where to set the merger line in the sand? As outlined in chapter 2, in its short life to 1991 the new *Trade Practices Act* had had both weaker and tougher tests, and was handed the weaker 'dominance' line by the Fraser Government.

The two tests in many ways make the difference between a passive and active competition regulator. With a dominance test, the competition regulator looks at whether the acquirer will be dominant or not. During the dominance test period the TPC used the yardstick of 45 per cent market share. Above that, and a merger proposal might have approval problems.

With a substantial lessening of competition test it must examine the overall market structure and make judgements about the future market. This more acutely puts the focus on what has become one of the most contentious issues of ACCC power — the definition of a market. The wider the market, the easier it is for a merger to go through. To take an example, the ACCC regards the free-to-air television networks and the pay-TV operators as being in different markets. So, a network could acquire a pay operator, other broadcasting regulations aside. But if these were regarded as being in the same market, a merger could be considered as substantially lessening competition, and would likely be barred. Similarly, the ACCC has always taken a relaxed view about the Packer television group acquiring Fairfax newspapers, despite concerns others may have about media diversity. The reason for this is that it regards television and newspapers as separate markets.

Fels may have been new in the job, but he knew instinctively that he wanted a return to the substantial lessening of competition test. He was backed by the TPC deputy chairman, Brian Johns, and senior staff. 'It's the right principle', Fels said. 'If a merger lessens competition it should be stopped. If you don't have that test then bank mergers are possible, oil company mergers are possible. Weak merger law has been a reason for Australia having a very concentrated economy.' Fels argued that if public benefits outweighed the fact that a merger would restrict competition then authorisation was always available. Authorisation, of course, enables merger parties to apply for approval on public interest grounds, even if their merger will lead to a lessening of competition.

The problem Fels faced in 1991, however, was that the weight of thinking was against him. The dominance test was in favour. What followed was perhaps one of the more significant business policy turnarounds in Australian history.

Only two years previously a House of Representatives inquiry chaired by MP Alan Griffiths had recommended retention of the dominance test. This reflected the conventional 'get big to compete overseas' wisdom behind the change to the dominance test in 1977, when John Howard, then Business and Consumer Affairs Minister, said:

> There should be no unnecessary impediment, legislative
> or administrative, to the attainment of rationalisation of
> Australian industry. It is in Australia's best interests to
> achieve economies of scale and improved international
> competitiveness.

Labor supported this. So did the bureaucracy. As late as the 1989 Griffiths inquiry Treasury's view was that in a small economy such as Australia only one or two efficient producers in any market were possible. 'In that situation efficiency considerations may require a relatively high degree of concentration', Treasury said.

However, dissenting voices began to arise. Labor's Economic Planning Advisory Council (EPAC) in 1988 expressed concerns at the high degree of economic concentration in Australia allowed by the current merger test, which was loose compared to international standards. It drew attention to overseas studies on the poor performance of merged companies. EPAC warned against the 'tacit collusion' of big groups, while consumer associations warned of a 'degree of public disquiet' about such power.

Under Fels' predecessor Bob Baxt, TPC managers had quietly lobbied the Griffiths inquiry for a more competitive test. The committee had appeared sympathetic, but Baxt personally killed it off. He told the committee that business deserved consistent, not ever-changing, rules. Baxt also believed that the dominance test, if properly applied, could be effective. He cited the TPC's wins in blocking the Arnotts/Nabisco merger and in the Australian Meat Holdings case, where the court ordered divestiture of an acquisition.

When Fels took up the cudgels with the 1991 parliamentary inquiry, chaired by Labor Senator Barney Cooney, the mood was beginning to change. Within government and Treasury there were mounting fears that the dominance test could allow mergers of the big banks. The four pillars (or 'pillows' as Fels jokingly calls them) could become two.

The pro-competition forces arguing for a tougher merger test were also blessed by a powerful new idea. In 1990 Michael Porter, a professor of business administration at Harvard who had been appointed to President Reagan's Commission on Industrial Competitiveness, published a seminal book called *The Competitive Advantage of Nations*. Porter turned conventional wisdom in Australia on its head, arguing that dominant domestic firms rarely led to an international competitive advantage. The rate of innovation was more important, and economies of scale were best achieved by exporting, not by having domestic market dominance. Porter went on:

> A strong antitrust policy — especially for horizontal
> mergers, alliances and collusive behaviour — is

fundamental to innovation. While it is fashionable today to call for mergers and alliances in the name of globalization and the creation of national champions, these often undermine the creation of competitive advantage.

Slowly, the debate began to turn, owing in no small part to Fels' efforts. He lobbied Treasury heavily. Although Treasury was sceptical of Porter — pointing out Sweden did not fit his thesis — it came out for a tougher merger test. Treasury had created a structural policy division in 1988, which by the early 1990s was arguing that micro-reform was necessary to kickstart the sluggish economy, and competition policy was critical to that. Treasury also feared that the weak merger test could see fewer banks.

Barney Cooney, an affable Labor senator from Victoria, must have felt like the ham in the sandwich during the inquiry as his own party, much less the Liberal and National Party opposition, began taking different sides, all armed with expert opinion. Within his party Attorney-General Michael Duffy supported retention of the dominance test. Duffy told Cooney there was no mood within the Labor Government for change. In meetings with Fels, Cooney indicated he himself was not interested in change. Fels asked Bill Kelty to speak to him. Cooney was hauled into a meeting with Kelty and Fels and told in no uncertain terms where the ACTU stood. 'I recall Bill Kelty being very sympathetic to Allan Fels' position', Cooney says.

Fels also set to work on other committee members. Democrat Sid Spindler was a big supporter, and so he should have been: it was a deal with the Democrats that had created the Cooney inquiry so soon after the Griffiths report! Fels talked with Senator Amanda Vanstone, a 'small l' Liberal who was also keen for change. The National's Senator Ron Boswell, although not on the committee, was an ardent supporter of small business and keen for the change. Boswell, in his usual practical style, offered to 'speak to' Senator Bill O'Chee, the Nationals' member on the inquiry. Whatever Boswell said to O'Chee it worked.

O'Chee voted for the change. But the Liberals' Rod Kemp proved more resistant, voting against any change.

For the Labor side, Fels called in the ACTU heavies. Apart from using Kelty on Senator Cooney, he asked Jenny George, the ACTU President, to speak to Senator Patricia Giles from Western Australia. Cooney appeared to be taken aback when at a subsequent inquiry meeting Giles said she was voting for change. Chris Schacht was another solid supporter for change.

Meanwhile, the Cooney inquiry faced a formidable array of outside experts anxious to retain the dominance test. Included in the line-up against change were no less than two former chairmen of the Trade Practices Commission, Bob Baxt and Bob McComas, a former TPC commissioner, Dr Warren Pengilley, the Business Council of Australia, the Law Council and, of course, the Attorney-General's Department. The main argument of this group was that the dominance test would facilitate industry efficiency and Australian participation in global markets — the very line Porter was demolishing.

The Cooney report, published in December 1991, seemed torn between the two sides, almost reluctant to make a judgement. It carefully noted the pros and cons of change, and then stated: 'There is no work of which the committee has been made aware which would compel it to come to a particular conclusion'.

So, no overwhelming argument for change. After paying due political obeisance to the recent Griffith recommendation for no change, the report then veers into a recommendation to support a more competitive test. It almost appears an afterthought. Justification for the recommendation was based on a few paragraphs citing the Porter thesis, the arguments of small business and the need to bring Australia into line with the competition tests of like-minded countries. Cooney says now that there was no 'bolt of lightning' that persuaded him and the inquiry. 'I was won over by the issue of competition and how it was going to improve things', he says.

The inquiry battle was won, but the power game was not yet over, despite the committee's recommendations. The government had to agree.

A few days before the Labor Cabinet was to consider the Cooney report, Fels received a telephone call from John Dawkins, then Treasurer. Apparently ringing on behalf of Prime Minister Keating, Dawkins wanted to explore compromises. What about retaining the wording of the dominance test but writing in some criteria that would move it closer to the competitive test? Fels listed the problems with that idea. OK, said Dawkins, what about the opposite: change the words of the test to substantial lessening of competition but write in criteria so that the old test continued to be applied? That's hopeless, Fels replied.

Dawkins asked Fels if he could think of a compromise. Maybe, said Fels, we could look at creating a test which would catch joint dominance or collective dominance. Over the next few days he explored these ideas with a few overseas experts, but quickly concluded that they were unworkable. Courts would be confused. The substantial lessening of competition test in the US had already created a lot of jurisprudence on the issue. Joint or collective dominance sounded like it was an issue of conspiracy rather than mergers. No go, Fels reported back to Dawkins.

Duffy, who had to write the brief for Cabinet to determine the government's position on the Cooney recommendations, was still not won over. 'I just cannot see any need for change', he told Fels, who immediately went to Duffy's office. There he found senior officials of the Attorney-General's Department urging Duffy to sign off on a Cabinet submission recommending no change, despite the Cooney finding. In front of Duffy, the officials and Fels staged an impromptu debate. The meeting, scheduled for just 30 minutes, lasted for almost three hours as Fels and Duffy's officials argued back and forth. By this stage Fels had his arguments highly polished. Duffy was won over.

Cabinet also agreed. After 15 years, the argument for scale so that industry could compete globally was lost. Although business mounted it strongly again in the late 1990s, it is unlikely to ever return. Duffy says the Cabinet decision was not greeted with enthusiasm within the government. 'I am still not absolutely certain it was the right

Beginning a lifelong obsession — a new cricket bat for the eighth birthday,
7 February 1950. Forest Place, Perth.

University of Western Australia Graduation Ball 1961 — *Left to right:* Allan Fels,
Mary Slattery (cousin), Anne Marie Lennon and her brother Tony Lennon.

Graduation day, University of Western Australia, 1965. Allan Fels and Mary Slattery.

Marriage to Maria-Isabel Cid at Iglesia del Espiritu Santo in Madrid, Spain,
7 April 1969.

At a ball. St John's College, Cambridge, England, 1969.
Left to right: Isabel, Allan and Elizabeth Heenan (nee Doherty). 'We ate swan, because St John's had a Royal Warrant entitling it to consume two swans per annum.'

The young Fels family in Perth, WA, December 1972.
Left to right: Allan, Teresa aged 6 months, Isabel and Isabella aged 19 months.

Isabella aged 5 years and Teresa, 4, in Perth, WA, January 1976.

Allan wearing a Spanish Basque *boina* or beret, at Teresa's pre-school creche, Monash University, 1976.

A fezzed Allan with a *sheesha* (tobacco waterpipe), relaxing after an Egyptian Competition Seminar at the famous Khan-el-Khalili bazaar, Cairo.

Santa Claus Fels at the Monash University Management School Christmas party, 1989. The tinselled blond fairy is Susan Grist, then Allan's Personal Assistant.

The prices watchdog. Allan Fels hones his skills as chairman of the Prices Surveillance Authority.

The perpetual paper trail. Allan Fels on his last day at the Prices Surveillance Authority, 30 October 1992.

The 'Untouchables' of the ACCC, 1995. *Left to right*: Paul Shertzoff, Allan Fels, Martin Foreman, Allan Asher.

Keeping an eye on the banks, 1995.

Allan fronts the media during a press conference on Telstra charges, 1996.

Allan the academic — the distinguished speaker at Deakin University Graduation Ceremony, 1996. *Left to right*: Chancellor Mr Jim Leslie, Professor Allan Fels, Professor Geoff Wilson, Vice Chancellor.

Make my day! Fels poses for the media during one of the many petrol crises.

Teresa, Allan and Isabel Fels at Teresa's wedding to Dr Simon Jones, Newman College, University of Melbourne, 4 April 1999.

decision', he says. On balance, however, he believes it the best decision. 'If Allan Fels had not been as committed to the change it would not have happened. He had a huge influence, and is entitled to put it down as one of his achievements.'

The critics still moved in on Fels. Peter Costello, then a rising star in the shadow ministry, mocked Fels' ability to reverse Labor's previous support for a loose merger test. The energetic Fels, he said, had proved a 'great Sir Humphrey Appleby to the Attorney-General's Jim Hacker, and managed to completely turn his own minister'. Only a few months before the Cooney report, Duffy had said the government was not convinced that there was any justification for reverting to the substantial lessening of competition test. What had changed? questioned Costello. 'What had changed was … Professor Fels as the new chairman of the Trade Practices Commission proved an indefatigable lobbyist, going around to the Minister, going around to other Ministers, going around to the Opposition, lobbying for a wider test which, incidentally, would increase the jurisdiction of the Trade Practices Commission to have a hand in determining the circumstances in which companies could buy assets or shares of other companies …'

Costello's clever 'good, bad and ugly' speech (Fels' role was bad, new unconscionable conduct powers good, and exemption of unions from new $10 million fines ugly) was bitingly accurate. For a regulator who in theory just administers competition policy set by government, Fels had shown himself a remarkably adept hand in actually changing that policy.

Two other changes at this time added to the TPC's growing armoury of powers. First, the Labor Government increased fines from the $250 000 they had been since Murphy's era to $10 million. The Liberals had been pressing for an increase to $5 million. Duffy went higher, following the Austel legislation where the Democrats had won fines of up to $10 million. If Duffy had not followed suit for the TPC the Senate may well have amended his new merger legislation. But the ACTU fought and won an exemption for unions, for whom most fines were left at the old $250 000, in a glaring piece of pro-union discrimination.

Second, the 1992 package introduced court-enforceable undertakings. The Griffith inquiry back in 1989 had suggested that the TPC's informal negotiating powers with merger parties be given some legislative backing. The change enabled the competition regulator to negotiate and then accept written undertakings to correct what it saw as undesirable aspects of a merger proposal, but applying to wider competition issues as well. These even included divestitures. These '87Bs' as they are called, have been a powerful instrument in many a merger negotiation. For example, in the 1997 Westpac/Bank of Melbourne merger the parties agreed to undertakings on trading hours, certain fee exemptions, and access to automated teller machines. In the 1994 Caltex/Ampol merger the Commission secured a set number of independent service stations.

Meanwhile, other winds were blowing through the Australian economy which would give competition laws a substantial boost. As has been mentioned before, by the mid-1990s the Hilmer reforms would stretch competition across most of the economy, including for the first time the professions, government agencies and a range of business not previously covered. These weaknesses in the reach of competition law had been recognised for some years. The 1977 Swanson inquiry after the election of the Fraser Government highlighted the lack of universal coverage of the *Trade Practices Act*, to no avail. Bob Baxt raised it, as did Fels in a Press Club speech shortly after becoming chairman.

The pressure for change, however, came from another direction. The Hawke/Keating government had begun internationalising the Australian economy, floating the dollar, deregulating banking and slashing tariffs. Yet the 1990s opened in deep recession, with Australia experiencing worrying current account deficit problems and high unemployment. Paul Keating's 'banana republic' remark struck a raw nerve. Was Australia heading into decline?

Keating began to explore wider competition fields with the states. Amazingly, given the normally tetchy state of federal–state relations, he secured agreement for a major inquiry into how Australia could lift its game. 'The engine which drives efficiency is free and open competition', Keating said. As a Labor prime minister, Keating was of a different stripe. The resulting Hilmer inquiry, chaired by Fred Hilmer, then Dean and Director of the Australian Graduate School of Management at the University of NSW, was a landmark for Australian competition policy.

The Hawke/Keating reforms such as floating the dollar and lowering tariffs mostly impacted the traded goods sector of the economy. Large swathes of the economy, from the professions through to agricultural marketing and many government agencies, were not affected. As well, the Trade Practices Commission really looked only at the market behaviour of firms, not underlying anti-competitive structures.

Rather than wrestling with the intricacies of new regulations, the Hilmer reforms went for processes to deal with moving competition into the professions, with abolishing restrictions imposed by egg marketing boards and other tightly government-regulated industries, and to create competitive access to monopolies in essential facilities and enforce competitive neutrality on government 'businesses'. Essentially, Hilmer was all about making competition a community and social value. 'If Australia is to prosper as a nation and maintain and improve living standards and opportunities for its people, it has no choice but to improve the productivity and international competitiveness of its firms and institutions', urged the report.

Hilmer proposed new powers for Fels' Commission in areas like the professions and in ensuring access to the deregulated energy and telecommunications markets. An entirely new agency, the National Competition Council, was created to cull the complex web of state regulations inhibiting competition. At one point, Hilmer and Fels had discussed an idea that the ACCC, to be formed in 1995, should take on running the entire national competition policy as well as its ongoing merger, anti-competitive policing and consumer functions. 'I thought it was too big an ask', says Fels. 'I thought we had enough challenges dealing with the wider jurisdiction we were getting with the professions and utility regulation. I also thought that politically I was stretching it. It's very important that the Commission be seen as powerful because as a regulator with power you tend to get results. I thought that on top of everything else, when we were constantly in conflict with major interest groups, that we then had to preside over the implementation of competition policy by governments, especially state and territory, that this was too big an ask. We'd be fighting wars on too many fronts.'

Fels' instincts were right. The Hilmer reforms set in train a complete overhaul of state statutes that in one way or another hampered competition — some 1800 different pieces of legislation in all. Not only was it a mammoth task, but inevitably it created confrontations with state governments. Fels had enough of those on his hands already with business groups.

Fels has often been accused of a mania for power. By declining suggestions that the new ACCC should also take on national competition policy oversight he showed something of the contrary.

Having decided on widespread reforms, with a new agency to run most of them, Hilmer then faced the dilemma of how to sell these potentially politically unpopular changes. Hilmer developed a series of little stories so that people could grasp the need for reform. One concerned McDonald's, the American hamburger chain. McDonald's sourced potatoes for the french fries sold in its Asian outlets not from Australia, but Idaho. Why? Because Tasmanian agricultural regulations meant potato-growing was dominated by small farms that could not be consolidated into the larger economic units necessary for quality control. The point, of course, was that regulation might protect a few small potato growers but it also stifled opportunity to develop new industries.

Hilmer's best 'story', however, was how he sold the reforms to the Labor Caucus, whose support was crucial for the Keating Labor Government. Whatever Keating might think of competition, some in Caucus were opposed. Hilmer asked one of the Caucus heavies for advice. 'Just tell them an anti-lawyer story', was the response. Hilmer stood up in front of Caucus and told the assembled Labor MPs that legal monopolies on conveyancing would suffer because of the reforms, with home-buyers paying less for transactions. 'That counted for more than all the policy discussions and definitions of competition', he says.

For Fels, the Hilmer reforms meant a lot of loose ends around competition policy were tidied up. The old Trade Practices Commission was renamed the Australian Competition and Consumer Commission. Finally, the PSA was swept under the same umbrella, with the entire show coming under Treasury. The states agreed to expand the reach of the *Trade Practices Act* within their domains, dropping the old 'shield of the crown' protection. The public utilities of the states and territories were now exposed to competition regulation.

Such state cooperation would come at a price. For the first time the states were given veto power over appointments to the new ACCC. That proved a political stumbling block in 2002–03 when Costello moved to replace Fels with Graeme Samuel, the head of the National Competition Council set up in the Hilmer process.

A final boost to the ACCC's powers in the 1990s was a costly one for Fels. The 1998 waterfront dispute posed a real test for the competition regulator on the politically sensitive issue of union secondary boycotts. But the close 20-year friendship between Fels and Kelty ended in bad blood. Such tensions with the unions might have been inevitable given the high emotion of the dispute and the role it thrust onto the ACCC, but the fallout with Kelty was personally wounding for Fels nonetheless.

The ACCC came late into the waterfront dispute, which ignited over Patrick Stevedores' bold plan to cut the powerful Maritime Union of Australia down to size. The Howard Government had strengthened the secondary boycott laws, moving them back into the *Trade Practices Act* and — perceptively given the waterfront blow-up — adding a new section preventing boycotts against international trade. Secondary boycotts were a powerful union tool. Many a company locked in a tussle with its own union suddenly found its postal and other services cut off as unions not involved in the actual dispute joined in to force a union victory.

The old TPC had been somewhat ambivalent in this area. There had been an unofficial agreement from the Fraser era between the TPC and Bob Hawke's ACTU that the TPC would act if a secondary boycott actually involved competition issues, but not if it was just the side-effect of an industrial punch-up. Employers were free themselves to take action under the secondary boycott provisions in such cases. Fels in his early days at the TPC had made the mistake of saying as much. Shadow Treasurer Peter Costello, with his legal background in the Dollar Sweets case, immediately jumped on him for not enforcing the law.

At a meeting with Costello, Fels explained this was a hangover from the late 1970s. Costello indicated he only wanted the law to be applied fairly and vigorously — with no favours to mates. This was clear indication of Opposition concern over Fels' friendship with Kelty. Costello went as far as to raise it, saying everyone knew about the relationship.

Fels denied any favours were given to the unions, and Costello accepted this assurance. Costello said the fact that Fels had a friendship with a union leader was not a hanging offence — provided the law was applied without fear or favour. It was to become a consistent message that Costello delivered to Fels, even after he became Treasurer with ministerial oversight of the ACCC.

As the waterfront dispute dragged on, with nightly scenes on television of clashes on the docks, the pressure on Fels and ACCC management to act became intense. Heat came from Workplace Relations Minister Peter Reith's office and his department. Reith was instrumental in organising the bid to break the power of the Maritime Union of Australia over the waterfront as a way to lift productivity and lower export costs.

Fels, however, was determined to play the dispute down the middle. He tried to also get evidence of collusion between the two major employers, Patrick and P&O. The ACCC issued Section 155 notices compelling the employers to divulge information. Nothing could be proven. While union boycotts were on television screens, any employer collusion was more difficult to uncover.

Pressure grew. Costello rang Fels after watching one of the many skirmishes on the docks on television. Costello had seen what he believed was a clear secondary boycott. 'Are you acting on it?' he wanted to know. Fels assured him the ACCC was collecting evidence. 'We're not caving in on it or going soft', said Fels.

The ACCC issued some stiff warnings to the MUA, some of which Fels learned later really upset the ACTU. Down on the docks, things were getting nasty. ACCC officers had a blazing 4 am row with MUA officials over a threatened union secondary boycott of tugs bringing ships into dock. The union backed away. The ACCC had been preparing to drop officers onto a ship by helicopter in order to get evidence.

The issue that finally drew the ACCC into legal action was the MUA's attempt to organise a boycott of cargo ships leaving Australia that had been loaded by Patrick with non-union labour. Within the Commission, Chief Executive Officer Hank Spier and commissioners including Alan Asher felt the ACCC just had to act, forcing Fels' hand. The ACCC sought and won a temporary injunction seeking big fines and permanent restraints against the MUA taking secondary boycotts.

But by the time the ACCC acted, the major parties were moving to a complex settlement after MUA wins in the courts against Patrick, which had set out to break union control over the waterfront. The settlement involved the MUA dropping its conspiracy case against Patrick, Reith and the National Farmers' Federation. The MUA refused to drop the case unless the ACCC dropped its action. Fels took the view that the Commission could not undertake such a landmark case and then suddenly drop it. 'We'll hang in', he told fellow commissioners. He was unaware that, behind the scenes, the government was shafting the ACCC, telling the parties that somehow it would get the Commission to back off.

The unions sought a meeting at the ACCC to negotiate a deal. Fels made it clear the ACCC was sticking to its guns, requiring a court-agreed injunction against further union boycotts, plus damages for exporters hit during the strike. The meeting became heated, and MUA chief John Coombs somewhat ostentatiously picked up his papers, stuffed them into a bag and walked out. This might have been a strong negotiating tactic when dealing with employers, but it did not work when the union itself had sought the meeting with the regulator. ACCC staff coming back from lunch were treated to the sight of ACTU Assistant Secretary Greg Combet on the pavement outside, imploring Coombs to come back into the meeting.

With the ACTU mounting a campaign to embarrass the ACCC as the recalcitrant blocking a final deal, the Commission saw that its future credibility was on the line. Tensions built up on the other side, as well. Companies financially hit when the strike blocked their exports had lodged many complaints with the ACCC. While many in the Commission believed these complaints had been orchestrated by the government, they still had to be dealt with.

As the pressure intensified, Fels had a private meeting with Kelty at a mutual friend's house in South Melbourne. Kelty was very critical of the ACCC's actions against the union, describing them as 'unjust'. Let the parties settle, and then take action, he argued — and there was just as much reason to move against the employers as the union. Kelty's main demand, however, was that the ACCC should drop its action against the MUA. Why not prosecute me? he volunteered. Kelty had been an active participant supporting the union on the docks.

Fels' response was that the ACCC was just doing its job, and would not back off. Moreover, it was the union, not an individual like Kelty, who was responsible. When it became clear that Fels was not going to budge, Kelty flew into a rage and threatened to end their friendship. The implication was that Fels' career could also be ruined. The ACTU had pretty much put him where he was, and with an election looming and the possibility of a Labor win, withdrawal of that friendship could be very career-threatening indeed.

Kelty's attempts to worry Fels into a settlement did not work. For a union leader with a reputation as a savvy operator, it was a very naïve pitch. Kelty was trying to use the old mates umbrella, but he must have realised it would be impossible for Fels to go back to his fellow commissioners — much less the government — after a private meeting with the ACTU and announce he had dropped the case.

As Fels resisted, Kelty became emotional about all the support he had given Fels in the past, implying he had been double-crossed. Eventually he walked out, declaring, 'That's the end of our friendship'.

⌐

Later, after the case was settled in a package deal in which the union agreed to the ACCC's terms and Patrick agreed to pay damages to exporters, Fels tried through mutual friends to make contact with Kelty, to no avail. For Fels it was personally very wounding. 'His family and ours were very close friends for 20 years', says Fels. 'We shared many causes. We fought many battles.'

Daughter Isabella also lamented the loss of contact with Kelty. 'Bill was very upset with dad because he thought that dad shouldn't have enforced the law against the unions', Isabella told the ABC's *Australian Story*. 'I was very sorry too because I got along really well with Bill Kelty, and I felt really close to him. We'd joke and we'd talk on the phone. I'm sad that that doesn't happen any more, that there's no contact.'

Fels and his family had learned that for effective competition regulators, principles can be very costly.

CHAPTER 6

'YOU'VE SAVED THE GOVERNMENT'

John Howard walked into a Cabinet briefing on the government's planned goods and services tax in 1999 just as Treasurer Peter Costello was finishing a statement with the words 'staff' and '10 million' close together. 'You mean Fels wants another 10 million staff?' exclaimed Howard, in mock horror.

Howard was quickly enlightened that the 'staff' and the '10 million dollars' were quite separate. 'We're only asking', Fels sheepishly joked. But if he had actually wanted huge numbers of new staff he might well have got them from a government desperate that its gamble on a new tax system would not cost it office at elections looming only 18 months later. The Howard Government lived in dread of what had happened after the introduction of a value added tax in Canada, when the government was wiped out at the next poll.

Overseeing the introduction of the new GST would prove the most politically risky and internally divisive task the ACCC had ever undertaken. If introduction of the tax was a disaster — and it was widely expected to be — the Commission's reputation as the consumers' friend, not to mention its image of professional competence, could have been trashed.

As it transpired, the arrival of the GST was an extraordinary success, although the Business Activity Statements drawn up by the

Australian Tax Office became something of a fly in the ointment. One minister would tell Fels: 'You've saved the government'. But in terms of hostility from both large and small business, and the Commission's internal harmony, the GST exercise was costly.

If the GST was a bear trap, Fels and the ACCC went into it with their eyes open. The first sniff came in a telephone call to Hank Spier from Costello's office before the 1998 election. Could the ACCC handle implementation of the planned new tax? Spier was interested but also sceptical. 'Why us?' he wanted to know. 'Because you've got an enforcement reputation', was the response. Why not the Australian Taxation Office? Spier asked. 'We want someone who will do the job and Tax will be too busy anyway', Costello's office replied.

Spier recognised the poisoned chalice of the new tax, but he also saw an upside — extra funding. Spier was in many ways the ACCC's corporate memory, having spent most of his working life at the competition regulator. He had seen the ACCC struggle to survive the years of underfunding and razor gang cuts. Funding promised by Labor when the ACCC was created in the mid-1990s never eventuated. As chief executive, Spier recognised the boon that extra funding could be for computers and videoconferencing to link ACCC offices around the states with Canberra, to give the Commission a more national enforcement approach.

Some commissioners were nervous about taking it on, although Allan Asher, curiously for someone with strong consumer sympathies, was in favour of the GST to remove the exemption of services from tax. Spier told the doubters that the ACCC's electronic upgrade 'will all be on the GST'. Moreover, the GST funding would overcome past neglect and put the ACCC on a proper funding basis.

Fels agreed with Spier's assessment. The two felt that if the ACCC was still enforcing the new tax law a year after its planned introduction on 1 July 2000, then they would have failed. Nevertheless, Fels agonised in his usual introspective way. 'We suddenly saw that we'd been given this very, very important role in the central policy of the government. The GST was the only issue for a while in government.

I could tell from the behaviour of ministers, bureaucrats and others that we were seen as tremendously important because there was a public suspicion that they'd all be ripped off', he says.

'From the ACCC's point of view I was concerned because it suddenly propelled us to the very centre of the political stage. Our reputation for years ahead would ride on how we dealt with the GST — it was a very risky thing. We might be seen as totally ineffectual, being given an absolutely major job by the government and failing. At another extreme, we might be seen as Stalinist, using draconian law to oppress business, all without much point. I was worried about us being bogged down in litigation for years ahead.'

At a meeting in Costello's office as the Treasurer was preparing some broad policies about the new tax to take into the 1998 election campaign, things were more hard-headed. Costello left Fels in no doubt of what he wanted from the ACCC — a 'really big stick' with not a lot of bureaucratic controls. Would there be an actual price control system, with full regulation requiring firms to notify price changes? 'No', said Costello. He wanted the big fine, and ACCC enforcement. 'We were seen as credible enforcers and able to put a lot of pressure on business to get results', says Fels.

Although Costello was criticised later for allowing the Tax Office too much bureaucratic leverage in devising the bungled Business Activity Statements, his instincts for the ACCC's actual price control oversight of the tax were spot on. Business, of course, would complain that the ACCC went overboard. 'Draconian' became an overworked pejorative. Costello and Howard, however, had one eye on Canada.

Costello's other options were to allow market forces to control GST prices — a course the ACCC believed Treasury favoured — or to create a new agency to handle the tax. Leaving it to market forces was politically too dangerous. The ACCC was a natural for the job. It already had the expertise of the old Prices Surveillance Authority under its wing, plus a track record in enforcement and a reputation of looking out for consumers. Consumers would see the Tax Office as about as friendly as a basket of rattlesnakes, while a new agency would lack the credibility of the ACCC, a credibility that government would lean heavily upon.

Costello's plans surprised Fels. Fines of $10 million for price exploitation under the GST! Modern price control systems usually have an administrative system in which firms apply for approval on their pricing. But Costello planned to introduce a general law that anybody could be fined $10 million for price exploitation — and wanted the ACCC to police it. Moreover, he wanted as few as possible prosecutions. The aim of the 'big stick' fines was clearly to frighten off potential price offenders. Later threats of 'shame notices' underlined the government's anxiety to publicise the results of non-compliance.

Fels began to realise the sheer enormity of the task. Costello was not just planning a 10 per cent GST. The new tax system was a complicated mix of removing the old wholesale tax and some state taxes, then adding a GST as well as a wine equalisation and luxury car tax, while also moving around a range of taxes and excise on petrol, diesel and alcohol. Later would come further reductions in petrol and diesel excise as well as beer excise, and the abolition of financial institutions duty and stamp duty on quoted marketable securities.

Fels estimated there were about one billion separate prices in retail alone. With the ups and downs of the new tax mixture, prices would both rise and fall. The potential for supplier and consumer confusion — much less price trickery — was enormous.

Fels took Costello's 'big stick' approach to heart. David Cousins, the former Prices Surveillance Authority chairman and another of the Maureen Brunt competition alumni from Monash, was brought in as a special GST commissioner. Cousins had been working with KPMG, and came to the job with the view that business cooperation was crucial.

As the GST gradually dominated the time of Cousins and his fellow commissioners, the ACCC engaged in a blitz of activity. Price guidelines, numerous explanatory guides, a web site, a prices hotline, and small business compliance guides poured forth. An everyday shopping guide giving estimations of how much prices might rise or fall was dropped into every letterbox in Australia, featuring Fels' smiling visage.

In two years the ACCC spent $20 million on 'consumer awareness', on top of the scores of millions spent by the government in television and media advertising. Fels became a household figure, with almost daily appearances in the media explaining GST activity. 'Keep an eye on those GST prices,' people would call to him in the street.

Nevertheless, the GST remained a monkey-on-the-back. A consultative group with the crucial retailers, chaired by Mitch Hooke (then chief executive of the Australian Food and Grocery Council), unearthed some thorny issues. One concerned a bundle of money — several hundred million dollars — that would be freed up between suppliers and the big supermarkets after wholesale sales tax ended. To whom should it go, the suppliers or the supermarkets? The ACCC decided this was a matter for the commercial players to sort out among themselves rather than a pricing issue for a regulator.

A bigger issue, however, was whether retailers should set GST-enhanced prices on dollar or percentage margins. The ACCC opted for percentage margins in draft pricing guidelines, but business exploded, saying this would effectively transfer to them some of the cost of the GST. A simple example shows how. Say a product sells for $6, with $5 in costs and $1 as the profit margin. If the elimination of wholesale sales tax and introduction of GST reduced production costs by 50¢ to $4.50, what should the new price be? If the original profit margin was expressed as a percentage, 20 per cent, the new price should be $5.40. But if expressed as a dollar margin — $1 — it would be $5.50. Magnify this example by the hundreds of millions of prices involved and you have some idea of the retailer profits at stake between percentage and dollar margins.

The ACCC eventually opted for the big picture of ensuring business compliance: it went for the dollar margin. In all fairness, business margins should not be squeezed to pay for the GST.

Retailing woes led to one of the few amusing incidents as the ACCC ran the GST gauntlet. A summit had been called between the retailers and government. Shopping counters would be the cutting edge for consumers of the new tax, and the government was anxious to minimise problems. Assembled in the annex off the Cabinet room were the Prime Minister, Treasurer, David Cousins, the heads of Coles and Woolworths, Dennis Eck and Roger Corbett, as well as the chief of the Australian Retailers Association, Phil Naylor and Mitch Hooke. Costello saw the meeting as the most crucial of the entire GST exercise. It went for five hours, covering everything from barcodes on products to dual ticketing.

But as it was about to get underway, there was no Fels. As the luminaries waited, Howard was handed a note. He read it, and then told the waiting meeting: Professor Fels is delayed giving a media conference!

Fels' famous penchant for publicity had finally resulted in him standing up the Prime Minister. Actually, Fels had a good explanation. He had arrived early at Parliament House and gone to the Treasurer's office. There he had quickly become embroiled in the GST flurry-of-the-day, this time on insurance. Nikki Savva, the Treasurer's press secretary, organised a doorstop press conference, and asked Fels to front it. Costello also urged him to do it. Fels took a bit of ribbing when he finally arrived in the Cabinet suite. Howard greeted him with, 'Thank you Professor Fels for sparing us some time from the media'.

Howard was being sarcastic, but the government couldn't really complain, given it was deliberately using Fels' credibility to 'sell' its confusing tax package. Such was Fels' profile that one cartoonist, adopting an old gag, depicted him walking down the street with Howard and Kim Beazley, the Opposition Leader. 'Who are those two blokes with Allan Fels?' an onlooker asks.

One aspect of this government embrace rankled with the independent purists at the ACCC: government insisted that all ACCC material on the GST be cleared by it. For an independent consumer agency, this set an unwelcome precedent.

As the 1 July 2000 GST introduction date approached, the politics intensified. The ACCC was embroiled in the government's indefensible

position on petrol pricing after a consultant's report predicted falls
after the swings-and-roundabout of the various tax changes, when
this was unlikely in country areas. But the major political heat came
over the so-called 'pricing rule'.

Assistant Treasurer Joe Hockey conceded in a speech that some
prices might rise more than the 10 per cent new GST. Hockey had
sought advice from Cousins' office beforehand, with airline frequent
flier points then rising by more than 10 per cent a burning issue. He
was informed there were bound to be occasions when a product
maker with no previous wholesale sales tax would have the
compliance costs of the new tax to pass on. It stood to reason,
therefore, that some prices could rise more than 10 per cent. But
when Hockey and Cousins conceded what appeared obvious, the
Saturday morning tabloid press's screaming headline — 'GST STING,
Business Allowed to Increase Prices on Top of 10% Tax' — put the
government in a panic.

Understandably so. This was manna for Labor. *The Daily Telegraph*
quoted Opposition Shadow Treasurer Simon Crean triumphantly
announcing: 'It's the first admission by the government that the GST
will be higher than 10 per cent'. The government could see their
GST disappearing down the drainpipe of price exploitation and
public hostility.

Hockey tried ringing around the ACCC to plan a response. Failing
to find Fels or Cousins, he located Spier at home and asked, 'What
can we do about it?' Spier was practical. 'Well, you know it's partly
true, Minister', he responded, 'can't we just fudge it?' The tabloid
coverage was dynamite to public acceptance of the new tax, as Hockey
knew. 'No. Can't do that', he said. 'I'll talk to Howard.'

Spier and Cousins conferred. The advice had been correct, if a
little too blunt for the tabloids. Then Hockey was back on the line.
He had spoken to both Costello and Howard, with the Prime Minister
flatly declaring: 'Change the policy'. Having promised at the recent
election that no prices would rise more than 10 per cent, Howard
could see their credibility was at stake. 'The Prime Minister has said

there's to be no price rises higher than 10 per cent', Hockey told the ACCC. 'I will direct the Commission.' An indignant Spier told him that he couldn't do that, at which Hockey said he would again speak to Howard. He rang Spier back, telling him that despite Spier's protestations that he lacked the power, he had already issued a press release that he would be directing the ACCC that GST price rises must be limited to 10 per cent. Hockey was sent out to suffer the cuts of the media. 'Joe, you're going to lose some bark on this', Howard had already warned him on the GST.

The ACCC was stuck with a political directive. In fact, it never received any written order from Hockey. Spier was right: the government lacked the power. But Howard's order had actually done the ACCC a favour in a way. 'Ten is 10 is 10' quickly became a mantra, clearing up much of the public confusion on how much prices could rise.

Nevertheless, the political flak, public contortions and business hostility the ACCC endured over the 10 per cent rule were all painful. In effect, the rule meant sections of business, particularly service industries where the old wholesale sales tax had not applied, were being asked to absorb some of the costs of the GST. They were told in so many words: go to 10 now if you have to, and come back for more later. The Reserve Bank later reported some 'rebuilding' of retailers' margins in the first half of 2001, indicating the margin depletion of the new tax.

Some disgruntled businesses threatened legal action on the basis that the 10 per cent rule was not legal. If you do that, the ACCC responded, you'll be seen by the public as price gouging, and remember Allan Fels is pretty good with the media. 'Do you really want to run this?' was the hard question. The answer, apparently, was 'no'. Not one legal challenge was launched against the price rule. Any legal action would likely have succeeded. The ACCC was playing with a particularly weak legal hand, as will be seen.

It was not just the ACCC engaging in some arm twisting. Dual ticketing of goods with pre- and post-GST prices also became an issue as the new tax approached. The ACCC had long opposed dual ticketing, arguing that it confused consumers. An earlier deal hammered out with retailers was that consumers would always be entitled to the lower price if an article had two price tags. Although the ACCC's pricing guidelines for the new tax allowed a short window of dual ticketing around the date of introduction, Woolworths proposed pre- and post-GST price tags well before that date.

Joe Hockey put a call through to Woolworths' chief Roger Corbett. Hockey's message was graphic: the government would not like to see a major retailer swinging from a light pole in Sydney's Martin Place, but if that was what it took to stop price exploitation, so be it. Back off or I'll unleash the ACCC on you, was the essential message. Woolworths complied, quickly removing the dual tickets in a massive internal operation. 'They were hauled off', says Costello.

Businesspeople could be dealt with behind the scenes. The Labor Opposition, however, was full frontal and highly visible. Labor's strategy was that public hostility to the new tax would be the key to their election win in 2001, so their response to the introduction of the GST in mid-2000 had all the atmospherics of an election campaign. Deputy Leader Simon Crean waved plastic bags of lettuce and children's clothing around in parliament in a bid to destroy the GST in public confusion. Aggrieved groups from small business to caravan park residents joined the swelling chorus.

In Labor's eyes, Fels and the ACCC were just doing the Howard Government's bidding. With the waterfront dispute still fresh in mind, some of the exchanges were bitter. At one Senate hearing, Stephen Conroy, Shadow Minister for Financial Services, told Allan Asher: 'You are running the biggest fear and intimidation campaign this country has seen for small business, and you can sit there with a straight face and say that you do not think these [dual ticketing guidelines] are frightening to people'. Senator Conroy mocked the three ACCC witnesses as 'like the three wise monkeys trying to pretend that 10 per cent is a legal cap'.

At one Senate Committee hearing, Labor accused Fels of misleading the Committee. At a previous session Fels had asked to leave at 6.20 pm to catch a plane. Outside, on the way to the airport, he was caught by the media, and gave an impromptu news conference. Labor had the conference timed — eight minutes. Fels could have spent that time with the committee, Labor argued. The fact that Labor was reduced to timing Fels' media conferences showed the level of desperation to score political points off the GST.

Labor enjoyed some success tying the ACCC in all sorts of knots over price confusion. But as the GST bedded in, Labor realised it had overdone the scare campaign, and that attacking the 'consumer's friend', the ACCC, was not smart politics.

⤶

As the ACCC worked up to the GST with a seemingly unending stream of pamphlets, education programs, media briefings, public hotlines and dire warnings to business, the public image was one of smooth professionalism. Internally it was a different story. Commissioners were seriously divided on whether to take a 'big stick' or a cooperative approach to business compliance with the tax changes. As well, there were agonising doubts over whether the new price exploitation laws for the GST would stand any legal challenges.

Worryingly, the legal advice was that they would not. The temporary price exploitation section added to the *Trade Practices Act* outlawed 'unreasonably high' prices in relation to the new GST. 'Unreasonably high' was not defined. But factors to be taken into account were the supplier's costs, supply and demand conditions, and … wait for it … 'any other relevant matter'.

'Any other relevant matter' freaked out the ACCC. A company could pretty much present *anything* as a reason for jacking up prices during the GST's introduction. Many accountants and lawyers, for instance, traditionally review their fee schedules at the start of the new financial year. With a new 10 per cent GST and no offsetting wholesale tax reduction, could they set fees above the 10 per cent and get away with it on the basis of past practice?

The ACCC pressed for some tighter definitions, but it was wasting its time. The loose wording had actually been drafted personally by Costello, for what he saw as a very good reason. The price exploitation laws, in Costello's view, reversed the onus of proof, declaring a price 'unreasonably high' unless otherwise proved. The lawyers had been 'stuffing around', Costello says, so he personally wrote the section.

Was there pressure to tighten it? 'Yes', says Costello. 'The lawyers said, "This is all too vague, this won't work". But my view was we were reversing the onus of proof. We were making it an offence to raise your price.' Costello saw his wording as a necessary defence for retailers.

The loose law left Fels and the ACCC as the proverbial GST emperor with no clothes. 'We didn't exactly publicise it', says Fels about his silence on the issue during the GST period. So was the ACCC's tough line, with threats of 'shame notices' to business, a bluff? 'I don't want to deny there was an element of that to it, but all these things are immensely complicated', he says. 'This law was not quite meaningless. It puts the emphasis on the fact that prices mustn't go above what is suggested by the tax changes. I mean, this is how we felt about it. The law is not meaningless, it's just very, very difficult …'

Allan Asher, chief of the ACCC's enforcement committee, believed the law was just unenforceable. The only way to make it work was to 'persuade business that we were just going to be all over them through a massive campaign, almost a blitzkreig, in advance of the law coming into force'. Asher says: 'It was a huge task of giving them the immediate apprehension of enforcement, and that that would induce compliance. It was always my view, and still is, that once some of these laws started to become unpicked in a court, it would be far too late. So the 10 per cent issue involved massive guidance and massive publicity. Sadly, it did cost us our relationship with small business for a while'.

In his usual energetic enforcement style, Asher had created a 'fast-track' legal system which would be used to nab GST offenders. This was designed to get alleged offenders into court within 24 hours.

Asher created teams in each state, using the cream of the ACCC's enforcement talent and signing contracts with private law firms and the Australian Government Solicitor to do the initial investigation, develop the documents and file the actions. Like much of Asher's energetic enforcement, this fast-tracking offended a lot of business.

Interestingly, Asher avoided the new GST price exploitation laws, and went for legal actions under old *Trade Practices Act*'s false and misleading conduct provisions. Was he deliberately avoiding the GST laws? 'Avoiding it absolutely', he says. 'It was an absolute loser.' And nothing was said about this at the time? 'Exactly', he says.

David Cousins, the GST commissioner, takes a slightly different view. The law may have been weak — and he tried to change it to bring more market forces into play — but the fact that it forced the ACCC to use existing false and misleading conduct powers may have saved some 'silly regulation'. In any case, trying to enforce a weak law would not have been sensible from the 'big picture' of GST implementation.

Cousins was alluding to another aspect of the ACCC's role in the new tax that has also gone unpublicised: the Commission was split down the centre on how to enforce the GST. On one side were the 'big stick' Asher forces, wanting to find a few examples to show business the ACCC was deadly serious. On the other was Cousins with his more self-regulatory style of compliance, pushing for voluntary agreements with major business groups.

Cousins had brought in some of his team from KPMG, and with their greater business orientation they began negotiating voluntary compliance deals with the big banks, retailers and food companies. The idea was that chief executives would put their name on a document saying exactly what their pricing response would be to the GST. Fels would also publicly sign off on these. Public voluntary agreements from the major corporations like Coles and Woolworths would send a powerful signal to all business of the type of behaviour that was expected. However, securing voluntary agreements was no mean feat. Business was being asked to hand over a lot of its confidential pricing information to the ACCC, information that many feared would be later used against them.

As these deals were being negotiated in the lead-up months to the GST, the tension crackled within the Commission. Asher was implacably opposed. 'I saw those [voluntary agreements] in much the same way that Martin Luther saw the selling of indulgences in the pre-Reformation period', he says. 'Going to all these big companies and saying sign up to a voluntary agreement is more or less giving them permission to steal, because we could not thereafter take enforcement action against them. I opposed all of those. I thought they were just contrary to what needed to be done. Deals like that with big business would ensure that we could only ever take action against the small-fry.'

Asher, of course, was instrumental in turning around an earlier ACCC culture of chasing small offenders to, as he puts it, 'picking on the biggies and the baddies'. For him and some others within the ACCC, voluntary agreements would compromise the Commission, setting it to chase small-fry while big business could do what it wanted. (Asher's Martin Luther comparison reveals another strand of the religious streak at the ACCC. While Fels is a committed Catholic, Asher is a strict Presbyterian, building churches in his spare time.)

With Asher running the enforcement side in Canberra, and Cousins and his GST team in Melbourne, the ACCC's telephone and video lines buzzed with tension. Asher's driving personality can be formidable in meetings. Many an ACCC staffer would wince in video conferences as Asher rode shotgun on enforcement. His aggressive style would create dangerous external enemies. Nevertheless, it was widely admired within the Commission after its years of keeping a low profile.

In the middle of all this, two watershed cases arose: Video Ezy and David Jones, the upmarket retailer. On 11 April Fels issued the ACCC's first — and only — price exploitation notice under the new GST laws, to Video Ezy. While the prosecution law may have been weak, price exploitation notices were undoubtedly a powerful tool. They constituted prima facie evidence of 'unreasonably high' prices. Any such court finding exposed companies to fines of up to $10 million.

The allegation was that Video Ezy sought to anticipate the GST — due on 1 July — by setting 'unreasonably high' prices several months before the new tax. The ACCC claimed it had received complaints of Video Ezy staff telling customers, 'The price rise is to introduce the GST now so that people get used to the idea of paying more. It won't be such a shock when the GST comes in'.

The notice was issued only after a vigorous internal debate. The Cousins forces believed this was rats-and-mice stuff being chased by the 'troglodytes' in the Canberra office. Better to concentrate on the big picture of compliance.

In return, the Asher forces regarded their Melbourne colleagues as 'gun-shy'. Asher believed there was no such thing as a small case or a big case. It was all a matter of symbolism. The litigation test for Asher was always the market impact — would a case ram it home to business executives that they could be liable for fines of up to $10 million?

With Video Ezy the ACCC got symbolism in spades. Video Ezy had 480 stores and 3.5 million customers, exactly the type of case that would make ordinary Australians sit up and take notice about the GST. Also, the ACCC had been running the line that it had 19 million price watchdogs on the beat, suggesting that every Australian would be carefully watching prices. The neighbourhood video store epitomised that consumer price watchdog concept.

The case also became the touchstone of business antipathy to the barking bulldog ACCC approach to the GST. For many in business it proved that the ACCC was really only after a few 'scalps' to frighten everyone else. Interestingly, Asher says that he had pretty much reached agreement with Video Ezy's lawyers on a deal before legal action was launched. The deal involved some free video hires to customers who might have been overcharged in pre-GST pricing. But he says Video Ezy was enraged by some remarks by Fels in talking to the media about the price exploitation notice, and the deal fell through.

The case the ACCC then brought against Video Ezy on 26 May involved not just the company, but three senior managers, including the general manager, Mr Peter Sciciuna, and a director, Mr Daryl McCormack. Video Ezy claimed it was being made a 'scapegoat'. But the ACCC claimed the company's actions went beyond the remarks of a few junior employees, indicating that its study of company documentation showed 'compelling evidence' of a breach of the Act.

Records of Video Ezy franchise meetings throughout 1999 are sprinkled with GST references. 'GST suggestion raised again to look at our prices', says one. 'GST. Now a good time to review our prices', says another. Whether these constitute a 'smoking gun' that would have persuaded a court was never put to the test.

Privately, the company complained that documents submitted to government to support a possible case against Video Ezy were incorrect and that no price exploitation had occurred. Chief Executive Robert Maidment sought the assistance of Dick Warburton, the influential businessman who chaired David Jones and was a member of the Reserve Bank Board. Warburton was also chairman of the Business Coalition for Tax Reform, and as such had fairly regular contact with Costello. Warburton reported back to Maidment that Costello had assured him the ACCC had a genuine case. Maidment strongly maintained the company's innocence.

The issue was batted back and forth as the GST came and went. Within the ACCC it was always intended to 'park' the case until the GST blew over. In April 2001, when the GST was becoming as stale as yesterday's newspaper, the parties announced an agreement. Cousins had held out against the prosecution proceeding. The ACCC dropped its action in return for Video Ezy agreeing to court orders that it had made some false and misleading representations to customers, offering reduced video hire in Townsville (the source of most complaints), sending letters of apology to customers and developing its trade practices compliance and staff training, as well as contributing to the ACCC's costs.

In effect, both sides withdrew from the battlefield with their colours still flying. Fels said the ACCC had developed a 'serious case', but decided it was not worth pursuing it over the next year or so through likely legal appeals. Maidment maintained that the company's actions did not amount to a breach of the price exploitation laws, but conceded the ACCC 'have a different view'. For his part, Costello believes 'there was something behind it'.

Was Video Ezy just a convenient scapegoat used by the ACCC to highlight its powers to discipline business for the introduction of the GST, as many alleged? Certainly the records of Video Ezy franchise meetings are ambiguous, with references to the GST that can be read several ways. Records of the ACCC's interviews with Video Ezy executives are not available. Nor are government records that Video Ezy claims show it was all a set-up. At the end of the day, however, Video Ezy put its hand up over some improprieties by staff and agreed to offer compensation.

Warburton, in his capacity as David Jones chairman, was also involved in an unhappy wrangle with the ACCC. The retailer had been negotiating a voluntary agreement with Cousins' team when some of the Canberra enforcement team began looking at prices in David Jones' advertising. The company found itself in the uncomfortable position of dealing with two arms of the ACCC.

After an internal debate, the ACCC decided, in somewhat complicated terms as outlined by Fels to the Senate, that it could not reach an unequivocal legal position that David Jones had breached the law. Cousins argued there was nothing wrong with the advertisements in question. The retailer offered to bring forward its GST advertising campaign to create greater consumer awareness, and set up a hotline for customers.

The debate was all in-house, except that it managed to find its way into *The Australian Financial Review*. Warburton was less than impressed. He let fly, accusing the ACCC of infringing against basic standards of justice by exposing innocent parties to public defamation while leaving them with very little — if any — scope for redress. The leak, however, had not come from the ACCC. Fels had been contacted by *The Australian Financial Review*, which already had the information, probably from the complainant.

As it happened, the day after the press leak Warburton and his David Jones team were involved in a video hook-up with Cousins and his ACCC group. Warburton asked for explanations, and pointedly asked how the leak occurred. Cousins could throw no light on it.

The Opposition took a different tack. Senator Conroy in Senate Estimates dropped a suggestion that David Jones had got off because Warburton was a friend of Costello's. Fels took exception to this. The ACCC, he said, 'has taken on much bigger and more powerful fish than David Jones or Mr Warburton'. The Commission had launched prosecutions against a 'who's who' of business that probably included friends of ministers in Liberal and Labor governments. 'But they have never complained to me, or it has never been a factor', he told the Senate committee. 'So the suggestion that this came into the David Jones matter is quite absurd and just ridiculous.'

Though the Video Ezy and David Jones cases resulted in a rather unhappy lead-up to the GST, the actual introduction of the tax went surprisingly smoothly. Still, the introduction date for the GST, 1 July, was a nervous time. In preparation for an arduous day, Fels went to a gym for a workout early in the morning. He bought a bottle of mineral water, but the gym owner was uncertain whether or not GST applied, indicating the widespread confusion about the tax. Perhaps there was no GST if the mineral water was consumed outside, as food was GST free? Fels went outside to drink it.

Fels had done a pre-recorded television interview to be screened on the Sunday morning before the GST's introduction and, unusually for him, managed to get himself in somewhat of a tangle over the dreaded 10 per cent price rise issue. Realising this, he arranged with the network to do a live broadcast instead. Fels shifted the interview to other matters, and the insurance industry woke that day to find the ACCC was taking a serious look at them.

The ACCC had put in advance planning to do snapshots of price movements. It had already monitored prices before GST, and in the wake of the new tax was able to report that price rises across a 'basket' of ordinary goods were broadly within estimates. In the three months after the introduction of the GST prices rose, on average, about 2.6 per cent, compared to earlier estimates of 3.0 per cent. Separately, the Consumer Price Index 'All Groups' rose 3.7 per cent in the September quarter, settling back to a 0.3 per cent rise in the December quarter.

⌐

The GST introduction was a mammoth task for the ACCC. It fielded 51 000 complaints, investigated about 7000 separate matters, obtained refunds of around $21 million, instituted court proceedings in 11 matters (Video Ezy was the only one brought under the temporary GST price exploitation laws) and accepted 55 court-enforceable undertakings from companies.

Business complained that profit margins had been squeezed, with some alleging that the ACCC was partly responsible for an economic slowdown which followed the GST's introduction. The Reserve Bank, however, gave this view no support. The ACCC could claim that its vigorous publicity style, and particularly the shopping price guidelines booklet just prior to GST, had reduced inflationary expectation from the new tax.

In political terms, the ACCC and Fels basked in a job well done. Both got a huge lift in their public profile. Howard ministers congratulated Fels. 'Allan did it brilliantly and business hated it', is Cousins' summary. 'The most amazingly successful operation, beyond my wildest imaginations', says Costello, who publicly thanked Fels for a 'magnificent job'.

The ACCC spent more than $50 million in its GST implementation. But as Spier had predicted, funding from government boomed, up from $38 million in the year before the GST to $57 million in the year leading up to the tax, and $75 million the year later. Also included was a new legal reserve fund that will build to $20 million. Fels is somewhat defensive about the funding increase being seen as a 'reward' for the GST. He points to the fact that it was awarded only following a review by the Department of Finance, regarded around the bureaucracy as scrooges. But Finance still reflects the government of the day, and there was no doubt the Howard Government was grateful to the ACCC.

While the ACCC benefited from this government largess after years of parsimony, there was some internal pain as well. Cousins decided not to take up the offer of another term as an ACCC commissioner, despite Fels' backing. Cousins had hoped that the GST exercise might somewhat temper the ACCC's hard line enforcement style, but events had killed off that hope. 'The enforcement policy was so locked in it was not going to change', says Cousins, who is now Director of Consumer Affairs in Victoria.

As successful as the GST implementation was for the ACCC, it left an embittered business community pondering what they could do about Fels. It also left the government wondering about the new public power of Fels. The high-profile regulator had been very helpful, but was he now too powerful?

CHAPTER 7

'READY, FIRE, AIM!'

One statistic tells the story of Allan Fels' era at the Australian Competition and Consumer Commission. In 1992, when he became chairman, the old Trade Practices Commission launched four or five cases a year against companies for various breaches of the Act. Now it launches about 40, with more than 70 to 80 cases running in any year.

Enforcement of the *Trade Practices Act* was the real engine room of Fels' ACCC. Apart from use of the media, it is the one issue that has pushed Fels into the eye of business.

ACCC enforcement roams across almost every nook and cranny of corporate life. A typical weekly meeting of commissioners will trawl across an incredible range of issues, from salmon farmers to Qantas and the future of Australia's digital communications.

In its 2001–02 annual report, for instance, the ACCC reported that during the year it had pinged Colgate-Palmolive for resale price maintenance, NRMA Insurance for misleading conduct, and the Maritime Union of Australia for harassment and boycott activity. In another cartel bust, this time in the electricity transformer industry, courts imposed penalties of $14.5 million against a range of companies, including Wilson Transformer, AW Tyree and Schneider Electric. Alstom Australia was fined $7 million. The

Commission also commenced proceedings against: Qantas, alleging misuse of market power; several milk wholesalers and petrol retailers, alleging price fixing; Wizard Mortgage, Mitre 10, Virgin Mobile and Total Communications for misleading price advertising; and Esanda, Commonwealth Bank and Westfield for alleged unconscionable conduct.

While Fels has been the highly visible public front of this marked change in the ACCC's culture, behind the scenes an unusual dynamic has been at work. Fels arrived at the TPC in 1992 to find that a former consumer activist, Allan Asher, had just assumed responsibility for the ACCC's crucial enforcement activities. Asher was no ordinary consumer activist. Enemies have called him a zealot, a label Asher would undoubtedly wear with honour.

After a stint as an accountant, Asher left the profession in horror at what he calls its 'infinite flexibility' to adjust figures for big clients. He spent some years as a financial analyst, before deciding to do law, drifting into a research job at *Choice* magazine while completing his degree. Asher had finally found his calling, rising to become advocate and chief executive of the Australian Consumers' Association. He left in 1983 to run corporate affairs for the Overseas Telecommunications Commission, quickly coming to the realisation that governments cannot run businesses. Asher was appalled at the way government had no idea how to deal with consumers. He was also shocked by the way dividends were ripped out of the OTC despite its obvious need for new capital to spend on fibre cable systems.

On holiday in Scotland in 1988, Asher received a surprise telephone call from Attorney-General Michael Duffy's office. A commissioner's spot was coming up on the Trade Practices Commission. The consumer movement was very concerned at the Commission's handling of big mergers such as Murdoch's acquisition of The Herald & Weekly Times Ltd, Coles/Myer and Ansett/East West. In fact, the ACA had put out a press release saying that Bob McComas as chairman was like putting a fox in charge of the chicken coop, an unfair comment. Would Asher like to be one of the commissioners?

The subsequent appointment was attacked by the Liberals as political. Asher had indeed been a member of the Labor Party some years before. He had left, finding the ALP too conservative and unwilling to embrace new ideas! McComas advised him to just shrug off the attacks.

Asher arrived not long before Bob Baxt took up the chairmanship. He recalls Baxt telling him that the TPC had a 'cowardly' image. In Asher's view, Baxt began to generate a more legal approach, but still the Commission undertook just a few cases a year. By the time of Fels' arrival in 1992, Asher was in charge of the Commission's enforcement and raring to go, particularly on consumer cases.

The two formed one of the more extraordinary regulatory duos ever seen in Australia: Mr Outside and Mr Inside. Fels with his media skills publicised the consumer messages of new cases, while Asher ran the internal enforcement committee, preparing the litigation. They turned the Commission's enforcement into an outcomes approach, picking up cases that would generate the maximum leverage to ensure compliance across an industry.

It was like an episode of Elliott Ness and his Untouchables chasing Chicago gangsters. Asher overturned the Commission's entire legal approach to enforcement. Previously the Commission would just accept the senior counsel selected by the Australian Government Solicitor to run a Commission case. No longer. Asher went out and personally interviewed senior counsel. 'That was quite revolutionary', he says. 'Many refused to work for us because some senior counsel, then and probably now, are so full of their personal pride and hubris that they don't believe that they should be told what to do.'

The Commission began staff training programs, telling them: 'You're the boss ... it's the Commission that decides what case we're going to run and we'll get lawyers who will run our theories'.

Within the Commission Asher junked the cautious mentality that wanted to 'research everything to death'. He regarded that as a failure, as while it might ensure fewer losses, it meant cases were weakened and possibly futile as they took years to get to court before consumers gained any relief. Asher's solution was to cut to the chase, instructing staff running complex investigations to forget all the peripheral counts of misconduct. 'Just grab two or three indicative areas of wrongful conduct and we'll go for those', he told staff.

'Ready, fire, aim', Asher called his new style, and the staff loved it. Asher seems to have been something of a terror to work for, remorselessly quizzing field staff in video meetings of the regular Friday enforcement committee. But the staff were devoted to him for the activist way he put the Commission on the map. Asher made the Commission an exciting place to work.

Asher just didn't pursue companies for breaches. He began a vigorous pursuit of executives involved. Fines had been increased in the early 1990s to $10 million maximum for a company and $500 000 for individuals. For Asher, even the new fines on companies were little more than parking tickets. 'A company might get fined $1 million and the chief executive would go along to the Melbourne Club or wherever he hung out on the weekends and get a bit of a chiacking from his mates', he says. 'But even a penalty of a tenth of that, if it was against him personally, that really started to count.'

Many an executive now found themselves defending personal legal action by the Commission. It stung. Mayne Nickless was upset when its then managing director, William Bytheway, was not only fined $40 000 but described in a TPC press release as having a 'central role' in the express freight industry cartel.

As well as executives, Asher also pursued appeals. McComas had declined to appeal following the Commission's loss in its first freight case. Now Asher began using legal appeals systems not only to combat opponents but to demonstrate to the Attorney-General's officers which areas of the trade practices law needed tightening.

A Commission insider at the time outlines the Asher thunderbolt: 'The thing he taught Fels was the benefit of activism and of using the courts as hard as they did. I'm not saying that Fels didn't come at it from essentially the same point of view. But Asher was the one who would pursue the nuts and bolts of a strategy. If he was involved in a case he would pursue people to the bitter end. He had the energy to keep doing it and to drive other people to do it. He was fantastic at litigation. His whole view was that you use the process and you resist other people using the process to frustrate you. Typically in litigation a lot of the time was spent in delay. People with deep pockets win because they use money to delay. Asher was magnificent at not letting that happen. The other side might do something, but he would always have a response. He'd always be trying to get Commission staff on the front foot. He changed the whole culture of the place. I mean, basically, he changed it'.

The culture change within the Commission accompanied the increase in its powers. Tighter merger laws, the ability to negotiate court-enforceable undertakings and higher fines were just the start. As the 1990s progressed, the Hilmer report saw the extension of competition law to the professions and government business. In 1998, following the Reid inquiry into fair trading, the Howard Government empowered the ACCC to stop unconscionable conduct by a corporation against small business. In transactions under $1 million the ACCC could intervene to stop a stronger party dealing with a disadvantaged smaller company in a harsh or oppressive manner. The GST also saw the ACCC armed with temporary price exploitation powers.

Another factor added to the burgeoning powers of the ACCC. The government decided not to create an array of smaller industry-specific regulators but get the ACCC to do the job. Fels' Commission assumed the primary role for competition and economic regulation of telecommunications services when the sector was opened up. As well, it was given the job of transmission regulator under the national third-party access code for the natural gas pipeline system.

Academic critic Professor Warren Pengilley slammed this aggregation of ACCC powers: 'When the Soviet Navy does not know what to do with its submarines' spent nuclear fuel, it simply throws it into the North Sea without much consideration for the long-term effects of its action', he said. 'We do much the same thing in this country in relation to regulation.'

Critics might carp, but there was method in the seeming madness. A single regulator ensures that competition regulation is consistent across various industry sectors. It also works against regulatory capture, when a powerful industry can dominate its regulator.

It was not as if Asher and his enforcement team didn't already have a big stick to wield. Murphy's original *Trade Practices Act* gave the Commission formidable power to demand information and documents. The Commission, or chairman, can simply issue a mandatory requirement for a company to produce records, or for executives to appear before the Commission for questioning. Called '155s' after the relevant section of the Act, these authorisations also enable the Commission to do 'walk-ins', or raids, to find material.

The Commission, however, cannot use this extraordinarily powerful investigative tool just for 'fishing expeditions'. It must have 'reason to believe' that the person has information about an offence, or a possible offence. That forces the Commission to have elaborate justification before issuing a 155, as it might need to justify its 'reason to believe' in a later court case.

It took both the business community and the courts some time to appreciate the full power of 155s. A TPC officer in an affidavit tendered in court told of the reaction of a corporate executive when served a 155: 'You ......, you can go and get ...... You are a pack of ...... I'm not accepting service you ......'. The judge considered the affidavit, and asked the TPC officer: 'Can you please explain the dots?'

The use of 155s has exploded in recent years as the ACCC has pressed its enforcement activities. In 1998–99 the Commission issued 84 mandatory notices for information or interviews. In 2001–02 that had grown to 438.

On top of 155s, as the merger test was tightened the Commission also gained the so-called '87Bs' mentioned in chapter 5, enabling it to negotiate court-enforceable undertakings. Previously it could make only voluntary agreements, some of which failed. The most spectacular of these was the Commission's failure to enforce the sale of SkyWest by TNT/News as part of the Ansett takeover of East West

Airlines. Both the Griffith and Cooney parliamentary inquiries urged that negotiated deals be made court-enforceable.

The ACCC regards merger agreements as a bit like marriage promises. The world is offered before the marriage, but afterwards it may be a different story. 87Bs help maintain the promises.

The new 87Bs added enormously to Asher's and Fels' growing armoury. They injected a new dynamic into dealing with business. Instead of a 'see you in court' stand-off, Fels and Asher could now directly strike deals that business was legally obliged to implement, and brush aside the usual phalanx of corporate lawyers. Almost every executive involved in negotiations with the Commission of recent years has a 'war story'. Interestingly, though, 87Bs allowed many transactions through that otherwise might have been blocked. 87Bs stretched across much of the Commission's work. Courts have even encouraged them when they lack the power to, say, order a compliance program. In 1999–2000, with the new tax regime looming, the ACCC struck 74 separate 87B undertakings, 16 of them in relation to the GST.

Asher wasted little time in going straight to the top. For example, AMP chiefs found themselves in direct negotiations with Asher over a Commission investigation of misleading insurance policies. Asher had drafted a class action for the policyholders, although it was unclear at the time — and still is — whether the Commission has the legal jurisdiction to file such actions. He handed them a copy of the proposed action, telling them the Commission would file it in court the next day unless AMP agreed to a settlement. AMP agreed on the spot and reimbursed policyholders more than $50 million.

For corporate Australia and the Commission, things were starting to get upfront and personal. Asher likened it to the end of the World War I-style civilities, when officers on opposing sides remained friendly to each other. 'It started to turn nasty because we were making it personal', he reflects. 'I think that's where some of the animosity started to develop between business and the Commission.'

By the end of Fels' second year as chairman, the Trade Practices Commission was taking on more than a dozen cases a year, and climbing. It was paying rewards for consumers and busting price-fixing cartels.

One of the biggest busts was in the air freight express business. The TPC had suffered a bloody nose when it lost an earlier case in this industry prior to Fels' arrival. In May 1990 it started investigating new allegations of price fixing. The case dragged on for four years, through appeals and objections. The nub of the Commission's allegation was that the three major companies, TNT Australia Pty Ltd, Ansett Transport Industries and Mayne Nickless Ltd, had for many years been party to an agreement to ensure no competition in the industry. As these three accounted for some 90 per cent of industry sales — including such brands as TNT Express, Comet, Kwikasair, Wards Express, Ipec Air and Jetpress Air Couriers — the benefits to the cartel of protecting itself from new entrants were obvious. Independents found it difficult to compete.

It was called variously 'the Peace', 'the Accord' or 'Détente'. Members of the cartel met periodically to fix prices, rig tenders, square-off for stealing each other's clients, and arrange to increase rates to provide 'cover' for each other with clients. Square-offs would entail both money settlements and 'burning' of clients to return them. 'Burning' meant hiking rates or poor service, both designed to offload customers anxious for time-sensitive deliveries. It was a classic cartel, and the Commission's investigations unearthed disturbing evidence of dubious standards of behaviour by executives in the late 1980s and early 1990s.

At one internal meeting of Mayne Nickless, Pat Kearns, then director of operations, said: 'I'm getting flak from TNT about stealing their accounts. You will have to toe the line. Leave TNT alone. Don't steal their accounts and when they are uprating, give them cover. They will do the same for us'.

At a cartel meeting at the offices of TNT in Mascot, Sydney, Paul Brown, TNT's General Manager and co-chair of the meeting of supposed rivals, opened proceedings with the following:

> Thanks you all for attending. We are here to discuss the arrangement and the problems associated with it. There

has been too much taking of each other's accounts and we are meeting here to settle the differences between our companies. We are also going to assure each other that you are going to abide by the arrangement between us, and you are also going to settle any individual disputes which exist between you at this time.

At another meeting in the Regent Hotel in Sydney, John Mullen, representing TNT and Ansett, said: 'We have all been out there doing silly things, and we have got to set some minimum prices, and we have to stick to them'. Such was the corporate mindset in at least one industry more than a quarter of a century after Barwick's landmark Act. Mayne Nickless was ordered to pay $7.7 million in penalties and costs. TNT and Ansett, who had dropped their defence of legal proceedings, paid agreed fines of $4.1 million and $900 000 respectively. Sixteen executives from the three companies also paid fines, with individual penalties ranging from $40 000 to $75 000.

Fels hailed it as 'the coming of age of competition law in Australia'. Clyde Cameron, the ex-Whitlam Government minister and shearer, sent Fels an extraordinary congratulatory note. 'Every time I see your photograph in the newspapers, I know I am looking into the face of a really great Australian whose soul is not for sale', he said. 'I wish we had a parliament of Allan Felses!'

The ACCC also won other headline-grabbing cases against several major cartels in the mid-1990s. The Federal Court in 1995 fined three big pre-mixed concrete suppliers and their executives $20 million for fixing prices in the Brisbane, Gold Coast and Toowoomba markets. Boral, Pioneer and CSR were each fined $6.6 million, while six executives incurred fines ranging from $50 000 to $100 000.

The cartel had met regularly, conspiring to fix prices and agreeing to maintain each company's market share at predetermined levels. They would not compete against each other's major clients, known as 'pets', or 'koalas'. An accountant was even engaged to monitor market shares between the three.

The concrete cartel bust showed the new-style ACCC direct negotiations with business on competition infringements. After assembling its case, the ACCC told the three companies it was happy to let the courts decide. Negotiations started for an agreed settlement. With the new fines running at $10 million per offence, and the ACCC listing numerous offences, a quick calculation put the possible total upwards of $450 million. The companies of course argued that fines should be much lower.

With the parties a long way apart on a settlement to take to the court, the three chief executives — Tony Berg of Boral, Geoff Kells of CSR and John Schubert of Pioneer — arranged a joint presentation for Fels and Asher in the ACCC's Canberra headquarters. The session lasted more than three hours as the three CEOs put the case for lower fines.

'They're still far too low', said the regulators. 'We're still way up here', indicating the upper end of the spectrum. In another three-hour session at the ACCC's Melbourne office, Fels and Asher put the case for higher fines. Finally, at 6.30 on a Friday evening agreement was reached: $21 million divided into three lots of $7 million. A court later set this at $6.6 million for each company, with fines for six executives ranging from $50 000 to $100 000.

If the concrete cartel fixed the price of pours at major Queensland building projects, a separate 'coffee club' also fixed the price of fire safety equipment. Penalties for the 'coffee club' finally ran to some $15 million as the ACCC brought 38 individuals and 20 companies before the courts. Tyco Australia (formerly Wormald), Grinnell Asia Pacific, F&H Pty Ltd, Sensor Systems and some of their executives were among the first fined in 1999.

Meeting in various clubs around Brisbane, the coffee club parcelled out tenders and fixed prices in another display of the cosy culture in some parts of business. Executives also agreed to give 'cover pricing' — submitting a high price for a job expected to go to another member of the 'club'. The group kept a computer record of jobs allocated.

Court documents revealed the mentality. 'It's easy to make money on organised jobs', one participant said to another. Jobs 'fixed' over the years included major public buildings such as hospitals and office and apartment blocks.

The coffee club case turned up the first example of organised document destruction to avoid ACCC detection. Ralph Harder, a former Wormald employee, told how an executive informed him of an ACCC investigation and ordered him to cull contracts Wormald had not won in the last seven years. In an affidavit to the court, Harder gives a colourful account of what happened next:

> That night Paul Terlecky and I loaded up two vehicles. I loaded a company car and Paul Terlecky loaded his own car. By the time we had finished loading the files into the cars, both cars were full. That was, the boots, back seats and passenger-side seats of the two cars were completely full of files … The files we loaded related to sprinkler and alarm installations and servicing … The next day (Friday) we drove the loaded cars to my brother-in-law's property at Edenville Road, Edenville via Kyogle. He was not aware we were coming until we arrived. We arrived at about 8 or 8.30 … and burned files all day. There were four huge bonfires.

Whistleblowers became important in enabling the Commission to unearth cartels. Not all whistleblowers acted out of moral outrage over price fixing, however. One dobbed in his company when he discovered the boss was having an affair with his wife.

In 2003 the ACCC developed a new leniency policy to grant immunity to a cartel whistleblower if he or she is the first to come forward. America and Britain have similar policies. American antitrust regulators say it puts enormous psychological pressure on cartel members, as they agonise whether their co-conspirators have sold them out to gain immunity. Maybe they should be the first to 'fess up, to get immunity?

Other big cartel cases came from contacts with overseas competition regulators. Fels assiduously pushed overseas links to get ahead of globalisation's capacity to easily spread cartels. In one case the Commission, tipped off by its overseas counterparts, broke up an animal vitamins cartel by big foreign-owned groups such as Roche, BASF, Rhone-Poulenc and Takeda. Fines in Australia were $26 million, while overseas the companies had to stump up more than US$1 billion.

Asher's case-driven style made a big impression on Fels. Indeed, Fels lists Asher as one of the five people who really influenced his career. (The others are his mother, Professor Bert Turner at Cambridge, Professor Maureen Brunt in Melbourne, and Bill Kelty.)

Inside the Commission, the power balance between the two Allans provided its own sense of theatre. They were certainly a contrast in styles. On the one hand, Allan Fels, with his Jesuitic public service streak, self-deprecatory humour, quiet manner and ability to see the big picture of where the Commission should be heading. On the other, Allan Asher, with his strong Presbyterian drive, stern manner and intense, serious countenance. But the combination clicked, as Asher plotted new enforcement strategies, and Fels, with his somewhat eccentric professor appearance, marketed the newly energetic Commission to politicians and the public.

Whatever else can be said about the Commission in that decade of the 1990s, it worked. Fels' sheer energy would never leave him caught asleep at the wheel like some of his regulatory colleagues with the big corporate collapses early in the next decade. *Bulletin* columnist Max Walsh makes a flattering comparison between Fels and the Australian Prudential Regulation Authority, caught short in the collapse of big insurer HIH. Walsh says Fels' crusading style and the culture he has encouraged within the ACCC is much closer to the open American culture than the clubby approach Australia inherited from Britain.

Ironically, Fels lost some of the ACCC's oversight of financial affairs after the Wallis inquiry created both the Australian Prudential Regulation Authority (APRA) and the Australian Securities and

Investments Commission (ASIC). Fels may have had a reputation as a big picture man, but unlike some of his regulatory colleagues in APRA and ASIC, the Commission was never caught short over details either, although there were mistakes.

Fels' informal but also hands-on style as chairman contributed to a collegiate atmosphere at meetings of the commissioners, held every Wednesday morning in Canberra. Appointed by a combined federal–state vote for five years, commissioners have a degree of independence from the government of the day, although, like the rest of Canberra, they usually have one ear cocked to the political breeze.

Given the workload of the Commission, meetings during the Fels era, which were held in the cavernous conference room on the Commission's seventh-floor headquarters in Dickson, stretched through the day. A lunch break usually saw the commissioners stroll across to the Chinatown restaurants close by for a quick — alcohol-free — meal. The formal agenda ran through items the Commission had to decide on, to reports from commissioners and senior staff on contemporary matters they were dealing with. Fels assigned commissioners areas of expertise. So if it was a big merger, Ross Jones would have taken the lead. On telecommunications through the 1990s it was Rod Shogren, who moved across from Treasury. On the professions it would have been Sitesh Bhojani and, on small business, John Martin.

Commission meetings were something of a passing parade. Staff came and went in relays as they presented cases to the commissioners, who sat looking out across Canberra's Civic Centre to Parliament House. A videoconference system linked in interstate staff. Secretaries buzzed in and out with messages. People often chatted in small groups away from the main meeting table. Mobile telephone calls often jarred the meeting, with the recipient jumping up to have a conversation in the hallway outside.

The Commission culture is that staff take the initiative, putting up proposals or suggesting new prosecutions and then arguing their merits with commissioners. The flow of paperwork is immense.

Behind the row of commissioners is a large cardboard box labelled 'confidential waste' into which they constantly dump papers.

Formal votes among the commissioners were rare. Usually Fels just took the sense of the meeting, keeping a weather eye on senior commissioners like Jones and Bhojani in summing up. Staff still chuckle about one meeting where he did take a formal vote, and lost.

Fels was happy to spend a lot of time talking issues out. Given that the Commission these days is virtually setting industry policy with its extensive regulatory powers in telecommunications and energy, and its ability to impose court-enforceable undertakings on merger parties, there was a lot to discuss! Despite the serious workload, the atmosphere could be informal, even somewhat chaotic. Jokes were not uncommon. Commissioners often passed scribbled jokes to each other as staff members who had joined the meeting via video hook-up looked on, puzzled by the laughter.

Every action recommendation that comes before the Commission carries a draft press release. This was ordered by Fels. While it has led to countless internal jokes about Fels' media passion, it has a purpose. Fels believes it not only concentrates minds on the issue, but forces the Commission to consider how consumers and business will view their actions.

The enforcement committee meets every Friday. It was chaired during the 1990s by Asher (and now by Sitesh Bhojani) and is open to any commissioner to attend. It works via a series of video link-ups with state offices, which drive the enforcement process. State offices are usually the recipients of most consumer complaints, although ministers can direct the Commission to launch an investigation. Around the Commission, these are known as 'mirror cases', as in 'we'll look into it, minister'.

There are inherent tensions between the Canberra and state offices as to who is running enforcement issues, and between the enforcement committee and the Commission itself. In the Fels/Asher era this led to some amusing cat-and-mouse games. Given Asher's activism, Fels largely delegated enforcement to him, only occasionally attending the enforcement committee itself.

'Fels loved Asher because he got things done, and he was out there getting cases into court, winning cases, and Fels liked that', says one insider. 'But every now and then Asher would do something he didn't like. This was one of those little themes of the Fels/Asher relationship. There was always this tension with Fels: "How do I let Allan Asher have his head, but rein him in?" Everything would be going swimmingly and then something would happen, and Fels would be very unhappy with Asher. He would try to institute some procedure where he was getting information out of the enforcement committee, but it never quite worked.'

Clearly the worry for Fels was that the enforcement committee would tie the Commission into a case, or that it could initiate cases other commissioners did not know about. That could be embarrassing if a minister picked up a complaint and asked Fels what was going on.

Fortunately there were few mistakes. One, however, caused red faces all round. In October 1997 the ACCC sought injunctions to stop the proposed merger between Foxtel and Australis, two of the three struggling pay-television operators. The Commission took the view that the merger would pretty much knock the third operator, Optus, out of the game. If Optus folded, competition in telephony would wither and prices to consumers rise as Telstra assumed an even more dominant role.

The pay-TV merger was proposed just as the telephony market was opened to full competition, and it posed an uncomfortable choice for the Commission. At that stage the ACCC saw the opening up of competition in local telephony as the single most important issue in competition policy.

As the Australia/Foxtel merger was being played out, a business columnist in *The Australian*, Bryan Frith, dropped a bombshell. He reported that the ACCC had accepted legal resources from Optus. It turned out that the Australian Government Solicitor had struck a deal with Gilbert & Tobin, solicitors for Optus, to second two solicitors to assist with the ACCC case. The financial arrangement was a shocker. The AGS paid Gilbert & Tobin at the standard AGS solicitors' rates of $250 a day. The sting was the top-up billing that Gilbert & Tobin then charged Optus for the solicitors to enjoy their normal fees. It was estimated that Optus, in effect, paid some $58 000 for the AGS to oppose the merger. Optus of course had a direct commercial interest in killing the merger.

In the event, Foxtel walked away from the proposed merger. But Optus's financing of ACCC's legal team left a nasty taste. The ACCC claimed it was not aware of the top-up fee arrangement by Optus until quite late in proceedings. The House of Representatives Standing Committee on Financial Institutions and Public Administration rapped the AGS over the knuckles for the top-up arrangement. It reported that the AGS later 'backed down' by altering its fee arrangements with Gilbert & Tobin to normal commercial rates. It was a very embarrassing incident for the ACCC.

Another, more minor, blemish was the Commission's entry and then withdrawal from running compliance programs for companies. Gardini & Co and the Law Council of Australia complained that the ACCC was conducting a business running compliance programs on 87B court-enforceable undertakings it had made with companies. As another operator of such programs, Gardini objected to the competition from the regulator. The Law Council raised issues such as the possibility that companies might seek to placate the Commission by choosing it to oversee compliance, and whether the ACCC was under a duty of confidentiality or free to prosecute if it found breaches.

It was a minefield, and the Commission advised the House of Representatives Committee, which acts as a watchdog on the competition watchdog, that it was 'totally pulling back'. However, it also advised the committee that it was 'copping a bucketing' from some companies it already serviced, as they now had to pay higher fees for compliance programs.

Within Fels' ACCC there was a philosophy that if the Commission was very active, and mostly successful, this would wash over the small mistakes. And the Commission was largely successful. It won 58.7 per cent of all cases between 1991 and 2002, losing just 4 per cent, while the remaining 37.3 per cent were settled. The Commission won 94 per cent of all cases that ended up in court. Almost all ACCC prosecutions in this period were for breaches of the corporate market power (Section IV) or consumer protection (Section V) provisions of the Act.

Blemishes aside, the ACCC's activist enforcement approach under Fels and Asher changed perceptions of the Commission. If performance can be measured by output and reputation, the Commission was no longer a bit player on the corporate and consumer scene. It had acquired a reputation for not shirking big issues, big business or big unions.

Fels makes no apology for this. To him, the ACCC is daily dealing with some of the most powerful groups in Australian society, including the big telecommunications groups, oil and banks. 'I believe it is important that we are seen by them as powerful, not weak', he says. 'We can more effectively achieve the results envisaged by the Trade Practices Act if we're seen as people who can't be pushed around.'

Asher left the Commission in 2000 after his second term expired. In his later years he had served as deputy chairman, and was acknowledged as the consumer representative. After leaving, he worked with the UK Consumer Association before joining the UK Office of Fair Trading.

Asher's slot as deputy chairman was not filled during the last two and a half years of Fels' term. The vacancy created considerable speculation about differences between Fels, Treasurer Costello and the states on possible contenders. At one stage, executive search consultants were hired, but to no avail. The Commission was left wondering whether the Howard Government really wanted to appoint a new consumer representative at all. Perhaps Asher's zeal had left a 'never again' attitude. Commissioner Sitesh Bhojani took over the enforcement committee, with seemingly little change in the pace of Commission actions. And it has begun testing new boundaries, including prosecution of the agents of companies involved in anti-competitive activities, as well as corrective advertising.

Pursuit of agents for 'accessorial conduct' has raised alarm bells around legal firms and advertising agencies, who naturally see themselves as just advisers rather than potential accessories to a breach of competition laws. Fels and Bhojani have been at pains to warn advertising agencies about the risks of false advertising to them, as well as their clients. In 1999, a West Australian legal adviser, Conal O'Toole, was found to have drawn up an anti-competitive conduct agreement for the local Real Estate Institute and was ordered by a court to refrain from engaging in any future similar conduct.

A Federal Court judge weighed in heavily behind the ACCC in its first action against an advertising agent, in 1998. Fining Adelaide agent Thomas Wightman $10 000 for his role in misleading and deceptive advertising for Nissan vehicles, Justice Von Doussa described the advertising industry as 'gatekeepers' who had a responsibility to consider whether the advertisements they prepare for their clients comply with consumer protection legislation.

Fine print advertising has been another campaign. In a 2001 win, the Federal Court ordered Target to run corrective television advertising after it advertised price reductions on 'every stitch of clothing' but did not sufficiently highlight the fine print exclusions of many items. The corrective advertising, run on television with a Federal Court signage, was embarrassing for Target's parent company, Coles Myer, which agreed to cooperate to keep a watch on future fine print advertising across the retail group. In corrective print advertising as well, Target also withdrew the criticism it had thrown at Fels during the case that his ACCC had adopted a 'sue now, talk later' approach.

Corrective advertising is one thing, but the ACCC has also gained amendments to its Act which give it power to seek court orders for penalty advertising, requiring wrongdoers to advertise their own sins. It remains untested as yet, however. It will be fascinating to see who actually writes the copy for any penalty advertising — the wrongdoer or the ACCC.

As the sun sets on Allan Fels' era, the unasked question around the ACCC is whether his activist enforcement policy, run first by Asher and then by Bhojani, will endure. An after-dinner speaker at a competition law function drew a witty but cuttingly accurate simplification of the various enforcement styles of the three outsiders who had been brought in as chairman after Bannerman. 'McComas spoke to everyone and sued no-one', he joked. 'Baxt spoke to no-one and sued everyone. Fels spoke to everyone and sued everyone.' What style will the next chairman choose?

CHAPTER 8

THE FULL FIVE CHANNEL BLAST

Attorney-General Michael Duffy was adamant. Visiting the Trade Practices Commission's Perth office in 1991 as Bob Baxt was exiting the TPC chairmanship, Duffy told staff he did not know who Baxt's successor would be. 'But I can tell you one thing', he added. 'The next chairman won't be another media tart like Baxt.'

Baxt, of course, had made the mistake of publicly criticising the Labor Government over its lack of support for the competition regulator. In what must be one of the great ironies of Canberra's control-freakery over the public service and its agencies, Labor went on to appoint a new TPC chairman who would make 'media tart' Baxt look shy and retiring.

Allan Fels' use of publicity — some would say his media obsession — would make him not only a household name but a media 'identity', whose views could be sought on everything from weight reduction to cricket. Use of the media and publicity would become the defining feature of Fels' stewardship of the competition regulator. Business critics might complain of 'trial by press release' and 'media manipulation', but Fels was never dissuaded from taking the media fight right up to his opponents, and usually emerged the victor.

It gained him a reputation, at least in consumer eyes, as a 'Robin Hood', an appellation pinned on him by Joe Hockey when the latter was Minister for Financial Services and Regulation in the Howard Government. And of course, the existence of a local goody in the form of a Robin Hood implies there is also a Sheriff of Nottingham, or baddy. Unfortunately for big business, it has allowed itself to be cast in that role.

Unlike many in business, Fels has never been afraid of publicity, or of bringing issues out into the public domain. His usual response to calls for inquiries into the ACCC was, 'good, at least we'll have arguments out in the open and know what people are saying, rather than the behind-closed-doors lobbying of politicians'.

Politicians, meanwhile, have been happy to trade off Fels' consumer champion image, as evident in the GST introduction. Not that Fels has objected. Behind his serious academic public demeanour, there is an almost childish delight in mixing it with the media and being able to create publicity. But is it skilful use of the media to win arguments, or just plain self-seeking? Opinions seem to vary depending on whether you are an ordinary villager or in the Sheriff of Nottingham camp.

Fels has not just used the media. He has mastered the media levers like no other recent bureaucrat or politician. Moreover, Fels actually seems to enjoy it. Any regulator who regularly spent part of his Sunday returning media calls must get a kick out of it. 'My first love', Fels jokes when a conversation drifts to the media. His 1990s career as TPC chairman did not start, however, with a high media profile. Indeed, as mentioned already, the government had a distinct hankering for a low-key chairman in the wake of Baxt. The public service committee that interviewed Fels sounded him out on just how he would go about raising concerns with government. The implied question: would he be a public agitator like Baxt? Fels' replies apparently provided him with plenty of room for manoeuvre.

In his early period as chairman Fels actually found it difficult to interest the media. His style then was to 'round up the usual suspects', as he called it. This meant singling out a few pro-competition journalists and commentators to try to get them interested in matters like the high cost of books. It helped kick along a few issues.

One incident in the early 1990s, when he chaired both the Trade Practices Commission and the Prices Surveillance Authority, brought home to Fels the relatively low profile of competition issues. Fels had called a press conference at the TPC to unveil the Commission's competition priorities for the next few years. It was attended by a single business journalist. Afterwards he drove across Melbourne to the office of the PSA for a press conference on the impact of the withdrawal of one- and two-cent coins, with the accompanying hot consumer issue of the rounding up and down of prices. The press conference was packed, and the withdrawal of the small denomination coins received saturation media coverage. The message for Fels was clear: consumer hip pocket issues were popular in the press.

Later, as the ACCC mounted a string of big cartel cases, and its powers extended first as a result of the Hilmer reforms and then of the GST, Fels' media appearances made him one of the most recognised people in Australia.

How did he do it? The first essential for anyone courting media coverage is access. Every major decision made by the Commission must be accompanied by a draft press release, a Fels initiative. All issued press releases carry a telephone contact number for the ACCC's public relations manager, Lin Enright. But releases on major issues also carried a pager number for Allan Fels. And Fels returned calls, briefing reporters or doing radio grabs.

Participants at ACCC conferences were surprised by Fels' willingness to break proceedings to take media calls. Fels' wife, Isabel, recalls him taking calls on the beach while on holidays. Enright had open access to Fels to pass on media requests for interviews. Fels' grasp of issues was such that he just handled these calls on the run, usually without prepared notes before him.

A second essential for media coverage is to have something newsworthy to say. In that regard Fels was fortunate. His staple diet was overpricing, consumer rip-offs, bureaucratic stuff-ups (like the

Olympic ticketing), or business malpractice. All are great copy for the media. There is an old expression around the Commission that 'you can never go too far wrong sticking it into Telstra, the banks or the oil companies'. All have managed to expose themselves to Fels' barbs by their own actions.

The third essential is to appreciate what the media wants. Years of dealing with journalists, and his own fascination with the media, have given Fels an understanding of how the media functions. He is also such an avid media consumer that he knows which business columnists are on his side, and which are being fed by big business.

Only a few newspapers like *The Financial Review* are interested in arcane arguments about the *Trade Practices Act*. Whether Section 46 market power provisions should apply a 'purpose' or 'effects' test in determining offences may be of crucial interest to business readers, but readers of ordinary newspapers want the thrill of the chase. The tabloid 'we name the guilty men' style requires colour to dress up usually dry competition stories.

Fels understood this, and tried to cater for it. If you listened to him talking one-on-one to a journalist you would have heard him utter words like 'angles', 'colour' and 'deadline', the standard jargon of the reporting trade. He would even offer to think about 'angles' for columnists on quiet days, and call them back. For journalists anxious to grab a story from a complex issue, Fels could be a godsend. Politicians who upbraid journalists for their attention to Fels fail to understand the sheer energy he put in to courting the media.

Why did Fels do it? Part of the answer may be that watching the academic Bert Turner and politician John Cain had taught him that the combination of controversy and publicity can advance careers. As well, Fels came into the job believing that regulators needed a media profile to show people they were on the job. The experience of his predecessor at the Price Surveillance Authority, Hylda Rolfe, who left lamenting that she had not spent enough time convincing the public, showed him the dangers of not being seen to be active.

'A wise regulator ensures that his or her organisation develops strong and transparent links with the media', Fels told a conference in Paris in 2001. 'It is vital that when certain business interests attempt to influence journalists in a way that promotes their particular arguments that the journalist contacts the regulator for the other side of the story. That is why the regulator's door must be always open. Being media-shy is a dangerous policy.'

For Fels, the media is a weapon. He understands that media coverage gives him and the ACCC power. In the long struggle with vested interests, monopolies and cartels, this perception of power is invaluable. It puts opponents off balance, opens doors to politicians and outguns critics. It also protects the ACCC: an activist, high-profile regulator is harder for opponents to shoot down.

High exposure in the popular media — tabloid newspapers, radio and television — was Fels' main aim. He consciously went for 'back of the book' stories, showing how much of the media industry jargon he had picked up. This means softer articles such as lifestyle. Fels had seen how the sustained attacks that had weakened business regulation by the old Trade Practices Commission had been in the serious newspapers and the business press. 'My approach was to go over their heads', he says. Fels chuckled as commentators in the serious press attacked him as a 'media tart' for using the more popular media.

Fels' media grabs are often a negotiating ploy to settle a dispute. When he publicises maximum fines of up to $10 million, as he often does, business quickly gets the message. Telstra has directly complained to the ACCC of publicity being used to 'ambush' the big telco. For Fels, the perception of power gets results. That is the major end of using publicity — results. Fels was always fearful of being ambushed himself by business, with its ability to influence some media commentators.

The constant media coverage makes Fels and the ACCC look omnipotent. Business opponents need to weigh up not just a court case in taking Fels on, but a media war as well. This media 'card' has sometimes been played by ACCC officials. 'Remember, Fels is pretty good with the media', has been a line used in negotiations to strike favourable settlement deals.

Media has become something that Fels deploys as naturally as he would any of the ACCC's formal powers. He talks about an issue being serious enough to warrant a 'full five channel blast', meaning hitting all the media buttons. The media-savvy ACCC has convinced many businesses that the Commission is just not worth crossing. During the GST, the threat of 'shame notices' for price exploitation was enough to make most think twice.

Sometimes the media coverage, however, implies power that the ACCC does not have. A case in point occurred in June 2000, just before the introduction of the GST. An ACCC publication stated that the ACCC 'can impose severe penalties for businesses that fail to pass on tax savings for lower prices — up to $10 million per offence for corporations, and up to $500 000 per offence for individuals'. The Commission may have been in full flight of warning businesses to be careful in their GST pricing, but the fact was that it could not fine any business or any individual. Only courts can do that.

Academic critic Professor Warren Pengilley pointed this out to the ACCC's parliamentary watchdog committee, which, in turn quizzed Fels. In a sarcastic moment, Fels 'congratulated' Pengilley for finding this slip among the scores of ACCC publications on the GST. The committee said this reaction suggested 'an intolerance of criticism'.

In the main, however, Fels simply shrugged off the avalanche of criticism from the business community. That's a point that needs to be borne in mind in assessing the media war between Fels and his business opponents. It is not as if the tussle between the ACCC and the big end of town is one-sided. Big business employs a phalanx of spin merchants, most at much grander salaries than Fels. All are anxious to sell their side of the story to the media.

There is a major difference, however. The aim of much of corporate public relations is to keep the company out of the media — except, of course, for some staged event or a product release. Moreover, corporate PRs are often employed to take the heat off chief executives who are too nervous to face the media. Business has just not twigged that Fels' sheer accessibility is a real winner in the media war.

And somehow, amidst the power and media parade that accompanied his job, he managed to retain a touch of humility. After announcing his early departure in late 2002, the following exchange took place with ABC business reporter Alan Kohler:

> *Kohler*: 'You've been described as the third most powerful
> person in Australia, the most boring person in Australia,
> and an evil genius. Are any of those close to being true?'
> *Fels*: 'There's a bit of truth in the second of those.'

This feet-on-the-ground image helped enormously with credibility. Fels may exude power but he cares little for the trappings. At a press conference on his early departure in late 2002, for example, the media had all assembled for a 'doorstop' interview at the Senate entrance of Parliament House, with television cameras trained on the spot where Fels' car was expected to arrive. Consternation ensued when one TV cameraman, looking up the road, shouted 'He's coming on foot!' (Fortunately Fels remembered where he had parked his car on this occasion. There had been a minor crisis within the ACCC a year or so earlier after he 'misplaced' a car.)

Some business leaders are realistic enough to recognise that Fels beat them in the media game. 'He's the most savvy media operator I've ever seen', says one. The fact that big business had to mount a sustained campaign with government to 'control' Fels is testament to his media success.

Nevertheless, business critics have not grasped Fels' aims. Business's constant bleat was about 'trial by media'. This 'such matters should be conducted in private' attitude is so very Australian. But Fels did not just use the media as a tool in a power struggle; he used it to win the broader war about a more competitive society. There are precious few business leaders with a credible public profile who speak on wider society issues, imbuing those issues with a business message.

Critics in business also make the mistake of playing the man, not the issue. Retailer Gerry Harvey, for instance, has stated he 'hates' Allan Fels and has likened the ACCC to Nazi Germany. Harvey says the very thought of Fels makes him so angry that he wants to go out and 'smack' a golf ball around — the implication being that he would like to do the same to Fels.

In contrast, Fels adopts a flat, factual delivery reminiscent of a schoolteacher, occasionally throwing in some irony or humour to sell his messages. Responding to businesses' claims that their reputations were being damaged by constantly being dragged into the media, Fels noted that this could indeed be so, 'But I also acknowledge that horse thieves and bigamists are generally not well regarded.'

The main failure of business critics, however, is that over the years they simply underestimated Fels. How could an academic-turned-regulator pose a threat even if he was good at the occasional media grab? Besides, if there was ever a problem it could be fixed in the traditional way — by lobbying political leaders. For a long time, business entirely missed that Fels had leap-frogged politicians to establish an identity with the public as a 'Robin Hood' consumer protector. This made him a difficult target who could not be handled by normal political lobbying — what politician is going to rein in the consumers' friend? The Fels phenomenon required a far more sophisticated campaign. It was not until the branch-office economy campaign of 2000 that business realised it needed new weapons to beat Fels.

Within the ACCC itself, Fels' use of publicity was the subject of much discussion, and even criticism, by other commissioners. Was the constant high profile necessary? Should the ACCC comment on prosecutions as well as announce them? Staffers worried that Fels' penchant for off-the-cuff soundbites was dangerous territory for verbal slip-ups, and they were right. His fondness for the media grab led to several occasions when Fels went just one step too far. Fels beat this off with the argument that publicity helps the Commission build up coalitions of support for the future. He meant that future unpopular decisions might go down more easily if the ACCC enjoyed broad public support as a result of publicity.

There is another dimension to Fels' proselytising on competition policy through the media. Deep within, he feared that a future government might backtrack on Australia's commitment to competition. As a relatively new policy, it is definitely not yet ingrained. Could it be wound back as quickly as it was rolled out in recent decades? The sheer amount of energy Fels put into publicity was certainly partly motivated by an almost missionary belief in the need to instil competition into the culture. He thus got nervous if the Commission was out of the media for a while.

'I've always had this educator idea, you know, the academic who's a lecturer', he says. 'I believe in the power of education and the importance of it. So I like always explaining things, and I'm confident that reason will work with the public. There have certainly been instances where I sort of just sought publicity to keep us in the public eye. I've always had it in mind that it's important for the perceived power of the Commission.' Fels concedes that sometimes this can be overdone, as in the case of the Commission jumping too enthusiastically into allegations of collusion between Tasmanian art galleries over bidding for a painting.

Business was not alone in struggling to adjust to Fels' media persona. Politicians were also left in the jet stream. Some ministers view media publicity as their job, not that of a regulator. Others are jealous. One junior Liberal minister complained to Fels, only half jokingly, that he had spent a year working up a big announcement only to find Fels had grabbed the top spot on the evening television news that night. In other situations, such as the introduction of the GST or the handling of sensitive commercial deals, politicians like Fels taking the heat.

ACCC publicity, and its image of consumer champion, is also a sign of power to politicians. It ensures the Commission better access to ministers. Such is the way Canberra works. No minister has ever tried to order Fels to drop his media open-door policy, although public hints have been heavy. However, his political masters have thrown the occasional barb: in July 2002, for example, Treasurer Costello told *The Financial Review* that Fels' use of media 'may have been excessive'.

The timing of this remark was revealing. Costello had just announced a review into the *Trade Practices Act*, to be headed by former High Court judge Sir Daryl Dawson. Fels' Commission was also under its heaviest public fire in the wake of the ACCC raids on Caltex (discussed later in this chapter). What should have been an ACCC coup, following a whistleblower's allegations about petrol price fixing, turned into a public relations disaster. Costello echoed widespread business fears that the petrol raids and the publicity surrounding them were a step too far.

'I think the concern of business is that [the ACCC] doesn't use its immense power for press [coverage]', said Costello as the Dawson inquiry into the future of the ACCC was underway. 'Now public education has its place, and that's important, but you've got to be sure the press is always secondary to the enforcement activity, and I think that's a legitimate issue that I hope will be teased out over the course of this inquiry.'

Costello was walking a fine line between responding to business pressure to rein in Fels and not attacking the popular consumer watchdog. Shadow Treasurer Bob McMullan was quick to play the politics, accusing Costello of aligning himself to the forces attacking Fels rather than defending the consumer regulator. Labor, of course, had veered from attacking Fels in the waterfront and GST to supporting him over petrol prices.

Given the extent of media coverage — and the level of criticism — it might be expected that Fels had a formidable media machine. In fact, it was skeletal. Apart from Lin Enright, a former journalist who worked as press secretary to Treasurer John Kerin, there was a feature writer for magazine articles, Tom Connors, and a speechwriter. Enright had an assistant for some years, but lost her in 2003.

This handful of publicity staff churn out an incredible 300 or so press releases a year, averaging more than one every working day. The range of issues covered by the releases reflects the broad canvas of competition law. In a typical week in February 2003, press releases reported on: misleading reporting by a furniture store; Will Writers Guild being ordered to pay $335 000 for misleading its franchisees; a weight-loss promoter being fined $9000; the ACCC not opposing a merger between Australian Cement Holdings and Queensland Cement Limited; competition in the pharmacy industry; and options for improving investment in electricity.

This press release cascade does have a formal purpose. The ACCC is actually required under Section 28 of the *Trade Practices Act* to publicise its activities. The ACCC's policy is not to announce investigations. It will put out a press release only when a prosecution is launched, or when a court makes a finding. Enright says her policy is that press releases must be 'moderately worded and accurate', a phrase used by a judge in a court case involving the ACCC's use of the media. Usually it was not the printed press release that got the ACCC into trouble. It was more Fels' habit of expanding on the release at press conferences.

Geoff Dixon, Qantas's chief executive, says Fels had a 'well-honed knack' of highlighting allegations against companies. This, he says, 'had the potential to extract an instant penalty and cause long-term damage to the company's reputation and brand'.

Dick Warburton, the Caltex and David Jones chairman who had unsuccessfully taken up the case of Video Ezy when it faced a GST pricing charge, articulated the business case against Fels in an interview with *The Australian*. 'He is very quick if it goes public to go much further than we believe anybody should go', says Warburton. 'There is nothing wrong with saying as [Australian Securities and Investments Commission chairman] David Knott does, "Yes, there is an investigation". Full stop. Whereas Allan will go on, "Absolutely, there is an investigation and I am going to stop all these price colluders and price fixers and blah, blah, blah", and immediately giving this huge inference of guilt. And the problem is, in the Caltex case, we cannot defend it because there is nothing to defend. There are no allegations, just these inferences.' Warburton was referring to the much-publicised ACCC raids on Caltex in April 2002. In that case the ACCC's hand had been forced by the fact that the whistleblower sent a copy of her allegations to *The Daily Telegraph*. The ACCC handles thousands of inquiries, and several 'walk-ins' or raids a year, without publicity. Media usually only comes into an investigation at the point of legal action.

Does the ACCC's open media style prejudice business by trial by media, as often alleged? It is difficult to find an unbiased answer to that. However, Dr Karen Yeung, lecturer in law at Oxford University, concluded there was no trial by media but that the media activities could be dangerous for the ACCC's credibility. Dr Yeung used the ACCC for a research paper posing the question: 'Is the use of informal adverse publicity a legitimate regulatory compliance technique?' Dr Yeung's research was conducted against the backdrop of changing use of media in the information society. The increasing sophistication in communications technology, she said, was accompanied by a 'professionalisation' of communications, in which politics, business and civil society routinely engaged media professionals. In turn, this had seen a spread of 'promotionalism' across political and institutional cultures. Public administrators had been caught up in this, with once media-shy government agencies now courting media attention.

Dr Yeung examined all the ACCC's media releases in 2001. Working on the basis that information about investigations was the most likely to unfairly prejudice individuals or companies, she found that only a tiny proportion of ACCC releases — 1.5 per cent — actually concerned the investigation stage. In only one case was a 'suspect' named where the suspect had not already identified itself.

Narrowing down to press releases about the litigation side of proceedings, Dr Yeung found that 26 per cent concerned proceedings on foot, while 74 per cent dealt with court judgments or negotiated settlements. Press releases pre-trial amounted to 10.3 per cent of total ACCC releases. 'This lends some weight to Fels' claim that 90 per cent of media releases arise after trial and therefore cannot be characterised as "trial" by media', she concluded.

The findings, however, were not all good. Turning to the balance and tone of press releases, Dr Yeung's analysis found that only 25.5 per cent of releases mentioned the views of the defendant, while only a few made it clear the ACCC's allegations were as yet unproven. 'These results seem to provide very clear evidence of media "spin control" by the ACCC, rather than what might be described as evenly balanced reporting', she said. On the other hand, when the ACCC announced formal court proceedings it took a cautious approach, not offering an opinion on the matter. Her conclusion about this mixed bag of findings:

> The ACCC's media strategy has a Janus-like quality. Viewed from the perspective of regulatory effectiveness, the ACCC's pro-active media usage has contributed to its credibility as a powerful, pro-active regulator, vigorously endeavouring to protect competition and the interests of consumers.
>
> But viewed from the perspective of constitutional principle, its pursuit of publicity may have a tendency to undermine its credibility as an even-handed law enforcement agency committed to ensuring that those at risk of violating the Act are fairly treated.*

The courts offer another unbiased view. Business is always able to resort to the courts to seek injunctions challenging ACCC actions, or to argue that excessive publicity that has damaged their company should be taken into account to lower any court penalty in a successful prosecution.

Justice Smithers of the Federal Court set the pendulum swinging one way in a 1977 (pre-Fels) case when he considered whether

---

* From: 'Is the use of informal adverse publicity a legitimate regulatory compliance technique?', Dr K Yeung. Paper presented to the Australian Institute of Criminology Conference, Current Issues in Regulation: Enforcement and Compliance, Melbourne, 03/09/02

penalties against Southern Motors Box Hill Pty Ltd should be mitigated by adverse publicity generated by the case. The Commission had issued a press release saying the company had sold a car twice as an 'ex-GMH executive car' when it fact it was an ex-rental car. Yet the particulars of the case when it came to court did not mention this allegation. 'In my view this is a case in which, by reason of the press release of the prosecuting authority, the danger of cumulative punishment ... is real and should be treated as part of the background against which penalty should be assessed', concluded Justice Smithers. 'And I have so treated it.'

Justice O'Laughlin, in a Fels era case in 1996, took a different view. Cue Design complained it had been adversely affected by publicity generated from an ACCC press release announcing proceedings against the company and alleging false and misleading price tags on new garments. The company cited television and newspaper reports naming Cue. 'I would have thought that a moderately worded, accurate news release, such as that published by the Commission in this case, serves a very useful purpose', said Justice O'Laughlin. 'To use the words of Smithers J it showed "appropriate restraint in tone and content". Without it, the media is left to make its own inquiries, and compile its own summaries. In doing that there is an increased risk that, by accident, inaccuracies might occur and greater harm could come to a defendant.' Finding that the publicity was due to Cue's actions, Justice O'Laughlin declined to reduce penalties.

The judge's point about a media left in the dark about ACCC prosecutions is apt. Without a media release, the press and television would turn feral in the hunt for 'facts'. The media may be less than perfect, but it treasures its watchdog role: ACCC cases would be hunted down. It would be more a case of 'mistrial by media'.

Another case involving claims for reduced penalties shows real chutzpah by a defendant. Nationwide News in 1996 complained to the court that an ACCC press release over a case involving a mobile telephone promotion had diminished its acquittal on 18 charges, while the media picked up on its conviction on six charges of misleading statements. Nationwide News is the publisher of *The Daily Telegraph*. Here was the tabloid terrier, the master of the punchy headline, complaining about selective reporting by a government agency! In any case, the ACCC press release *had* actually mentioned both the convictions and the acquittal. The court dismissed any idea of a reduced penalty, noting: 'The fact that some of the media might have chosen not to report on the dismissal of the charges does not mean that the Commission's press release was unfair'.

Similarly, Justice Von Doussa dismissed a claim by Nissan for mitigated damages after the car company complained of an ACCC press release while a case was still pending. 'Overall, I do not think the substance and effect of the release was unfair, or that it led to "adverse" publicity', said Justice Von Doussa. 'I do not propose to make any allowance for adverse publicity in fixing penalty.' The judge did say, however, that inaccuracies in the press release would be a consideration in determining costs.

Attempts to sue the ACCC for defamation arising from its press releases have failed. The Federal Court dismissed a claim by Giraffe World Australia that it had been defamed by the ACCC issuing in a press release posted on the internet and informing NSW Fair Trading of actions against the company for misleading advertising of a health care mat. The court also found Giraffe World guilty of breaches of the *Trade Practices Act*. Courts have also said it is reasonable for the ACCC to state in press releases that a case is seen as a potential test case.

Court comments on ACCC publicity, however, have not been all favourable. Far from it. In September 2002 Justice Hill in the Federal Court fired a legal shot across Fels' bows over a speech and magazine article on ACCC action against advertising agencies. 'It might be said that while the Commission is entitled to tell the public that proceedings have been brought and the general nature of those proceedings, there is a danger that wide dissemination of the fact before a hearing might in a particular case injure, perhaps irreparably, the person against whom the proceedings are brought', he said.

Much more colourful were Justice Finn's comments in a 1999 Federal Court action brought by the Electricity Supply Association of Australia (ESAA) against the ACCC over electricity contracts. While Justice Finn dismissed the ESAA's action, he took a dim view of Fels labelling comments by the ESAA's senior legal adviser as 'absurd' while also raising the threat of legal action against views on electricity warranties that might differ from the ACCC's:

> The stances so taken may constitute good public theatre. Whether they represent good public administration is another matter. There is a very real prospect that the view the ACCC has taken of Division 2 of Part V will be found to be incorrect. At the moment, as the ACCC's counsel in this proceeding properly acknowledges, whether and if so how the implied conditions apply to electricity supply contracts is a matter of debate about which there can be respectable opinions on both sides of the argument. To describe the opinions supporting one side of the debate as 'absurd' borders on the mischievous.

There was more. Justice Finn elaborated on the ACCC's threat of proceedings against the ESAA or its suppliers. 'The stance taken by the ACCC, in at least some of the instances in which threats were made against ESAA and the suppliers, could quite reasonably be interpreted as simply an attempt to stifle debate', he said. 'It could be censurable for so powerful and influential a public agency to take such a course.'

Ouch! Just as well the ESAA lost the case. Still, if Fels chooses to mix it in the public arena with tough language, he has to expect the same in return. Fels knows that in using the media he walks a very exposed high wire. Not only can opponents seek legal redress, but looking over his shoulder are a raft of appeal bodies, reviewers and political masters, including the Australian Competition Tribunal, a division of the Federal Court, the Ombudsman, parliamentary committees, and the Treasurer, not to mention specially appointed reviewers such as the recent Dawson, Uhrig and Wilkinson inquiries.

⌐

The publicity case that will probably come to epitomise Fels' legendary use of the media was the Caltex raid. On Wednesday 24 April 2002, The Daily Telegraph's front page banner headline trumpeted 'PETROL RAIDS', with the kicker line of 'Exclusive. Biggest ever fuel price fixing inquiry sparked by whistleblower's letter'. The front page splash included a photo of four ACCC officers carrying cardboard cartons, with the caption: 'ACCC officers carry boxes of documents from Caltex headquarters in Martin Place yesterday'.

For the media, the story hit some hot buttons: petrol prices, collusion by oil companies, corporate raids and whistleblowers. It touched that 'Aha, we always thought so' cynical view of ordinary Australians that something lay behind the seemingly ever-rising petrol prices. Caltex in fact later did a survey which revealed that 74 per cent of those who could identify Caltex as being investigated believed the allegations of price fixing were true.

The raid originated from an anonymous letter on green paper and italic printing received by the ACCC in early December 2001. The whistleblower alleged that certain people during their employment with an oil company had seen material that strongly suggested Caltex, Shell and Mobil had discussed and made agreements on the sale of petroleum products. While the allegations mainly concerned bitumen in relation to contracts with council, they also touched on petrol.

Some of the material supplied was on oil company letterhead. For the ACCC and its Prices Surveillance Authority, which had chased petrol pricing around the political plate for years, it must have seemed like the holy grail had arrived in the post. But more information was needed. The ACCC advertised for the whistleblower to make further contact. She did, writing again just before Christmas. A man, believed to be the informant's husband, rang and spoke to an ACCC officer. Another call, unfortunately, was missed. The usual checks were made on fax numbers and people mentioned to ensure the information was accurate. It seemed to check out.

Legal advice was sought, and it confirmed that on the material received so far the ACCC had 'reason to believe' a breach of the *Trade Practices Act* might have occurred, and therefore could issue a Section 155 notice to enter premises and collect information.

Still, more information was sought. The ACCC advertised again. *The Daily Telegraph*, reporting the new attempt to contact the whistleblower, cheekily added to its story a footnote along the lines of 'and send us a copy as well'.

Staggeringly, the whistleblower did. The ACCC was astounded to take a telephone call from *Daily Telegraph* reporter Kathy Lipari claiming she had a copy of the second letter received at the Commission. The informant was obviously frustrated at the apparent lack of action since the first contact almost three months before, and had now copied in the press to stir the ACCC along.

'I would like to express my disappointment at the lack of action taken regarding the information that I have provided to the ACCC,' the whistleblower's message said in its trademark italic type. 'I have given you several pieces of information regarding inappropriate behaviour by [blank]. I have also provided you contact details of another lady who is no longer employed by [blank] and two gentlemen, who with some persuasion could provide you with additional information. I have also sent numerous copies of correspondence to your office. I will [now] provide you with another piece of information … [blank].'

Fels and the ACCC's chief executive Brian Cassidy were horrified. If *The Telegraph* published this letter it could scupper the entire investigation. Documents could be destroyed, as in the coffee club case involving Ralph Harder, where critical documents were quickly loaded into cars, taken out into the bush and burnt.

Both Cassidy and Fels implored Lipari not to publish the letter. Eventually a deal was struck: if *The Telegraph* held off, the ACCC would brief it on any future action, though there was no agreement about an 'exclusive'. The newspaper agreed. But this still left the ACCC in a dilemma. *The Telegraph* could publish at any time. And there was always the niggling worry that documents might disappear.

Under this kind of pressure, it was decided to do a 'walk in' under Section 155 notices to get more information. This would be a big operation. The ACCC would need to move on eight premises simultaneously: the head offices of Caltex, Mobil and Shell; the Caltex terminal at Banksmeadow; the Mobil terminal at Spotswood; a Caltex distributor in Smithfield; and two distribution companies in the Newcastle area. It would require some 90 people all up, including ACCC staff, lawyers and IT experts, as well as Federal Police to ensure entry to the premises. The raiding party would also have to take in copying equipment and boxes to carry away documents, as raided companies are under no obligation to provide such assistance to the ACCC.

Fels gave the go-ahead for 23 April. He had been in Alice Springs, but flew to Sydney to be present. Just prior to the raids, the ACCC informed the lawyers of each of the companies, and gave them copies of the 155 notices. Interestingly, the lawyers gave the ACCC assurances of assistance. The ACCC was surprised the companies did not immediately seek to challenge the notices. Caltex took the view that if they had done so it would have indicated they had something to hide.

On the evening before the raid Cassidy called Lipari. The Commission was now in a position to talk to her about the letter. Could she come in tomorrow morning? 'Is it a raid?' asked Lipari. Talk to you tomorrow, was the reply. The ACCC never publicises its 'walk-ins', but was under an obligation to Lipari, as *The Telegraph* had honoured its part of the bargain by not publishing the letter.

When Lipari arrived at 11.30 am the next day, the raids had been long underway. Fels and Cassidy briefed her. *The Daily Telegraph* was keen for an exclusive. Fels and Cassidy could give no such guarantee. The ACCC did not announce its raids. But given the scale of this operation they felt certain news would leak out. Lipari was told that if they were contacted by other media the ACCC would have to respond.

What about a photograph, Lipari asked? Cassidy knew that some ACCC staff would shortly be returning from Caltex head office in nearby Martin Place. The document search there had not been going as smoothly as elsewhere. Issues of documents protected by legal professional privilege had arisen. The ACCC offered *The Telegraph* the opportunity to photograph the returning staff. As it happened, they were bringing back unused, empty ACCC document boxes.

News of the raids did not leak out that day. Later in the afternoon Lipari contacted Cassidy. Had the ACCC been contacted by any media organisations tipped off about the raids? No.

The Telegraph realised it had an exclusive, and splashed with three pages, including maps of the raid locations, copies of the ACCC's advertisements to contact the whistleblower, and Lipari's own story of how the paper had worked in cooperation with the ACCC to ensure the investigation was 'not jeopardised'. It also ran the photograph, with the caption 'ACCC officers carry boxes of documents from Caltex headquarters'. In an accompanying article, columnist Ray Chesterton tapped popular anger, comparing the simultaneous petrol price movements to synchronised swimming, and concluding there was 'no other explanation' apart from collusion.

Fels was staggered by the response of the rest of the media. By early evening *The Telegraph* had put its exclusive on the internal News Limited system, and Fels was fielding calls from other Murdoch papers. By the time he arrived in Melbourne about 10 pm the television stations and desperate Fairfax newspapers were chasing him. Stopping at The Herald & Weekly Times on the way home to pick up an early copy of the *Herald Sun*, one of the News Limited chain, he was besieged for more information. Faced with saturation media coverage, Fels called a press conference for the next morning.

A few days later Fels attended a dinner organised by Reserve Bank Governor Ian McFarlane. Dick Warburton, the Caltex chairman, was also present. 'I hope you're not planning any more raids', Warburton asked Fels, amid jocularity among the diners. But the jokes disappeared a few days later when Warburton called to see Fels in his office. Caltex had worked out that the boxes in the front-page photo were empty. He was quite angry. The incorrect caption enabled Caltex to mount an effective media onslaught on the ACCC about the raid, particularly in the Fairfax newspapers, which were smarting about *The Telegraph*'s scoop.

The incorrect caption, even though written by *The Telegraph*, would become business's rallying cry on everything they saw as wrong and damaging about ACCC publicity. Little matter that ACCC officers *had* carried away documents later in the day.

'The caption was false', Caltex said in its submission to the Dawson inquiry. 'This was well known to the ACCC yet no action was taken by the ACCC to correct the gross misrepresentation of the actions of its officers, for example by requesting *The Telegraph* to print a correction or apology. The false information that the boxes contained Caltex documents was very damaging to Caltex's reputation as it implied substantial (presumably incriminating) evidence had been collected.'

Caltex was also upset when Cassidy told a Senate inquiry that one reason behind the raid was the ACCC's fear of document destruction. 'Caltex complains that its reputation has been damaged', said Fels. 'The ACCC is not responsible for the reputation of an oil company — this is a matter of public perception — but the ACCC is responsible for the enforcement of the *Trade Practices Act* and will continue to do its job without fear or favour.' Later in 2002 Caltex moved to block in the Federal Court further ACCC 155 notices seeking more documents.

If the ACCC had its time over again it would not have given Lipari the photograph opportunity. That was the step too far. The Commission had felt it had to give *The Telegraph* information, as it had cooperated to suppress details of the whistleblower, but the photo op made it look too cosy.

The sheer size of the raids, involving 90 people and police, has been an issue of internal debate in the ACCC. Around the oil industry colourful stories are told of policemen, hands near their guns, telling staff it would be inadvisable to make telephone calls during the raid. Such stories are apocryphal. Both the ACCC and Caltex say that police did not actually enter buildings, and left after ACCC staff gained entry.

For the ACCC the raids had not gone well from the start. Copies of the 155 notices were faxed through to Caltex's general counsel, Helen Conway, upside down so that she received a sheaf of blank pages. This left the ACCC raiding party milling about in the Caltex foyer until Conway had read the correctly faxed documents and admitted them. She described the ACCC team as striding around the foyer like pumped up footballers before a big game.

The ACCC collected a huge amount of information at the various sites it raided, including the Caltex headquarters, offsite storage locations, the other companies and refiners. In all, it was some 75 computer loads of detail. But as this information was sifted in subsequent months the dawning reality was that it contained no smoking gun. 'In these sorts of cases, and particularly a case involving big oil, you've got to have pretty good evidence', says Fels. 'We had some information but you could see it was not going to carry us through a big law case.'

The ACCC had lost an earlier attempt to pin price fixing on some of the oil companies after uncovering what it believed was an incriminating email and receiving a letter from a whistleblower in December 1994. The letter was a corker, alleging that price fixing among the oil majors went right up to the top. It detailed meetings in hotel rooms under the cover of industry functions. The whistleblower said the price fixing arrangement was on a single sheet of A4 paper covering the 12 points of the deal. The letter listed six, drawn from the whistleblower's memory.

'If you were to find internal documents in different companies, all in the June/July 1991 time frame, with similar wording, or addressing the same issues in the same order, with the same general approach, that, it seems to me, would require some explanation', the informant wrote. The four-page letter detailed how the price fixing arrangement broke down, due to the real competitiveness in the industry, distrust between the companies, and the incompetence of some senior executives. 'Even though it failed there WAS an agreement', the whistleblower said. The court, however, struck out an attempted prosecution based on an email.

As the 2002 inquiry against Caltex, Mobil and Shell ground on without much result, the ACCC stepped up action to locate the whistleblower. At one stage it believed it had identified the woman, a Caltex employee, but when this proved incorrect apologised to her. The ACCC's tenacity in trying to identify the whistleblower in the Caltex affair was odd. It knew from the earlier case that whistleblowers are frightened of detection. 'I could not afford the dismissal which would be the inevitable consequence of my being identified as having assisted you', said the 1994 informant, apologising for the anonymity.

New Section 155 notices were issued seeking details of staff. Caltex objected. For the ACCC, and future recipients of 155 notices, the case involved an interesting legal point: the ACCC might have the power under these notices to investigate price fixing, but did they also give it power to seek details of staff?

The issue was not tested, as on 28 March 2003, almost a year after the raid, Fels pulled the plug, announcing that the ACCC had 'finalised' its investigation and 'will take no further action'. The material collected was inconclusive, and the whistleblower had not come forward again. With his own departure looming, Fels felt he had to finish the oil raid controversy one way or another without leaving it on his successor's plate. If there was going to be a negative card out of the incident, he wanted to take it himself.

'Unfortunately, whistleblowers often are not of an investigatory mind so they don't give us information about where the linked information can be found', says Fels. 'In this case we almost needed to be told "go to filing cabinet 14 on floor seven".' There were also growing doubts about the whistleblower's identity. The written messages appeared to come from a woman, but a man had made the telephone calls.

In retrospect, Fels concedes the raid was disproportionate to the material supplied by the whistleblower. He also believes the ACCC should have worked harder on the case background before the raids. 'We should've looked at what we had', he says. 'We should've discreetly studied the industry and figured out what we were really looking for. You tend always to say this after an investigation that leads nowhere. There are other instances where we've had something, we've blundered in and major results have occurred.'

Fels is pragmatic on what the raid did for the ACCC's image. Public reaction was mixed between those who believed that at least the ACCC was trying, and those who saw it as a blunder, but one in the long run of little significance. Big business, however, saw it as a substantial win, underlining its argument that the ACCC overdid publicity and was out of control. 'It's probably encouraged them to fight us more', he says. 'It's encouraged them not to think we're invincible. They were starting to see us as invincible almost.'

At the Canberra end, Fels believes the failed raid could feed the business campaign that the ACCC should not be given any more powers. On a positive note for the Commission, however, it might also encourage whistleblower protection legislation.

Fels refused to take a backward step despite the business outrage over the raids. 'In recent weeks there has been a set of virulent, seemingly semi-coordinated attacks on the administration and media practices of the ACCC', he told the National Press Club a few months after the raid. 'The ACCC will not be intimidated nor diverted from carrying out its proper functions of applying the *Trade Practices Act* without fear or favour to whomever it applies, no matter how powerful they may be politically or economically.'

The failed investigation left Fels exposed, however. Treasurer Costello said: 'I think this has highlighted the issue of how regulators should deal with the press, and I think that the lesson here is that regulators should be perhaps understated in their dealings with the press'.

This was a distinct hardening of Costello's view of Fels' dealing with the media. Costello seemed caught between wanting to encourage the competition regulator and responding to business critics. Previously his line had been 'enforcement first, media second'. Now he wanted an 'understated' media profile. This was a marked contrast to the government's riding orders for the GST when it wanted the ACCC to be very high profile in the media. But that was when the ACCC and Fels' high profile were needed to save the government.

CHAPTER 9

'THERE SHOULD BE CHEAPER CDS BY CHRISTMAS'

— Allan Fels in 1993, 1994, 1995, 1996, 1997

I f Allan Fels enjoys a charmed life with working journalists, relations with the business end of the media and publishing industries have been terse. Poisonous, in fact, might be a more accurate description when it comes to the publishing and music CD industries, as well as Telstra, the big media/communications company.

All three have enjoyed cosy monopolies in Australia, in various forms. Fels has stuck his competition stick into all their nests, provoking hostile responses. The book industry, for example, has demonstrated that it is prepared to cut off its commercial nose to spite its face when it comes to Fels.

This book is a case in point. With Fels' Robin Hood image and his ranking as one of the most powerful people in Australia — not to mention his being the only Canberra regulator ever to make Sydney society's A-list — his story would appear to have all the ingredients for a popular book.

That's not how many publishers see it. An author's proposal for this book drew a consistent negative reaction around publishing houses, although some of the smaller university presses were interested. Some commercial publishers did not even want to entertain a proposition about the book. Then Penguin, a major global publisher, expressed great interest. After the usual discussion on content, Penguin's

Publishing Director, Robert Sessions, was 'delighted' to offer a contract to publish. But a month later, Sessions had to withdraw the offer.

Sessions said he did not enjoy the support of his fellow directors, who felt they could not support a book about Fels. The directors felt Fels had tried to scuttle their industry, whether unwittingly or by lies.

Sessions was extraordinarily frank in his response, claiming that he did not necessarily share the view of the other directors. He wrote that the decision was not a veto but said that it would be too difficult to work with a team that was so implacably opposed to the book. The book proposal was dead despite Sessions' own belief that it would work.

The experience provided an amazing insight into how far some sections of business were prepared to take their hostility to Fels. A publishing director believes a book project is commercially sound and has every prospect of success, yet his fellow directors loathe Fels so much they will not publish it. Paradoxically, the wider publishing industry, as expressed in the Australian Publishers' Association, is now arguing that the industry is doing so well after the initial round of Fels-inspired changes that it does not need the next round.

Fels generates antipathy in the book and CD industries because he has turned them upside down, breaking down lucrative import cartels and forcing lower prices. But Fels' aim of fully opening the Australian book market to parallel imports — copyright books that can be imported without the permission of the Australian copyright holder — has been blocked, at least for the moment. In March 2003 the Senate, in a deal negotiated between the Democrats and the government, agreed to lift the restriction on parallel imports of computer software. The Democrats' 'price' for agreeing to the software relaxation was that restrictions on book imports remained.

Fels has a deep personal interest in the book and music industries. He is an avid consumer of the printed word: the private room behind his Melbourne office was always strewn with newspapers and books, as is his home study. He particularly keeps a keen eye out for new foreign literature on competition and economic policies. Music CDs are another favourite. Fels also keeps a cardboard box full of cassette tapes on philosophy and history, playing them in his car and swapping tapes with New South Wales Premier Bob Carr.

So it was of unusual interest to him when in the late 1980s the Prices Surveillance Authority turned up an odd finding. The PSA had been looking at price movements following a rise in the value of the Australian dollar. Normally, prices of imports would fall. But book and CD prices both stood out, showing no response to the stronger dollar. This was sheer greed by the British publishers who monopolised the Australian market. It would turn out to be very costly for them.

Fels approached Nick Bolkus, then Assistant Treasurer in the Hawke Government, with a proposal for the PSA to do a major study into book prices in Australia. Bolkus agreed.

Books exactly fitted the idea of what the PSA should be doing — bark, but not much bite. In Britain, Fels had watched as the Prices and Incomes Board struggled to find a useful role, eventually using its power over prices to press for improvements in management efficiency. Similarly, the PSA had to show it was on the prices beat without scaring away investment. Books were high profile and a clear case of a rip-off: perfect territory for the PSA.

About the same time, sections of the media were also starting to take an interest in the Australian book market. The late Robert Haupt, a Fairfax journalist, began campaigning against the absurdity of the global segmentation of the English-speaking market which handed Australia on a plate to British publishers. US publishers, with their longer book runs and cheaper prices, had agreed not to enter the market in an agreement dated back to 1899. Before that, Australia had been an open market for books.

While the existence of this global carve-up was reasonably well known — particularly after Haupt gave it few caustic broadsides — the details of how it actually kept prices high for Australian readers were still a mystery. But the PSA inquiry got a lucky break in the form of a whistleblower. Ken Wylder, a retired chief executive of the major British publisher Collins, telephoned and offered confidential details of how the cartel worked to keep prices up for Australian book readers. Wylder not only detailed how London meetings would dictate prices of Australian books, but pointed the PSA to the cartel's global price discrimination, the key to high prices in Australia. This is classic monopoly power — dividing markets and charging each sector the maximum price it can.

Wylder showed the PSA that the real comparison to make in the pricing of local books was not the British or American price for the same book, but the Canadian price. This is how it works: first, the British publishers 'own' the Australian market courtesy of the 1899 British Publishers Traditional Market Agreement with their US counterparts. Second, the Australian *Copyright Act* prohibits parallel imports; that is, imports of a non-pirate copyright book without the approval of the Australian copyright holder — the British publisher.

With their copyright import monopolies in the Commonwealth, the London publishers would price what each market could bear. Canada, where cheaper US books were more easily available just across the border, had a comparatively low price. Australia and New Zealand, where no such troublesome US competition existed, could bear higher prices.

And the PSA, following Wylder's pointing, found that that was the case. Identical paperbacks supplied by British publishers sold for A$11.95 in Australia and A$7.05 in Canada. The same book, although produced by a US publisher, would sell for A$5.45 in America. The PSA inquiry showed that the British publishers were marketing books in Canada at prices generally below or close to UK prices, despite the freight costs, to meet potential US competition.

In contrast, the same books marketed in Australia were about 30 per cent higher than British prices. 'Oh, we separate those Aussie mugs from others', is how Fels describes the view of the British publishers. 'We know we can charge them a high price, not so much because they're Aussie mugs but because they're a long way from anywhere.'

The PSA recommended the government change the *Copyright Act* to allow parallel imports. In effect, the PSA wanted to bust open the old British publishers' monopoly, opening the local market to cheaper American editions of the same books. Fels and the PSA argued this would not only lower prices, but speed up availability. The British publishers had been notoriously slow in publishing books in Australia that were not bestsellers.

Fels developed a few gimmicks to sell the message of high-priced books. He would hold up to audiences three copies of Jackie Collins' bestselling bodice-ripper *Hollywood Wives*, one copy published in the US, one in the UK and one in Australia. He would joke with audiences that he had read all three and the words were exactly the same, although he had had to consult with university medical schools for explanations of some parts. Fels would then slip in the point that there was one major difference — price.

By 1990–91, with an election looming, the PSA's exposure of high book prices had created media interest — fuelled by the campaign by well-known authors against parallel importing. Thomas Keneally and Morris West joined the fray, with West writing in *The Australian* in 1989: 'Copyright and the rights arising out of copyright are the inalienable property of the author. To expropriate this property under any pretext is a fundamental invasion of human rights.'

The authors and book publishers lobbied the Hawke Government hard in the first example of 'Hollywoodisation' of a policy debate in Australia. This would achieve new heights when the big rock stars began lobbying against similar parallel importing restrictions being lifted on CDs.

The Hawke Cabinet decided to appease the authors with a compromise that gave publishers a 30-day window within which the book had to go on sale in Australia. If not, or if a protected book ceased to be available for 90 days, the publisher would lose import protection and parallel imports would be allowed. The 30/90-day compromise addressed book availability, but did not confront the price effect of import monopolies head on. In retrospect, Fels sees

that the PSA's highlighting of the twin problems of delayed availability
and price gave the government a convenient 'solution' that in reality
did little to end import monopolies.

The book debate, followed by an even more politically traumatic
debate on CDs, put the copyright versus consumers' rights battle
firmly in the public arena for the first time. The PSA, later folded
into Fels' ACCC, was not proposing to extinguish copyright; it only
wanted cheaper overseas copyright versions of books or CDs to be
made available to Australians.

Authors and musicians argued that cheaper versions of their
material would be 'dumped' in Australia, paying them less in royalties.
The irony was that many of these writers had benefited from
government grants funded by taxpayers, but were now saying that
those taxpayers could not share in their success by cheaper book
prices. In effect, they were arguing that their copyright should
determine book prices in Australia, and that meant import
monopolies should be left in place.

Sensitive issues were in play. Authors and musicians also argued
that the big book and music publishers fostered local talent, and
removal of their import monopolies could directly impact on
Australian culture. The argument that Australian culture is protected
by import monopolies is a curious one. As Fels kept pointing out,
surely a culture is enhanced by widespread and cheap access to books,
music, and computer software. Handouts to writers and musicians
should be through direct government cultural payments, not forced
subsidies from consumers.

Fels wrestled with the intellectual property rights issue through
his entire period as competition regulator. While holders of
intellectual property rights claimed these were 'absolute', as Fels told
a conference in Rome in 1991, all property rights had limits placed
on them. 'All rights are limited because they cannot be extended
without affecting others', he said. 'The question is how far should
[intellectual property rights] extend? Moral arguments of rights
versus obligations are inherently difficult to resolve. Economic

analysis provides a useful set of tools for determining these boundaries. In general a freely competitive market maximises society's total economic welfare.'

The campaign on CDs offered a replay of the books debate, although it went on much longer, with rock star involvement adding new media and political intensity. The quote heading up this chapter — 'There should be cheaper CDs by Christmas (Allan Fels in 1993, 1994, 1995, 1996, 1997)' — is a Commission in-house joke about Fels' long campaign to secure reforms.

The basic ground rules were the same as books: copyright conferred on a few global record companies an import monopoly into the Australian market, with comparatively high prices the result. The PSA found that a popular CD which sold in Australia for $27 cost $23 in Canada, $18 in the US, $21 in Japan and $24 in New Zealand.

Again, the recommendation to government was to allow parallel imports. Again, the local artists flew to the defence of the global producers. Midnight Oil's Peter Garrett led the charge, saying record companies could only invest in local bands if they had the import monopolies on big international musicians. Fels was stunned by Garrett's admission at a media conference that he bought many of his own CDs overseas.

Consumer prices versus subsidies to some local artists. Which way to promote 'culture'? With CDs, however, there was a twist. The Musicians' Union came out in favour of allowing parallel imports. John McAuliffe, the union's federal secretary, demolished the argument that import monopolies and high prices were necessary to foster local talent. He pointed out that record companies invested in local artists because of commercial considerations and the local content rules on radio. Local content rules were working as an indirect subsidy to Australian artists, forcing radio stations to buy and air their works. It backed Fels' argument that there were other ways to boost local artists than handing record and book companies lucrative import monopolies.

Despite such union logic, the debate raged through the Hawke and Keating Labor governments, coming before Cabinet at least five times. Within Cabinet, Attorney-General Michael Duffy, with three CD-buying teenage daughters, backed Fels' reforms. On the other side Senator Graham Richardson, the influential right wing numbers man who for part of that time was also Minister for Communications, strongly campaigned for the status quo.

Ministers wavered as the campaign intensified. Shortly after publishing the PSA report on high CD prices, Fels bumped into Paul Keating, then Treasurer. 'Oh, that's great', Fels recalls Keating telling him. 'That's just what we want you to do, cut CD prices. That's great for consumers.' Fels believed Keating was sincere, but he never heard from him again on the subject. Press reports indicated Keating was later lobbied against the reforms at his local record store in the Canberra suburb of Manuka, where he shopped for classical CDs.

Fels and Jill Walker, the PSA officer who wrote the CD report, attended a formal dinner of the Australian Record Industry Association at which the two became Daniels in the lions' den. Industry leaders made speeches ranting against the competition regulator. With the rock star-led debate capturing headlines, and seemingly influencing Cabinet, Fels went into his 'full five channel blast' publicity mode. He debated Molly Meldrum and rock stars on television, was photographed examining CDs in stores, and published newspaper feature articles with Peter Garrett, each outlining their case.

For Fels, the celebrity support for the big music companies' import monopolies was disappointing. In its package of reforms, the PSA had recommended a music industry council to provide subsidies to young performers as well as vesting copyright in artists. (Normally that is held by record companies or composers.)

Fels' publicity stunts on CDs led to a Keating outburst that he was nothing more than a 'media nymphomaniac'. Undeterred, Fels went one step further: he began criticising the Labor Cabinet for stalling on CDs. 'Fels raps Cabinet on CD delay', headlined one article in *The Australian*. 'The time has come for Federal Cabinet to bite the bullet on this issue and to stand up to the vested interests which have for far too long stood in the way of the public interest', he wrote in a Trade Practices Commission newsletter. 'A decision on the Copyright Act is a test of the government's willingness to uphold the proper public inquiry process and to undertake necessary micro-economic reform.'

This was close to insubordination — a regulator publicly telling Cabinet it was failing in its job. It showed how far Fels was prepared to push a consumer line. This was pioneering territory for a regulator. Whether brave or foolhardy, it would come as no surprise to Fels that first the Labor Cabinet and later the Howard Cabinet would begin to wonder if he was beyond control.

The Keating Government proved incapable of coming to a definitive decision on CDs. In 1996, the incoming Howard Government had no such qualms. If Labor was opposed to the reform, Howard was for it. The campaign took some nasty turns. The music industry prepared advertisements slating Howard for 'killing' the industry, and made sure they were sent to Howard's office. Around the industry there was talk of a private investigator being hired to dig up dirt on Fels. (They could have saved themselves the trouble. If there was any 'dirt' on Fels it would have already been found and published, such was the mounting antipathy of business.) Fels publicly deplored reports that the record companies were leaning on radio stations not to run news reports of the CD pricing issue.

Howard could guarantee the numbers for the copyright amendment bill's passage through the House of Representatives, but lacked a majority in the Senate. A powerful phalanx of lobbyists, including US record companies and even the Christian Music Association, descended on the handful of independent senators who could swing the vote either way.

Fels, who reserves any personal lobbying of politicians to major issues like merger policy, obviously decided the CD vote was crucial. He canvassed two key swing votes, the Labor defector Mal Colston, then a Queensland independent, and Brian Harradine, the

Tasmanian independent. Colston's son, then on his staff as an assistant, was a music fan and told Fels: 'I'll get dad to vote your way on this one'.

The vote was shaping up as very tight, with Labor, the Democrats and Bob Brown (Greens) likely to oppose reforming the CD market. Even Colston was uncertain, and if he and Harradine voted 'no' the bill would likely fail. Fels discussed with Colston's office the possibility of the Senator being 'ill' for the vote. Colston was reportedly suffering from cancer.

At 12.37 am on 11 July 1998, the Senate voted. Colston did abstain, and Harradine voted 'yes', after saying he had paid particular attention to the consumer movement on CD prices. The reforms passed by just one vote — 33 to 32.

It was not the end of the issue. Within a year the ACCC was investigating allegations that some of the big record and music companies had cut off supply to record shops that stocked cheaper parallel imports. In September 1999 it instituted proceedings against Sony, Warner and PolyGram, later taken over by Universal. The ACCC alleged that trading accounts of record stores had been closed, and the record companies had threatened to withdraw trading benefits from stores stocking parallel imports.

Charges were also brought against executives of the record companies, alleging they were 'knowingly' involved. The case against Sony was settled out of court, with Sony, without admitting guilt, giving undertakings not to block supply, to implement a Trade Practices compliance program, and to pay $200 000 of the ACCC's costs.

In March 2002, Justice Hill in the Federal Court fined Warner and Universal and some of their executives more than $1 million for breaches of the *Trade Practices Act*. 'It must be accepted that the conduct engaged in here was serious', Justice Hill said. 'It was a deliberate attempt to subvert the consequences of legislation designed to permit parallel imports of non-infringing copies of compact discs.'

Justice Hill also exploded the industry claim that parallel imports would lead to market failure. 'The dire predictions of reduced competition through to reduced production and ultimate market failure have simply not happened', he found. 'If anything, the evidence shows a continued increase in titles, promotion and production and at the same time at lower prices.' Universal and Warner have appealed.

Attorney-General Daryl Williams pointed to the same evidence of lower CD prices when in March 2002 he moved to end Labor's 'use it or lose it' 30/90-day system and allow parallel imports not only for books but also computer software. This followed another ACCC review showing that, on average, Australians paid around 44 per cent more for paperback fiction than US readers in the 12 years from 1988 to 2000. Packaged software, on average, was 27 per cent higher in Australia, while popular PC computer games were 33 per cent higher.

Publishers strongly disputed Fels' claims, saying he was using the wrong comparisons and failing to take into account the new large-size paperback that was now printed in Australia to meet the 30-day rule. These 'trade paperbacks' had actually led to cheaper prices, they claimed. The publishers won this round, with the Democrats in the Senate doing a deal to approve parallel imports of computer software provided the government left the book industry alone.

'Allowing further parallel importation of books may result in overseas publishers dumping books written by our highest profile authors', said Senator Aden Ridgeway, the Democrat spokesman. In a choice between prices and availability for consumers versus the incomes of authors, the Democrats, it appears, preferred the latter.

The century-old division of the world by book publishers is being replayed in the digital age. In 2000, Fels' ACCC began investigating whether regional playback controls installed in all DVD players enable copyright holders to charge higher prices in areas like Australia. The California-based DVD Copy Control Association requires all makers of DVD players to install these control systems, which effectively divide the world into six regions. Australia is in Region 4. DVDs made for Region 1 will not play in Region 4, and so on. It means an Australian buying a DVD player or disc overseas will find them of little use in Australia, unless he or she has the player modified to accept discs from any region.

A similar situation is evident in PlayStations. A 2002 Federal Court case established the right of Australians to modify their Sony games consoles to play imported and copied games otherwise barred by regional coding restrictions.

⌒

Australian governments may have been prepared to tackle the import monopolies of global publishing and record companies, but when it came to media monopolies within Australia it was a different story. Successive governments have moved to protect newsagents and bolster the position of the big media players. It's all a question of power. While Australia has some of the most concentrated media ownership of any comparable country, governments on both sides have paid only lip-service to the idea of media diversity.

Cross media rules and foreign ownership restrictions have kept media ownership largely out of Fels' domain. Newsagents and their various exclusive arrangements, however, are very much in his regulatory purview. But when it came to the crunch over deregulation, the Howard Government threatened legislation to override the ACCC. It was no novelty. The Fraser Government also bent the competition regulator's ear over newsagents in 1979.

Newspaper publishers and newsagents rushed to apply for authorisation of their sales and distribution agreement in 1974 when Lionel Murphy's *Trade Practices Act* was introduced. They feared — with good reason — that their newsagency arrangements might be seen as anti-competitive. The publishers, in effect, controlled distribution of their products via 'authorised' newsagents, who were granted the sole right to sell a publishers' products within a defined territory, provided they also maintained home delivery.

After examining this system of little geographical monopolies, the Trade Practices Commission found it highly anti-competitive, and could see no offsetting public benefit. But it did not count on the Fraser Cabinet. Wal Fife, then Minister for Business and Consumer Affairs, gave the TPC a special submission from Cabinet, arguing that in a democratic society there was a public benefit in maintaining a low-cost system of distributing newspapers and magazines, both for home delivery and over-the-counter sales. The Commission folded under this pressure, authorising the anti-competitive newsagency system. For years around the newspaper business Wal Fife was put on a pedestal.

Fels decided to open the issue for review soon after his arrival at the TPC in 1991. Fels was aware of the political sensitivities, and also of the deep worry of newsagents as to what he might do. Although declaring there had been a material change of circumstances from the Fraser era decision, the TPC only tinkered at the edges, promising future reforms. The 7-Eleven convenience store group, anxious to sell newspapers on the same terms as newsagents, appealed to the Trade Practices Tribunal. Surprisingly, the Tribunal took a very hairy-chested view of the newsagents systems, proposing speedy and total deregulation within a few years.

In 1996, Fels' ACCC was about to begin another round of reviews of the newsagency system when it received a letter from John Howard, then leader of the Opposition. With an election approaching, Howard asked Fels to hold off until the new government was in power. Fels agreed, aware that Howard had promised to look after newsagents.

A year after the election, as the ACCC was working its way through proposals to deregulate the industry, Fels was sitting next to Health Minister Michael Wooldridge on a plane flight. Wooldridge was an old MBA student of Fels, and the two fell to chatting. Both were having problems with small business: Wooldridge with pharmacists and Fels with newsagents.

One of Fels' headaches at the time was dealing with the 'look-alike' newsagents, the small stores which could not get direct supply of newspapers and magazines from publishers. They were forced to become 'subagents' of the local 'authorised' monopoly newsagent. Subagents received only half the 25 per cent commission paid to newsagents for the sale of each newspaper or magazine. The authorised newsagent received the other half of the commission of subagents' sales.

Fels apparently left Wooldridge in no doubt that he intended to deregulate the industry. A few days later Fels took a telephone call from Treasurer Costello's office. What the hell had he been up to? Cabinet had just had a huge discussion about newsagents and small business triggered by Wooldridge's reporting that Fels was out to get them.

Costello himself left Fels in no doubt that Cabinet was taking the issue very seriously, saying a legislative override was possible if the ACCC was not careful. Later, when the ACCC's deregulatory plans on newsagents were clearer, Fels went to see Costello. Fels drew Costello a little diagram, explaining the various possible deregulatory steps, including the geographical monopolies of newsagents. Costello made it clear that full deregulation as the ACCC eventually planned would draw a legislative override from Cabinet. But Costello left it unclear where Cabinet would draw the line.

Also left fuzzy was the issue of the extent of the legislative override. Would it be just newsagents, or apply to all ACCC authorisations of small business anti-competitive conduct? If the latter, it would impose a new political check on a supposedly independent agency. Moreover, it would lead to a mammoth lobbying hit on Cabinet by every industry facing a possibly negative ACCC decision. Cabinet, not the ACCC, would become the regulator for a large section of the *Trade Practices Act*.

Not since 1977 could the Minister overrule Commission merger decisions. Up until the mid-1980s the Minister had had to consent to all Commission consumer actions, opening many opportunities for interference. But this type of political oversight was a thing of the past.

Costello's override threat left Fels between a rock and a hard place. The Trade Practices Tribunal had already decided that the newsagency business should be fully deregulated. Now here was Costello, saying that this could trigger a new general override power which would threaten the independent basis of the ACCC. Fels and his fellow commissioners decided on a tactical retreat. The Commission issued a final decision containing only mild reforms.

It was somewhat of a cultural shock for the ACCC, which had always regarded the Trade Practices Tribunal as all-powerful. In effect, Fels and the ACCC ticked the newsagency system for another few years, until 2001. Fels dressed this up as best he could, saying both the government and the Tribunal agreed on a 'period of transition' before any change.

In 1999, the ACCC edged the reform process forward another step, ending the old Newsagency Council controlled by the publishers and, instead, instituting direct contracts between publishers and newsagents. It also gave the Australian Newsagents' Federation the power to negotiate with the big publishers in behalf of all newsagents.

Effectively the old newsagents monopoly was re-sculptured. Geographic monopolies were retained, but in direct distribution contracts between individual publishers and newsagents, now on tighter performance leashes. Newsagents can thank persistent political intervention over decades for resuscitation from a near-death experience.

Around the industry, Howard is credited not only with hauling in the ACCC, but also telling Lachlan Murdoch that media policy could be in jeopardy unless the big publishers accommodated the newsagents and signed contracts. At one stage of the tortuous newsagency negotiations News Limited had considered launching a direct home delivery system, avoiding newsagents. All major publishers have now signed contracts with newsagents.

For Fels and the ACCC it was a long march from its declaration in 1979 that 'there is no public benefit in subsidised home delivery of newspapers'. That might be the cold economic rationalism, but the concept of endangered family small businesses still tugged at political hearts. Howard's father had run a service station in Sydney's Dulwich Hill.

⌒

If newsagents were the Australian commercial equivalent of a protected species, Telstra was the monopoly that refused to be slain. The relationship began with great hope in 1997 after the ACCC was handed industry oversight upon the full deregulation of telecommunications, but things quickly soured.

At one point Telstra's Bruce Ackhurst, then in charge of regulatory affairs, would tell the ACCC's Rod Shogren that Telstra just did not trust the regulator. The reason: ACCC publicity. Telstra felt it was being ambushed, and that the ACCC unfairly used publicity. For the ACCC it was a familiar whinge. Although most of the issues between the ACCC and Telstra dealt with treatment of customers, Telstra felt they should still be handled in private.

Fels had had earlier indications that Telstra could be difficult. In the early 1980s, as Labor was planning for a 1983 election win, the ACTU had asked Fels to cast an eye at Labor's embryonic idea of a prices and incomes accord. Fels advised them to include the big public utilities such as Telecom (as it was then known) and Australia Post.

Later, as Director of the Graduate School of Management at Monash, he bumped into Mel Ward, then Telecom's chief executive. Fels told Ward that Henry Ergas, an Australian economist at the OECD in Paris who specialised in telecommunications, had agreed to work at the university for a few years. Ergas had also done some work for Telecom, and Ward was enthusiastic about the appointment, offering to donate $250 000 a year for three years for research. But when Ergas published research highly critical of Telecom, the funds stopped.

When Fels became chairman of the TPC, Ward came to see him. Telecom, he said, was a big business, and if the competition regulator had problems with it Fels should feel free to call him to fix them. Ward implied that was the way things had been done in the past. Fels' reply was 'no, that is not the way we will do things'. If Telecom broke the law, the Commission would apply sanctions, as it did to others. There would be no special deal for the biggest company in

Australia. Over the years several chief executives tried this 'just ring me' approach. Fels' reply was always the same.

Although Telstra and the ACCC had a few consumer skirmishes through the 1990s, the telco did not come directly into the ACCC sights until 1997, when the Commission was handed the specific task of regulating the new open telecommunications market. (Between 1992 and 1997 when Telstra and Optus had had a duopoly, regulation was handled by Austel, which was then split between the ACCC and the new Australian Communications Authority, which would look after licensing and management of the radio frequency spectrum.)

In theory, the newly deregulated industry was supposed to run with a modicum of self-regulation. The key was access: how smaller new players could get onto the networks of the big players like Telstra. The ACCC was empowered to ensure an access regime, supposedly guaranteeing such entry, and to issue competition notices for anti-competitive behaviour. Competition notices, with stiff penalties of up to $1 million a day — cumulative — were supposed to be show-stoppers.

Telstra, however, quickly found ways to stall these, and it was not long before they were in dispute over fines theoretically stretching out to telephone book numbers. One of these was settled in an airport lounge meeting between ACCC Commissioner Rod Shogren and Telstra's Bruce Ackhurst, who, incidentally, had been a student of Fels at Monash. As Fels says, Telstra found ways to negotiate, arbitrate and then re-arbitrate. Despite ACCC intervention, bids for access to Telstra's cable network by competitors to Foxtel pay-television (50 per cent owned by Telstra) remained unresolved for years.

Fels' level of frustration with Telstra's dominance was evident in a speech to the Australian Telecommunications Users Group (ATUG) in March 2003. Telstra, he said, had 'overwhelming dominance', and he termed it 'one of the most horizontally and vertically integrated telecommunications companies in the world'.

Telstra's primary market power comes through its control of the local telephone loops to homes, where it retains some 94 per cent of the wholesale market despite more than a decade of deregulation. In his ATUG speech, Fels also ticked off Telstra's other powers: two mobile networks (GSM and CDMA), a forceful presence as the largest internet service provider, largest provider of wholesale data and internet services and a 50 per cent shareholding in the major pay-television cable network, Foxtel.

'The existence of such extensive market power is a major risk to competitive outcomes as it has both the ability — and importantly the incentive — to try and thwart entry into complementary and substitute markets by other companies', he told the ATUG audience. 'Telstra has demonstrated a willingness to use its market power to game the regulatory regime and delay competitive outcomes.'

It was unusually blunt language by Fels, admitting, in effect, that Telstra was winning in its long battle with the ACCC to retain its dominance. What had gone wrong? The reality is that any competition regulator, even one with the publicity powers of Allan Fels, was going to be pushing it uphill to create a more competitive communications market. The Hawke Government had launched deregulation by muscling up the old Telecom with the Overseas Telecommunications Commission, rather than using OTC to create a new competitor, as Treasurer Paul Keating wanted. The new competitor, Optus, was instead launched from the base of Aussat's small satellite operations.

On top of this, the fact that the first period of deregulation was a duopoly, with Telstra facing only Optus for five years, meant the first period of supposed 'competition' was fairly light. Also, successive governments have declined to force the structural separation of Telstra — that is, hiving off its core telephone cable network from its various retail functions. (The structural separation of incumbent monopolists in telecommunications deregulation is advocated by the OECD as the best way to create a competitive market.) The result in Australia is that Telstra has enjoyed a comfortably padded base from which to ward off competitors.

The ACCC–Telstra sniping continued unabated over the years. At one point Communications Minister Richard Alston called both

Fels and Telstra chief Ziggy Switkowski to his office. Alston chose his words carefully. He needed to. The government is the majority shareholder in Telstra, and the ACCC is the industry regulator. Was such public disagreement necessary, he wanted to know? After all, Telstra and the ACCC were both really under the Commonwealth umbrella.

Fels and Switkowski had a blunt exchange of views. Switkowski said Telstra was responding to ACCC attacks, and had decided to increase its own PR efforts. Fels said all that meant was an escalation of the 'arms race'.

Things cooled for a while. But it is not surprising that the ACCC would sup with a long spoon when Foxtel and Optus came calling in 2002 with a scheme to merge their pay-television content. The ACCC had already rejected an earlier merger by Foxtel and Australis, a pay-TV group, on the basis that the merger could damage Optus. Australis later collapsed, with Foxtel picking up most of its subscribers in deals with the liquidators, a sort of posthumous merger. Fels suffered considerable criticism over the collapse, but maintained that neither Foxtel nor Australis had ever mentioned this possibility in the months of negotiations, and that it was not the ACCC's job to second-guess merger participants.

If Telstra had not been a 50 per cent owner of Foxtel (Kerry Packer's PBL and Rupert Murdoch's News Limited split the other 50 per cent), the content merger with Optus would have sailed through.

But Fels and Commissioner Ross Jones, who would negotiate with the parties, saw this as a last chance to prise open some form of access for both pay-TV content providers and rival telephone groups to Foxtel's network and programming. If the old Trade Practices Commission had failed in preventing the print dominance of Rupert Murdoch when it approved (with only minor qualifications) his 1987 acquisition of The Herald & Weekly Times, could Fels' ACCC now prevent similar dominance of the electronic future?

The negotiations extended over months, and were accompanied by some off-stage fireworks. Competitors like Fairfax and Kerry

Stokes' Seven Network lobbied intensely against it. At one stage a plan was floated, and rejected, for Stokes to buy an equity slice of Foxtel. Accusations flew that the ACCC lacked commercial negotiating savvy, and that there were some extraordinary political interventions — in short, about par for the drama-laden media industry. There were also more serious tensions about whether Optus would stay in the telephony market if the merger was rejected, and whether Telstra would stay in the merger if the ACCC tried to impose tough conditions.

If Optus had folded its small operations in local telephony and retreated basically into mobiles, as it threatened, it would have been a severe blow to ACCC hopes for a competitive future telephony market. Telstra's willingness to stay in the merger was another worry, as it appeared to offer only low benefits to the dominant carrier. Optus's chief executive Chris Anderson had earlier floated the idea of a content merger provided Foxtel picked up Optus's horrendous movie contracts, estimated at some $600 million, and this stipulation remained in the new proposal.

The three Foxtel partners, Telstra, PBL and News, were in a stand-off about the future of the pay-TV operation when the original content-sharing with Optus was proposed. Telstra saw Foxtel strictly as a defence for its telephony business, wanting to use it to 'bundle' cost-attractive telephone and pay-TV offerings to customers. News and PBL, however, wanted Foxtel to operate as a stand alone pay-television business more on the lines of Murdoch's successful BSkyB in Britain, and blocked any Telstra bundling until it was allowed to operate more independently.

The appointment of Sam Chisholm as Foxtel chairman started to break the logjam. Chisholm is an aggressive Kiwi who had driven BSkyB to a premier position in the UK television market with a single-minded subscriber pitch on movies and sports. Chisholm and new Foxtel chief executive Kim Williams focused the Foxtel partners on the future potential of pay-TV, the digital world of interactivity and the way BSkyB had become a television gateway. The merger was

Joviality at an ACCC/SOCOG meeting.

It's no laughing matter where the press is concerned.
Allan Fels with SOCOG's Jim Sloman.

GST takes wings thanks to Fels' price campaigning.

Have we got a tax for you? Allan Fels on the GST sales trail with wife Isabel.

Internationally speaking: Fels at an OECD Paris meeting of the
Competition Committee, 2001.

Always in the picture. Fels at a press conference, 2001.

Allan Fels with Bronwyn Bishop, kicking up their heels at the 2001 Press Gallery Midwinter ball.

Professor Allan Fels AO Chairman ACCC 2002
Artist: Irene Clark
96 × 127 cm
oil on linen
Finalist in Portia Geach Memorial Award 2002
Reproduced with permission of Irene Clark and Gallery 101, Melbourne

THE Daily Telegraph

Wednesday, April 24, 2002

$1*
Including GST S

ANZAC COMMEMORATIVE SERIES
— Remembering Gallipoli —
Images from the front lines P36

EXCLUSIVE

PETROL RAIDS

ACCC officers carry boxes of documents from Caltex headquarters in Martin Place yesterday.

Picture: ROHAN KELLY

Whistleblower sparks massive price swoop

By KATHY LIPARI

THE largest corporate raid by Australia's competition watchdog took place across two states yesterday following allegations of price fixing by the petrol giants.

A team of 90 Australian Competition and Consumer Commission (ACCC) lawyers, investigators and IT experts marched on the offices of Caltex, Mobil and Shell and other distributors in NSW and Victoria.

The ACCC is investigating whether the companies have:

INSIDE
- ■ **Green letters sparked raids**
- ■ **Allan Fels strikes again**
- ■ **The petrol price equation**
   — **Reports: Pages 4-5 —**

- ● ACTED together to price competitors out of the market;
- ● ENGAGED in price fixing of petrol;
- ● ENGAGED in market sharing.

Last night a spokeswoman for Mobil said:

"It's Mobil's policy to fully comply with the Trade Practices Act at all times, we fully co-operate with the ACCC investigation."

If the allegations prove correct, the companies and some executives could face tens of millions of dollars in fines.

The ACCC investigation was triggered by an anonymous letter from a female whistleblower mailed to the commission in December last year.

ACCC chairman Allan Fels said the allegations were very serious, prompting raids of documents, computer hard drives and laptops in 10 locations including Sydney, Newcastle, Melbourne and parts of both states.

The actions of distributors, including Metropolitan Fuel Distributors in Smithfield, Bowen Petroleum Services, Hexham and Midcoast Petroleum, Sandgate also are involved in the ACCC's investigation.

Investigators were sorting through boxes of information last night and will continue seizing evidence today.

"We have concluded that there may have been a contravention of the Trade Practices Act," Professor Fels told *The Daily Telegraph* yesterday.

"It principally applies to Section 45 of the Act which is about collusion. We have

Continued Page 4

Why Mad Max met the Liberals' young turk in Macquarie St — Page 3

Weather
Mild to warm in the east. Warm in the west.
— Page 57

dailytelegraph.com.au   Business: P39; Comics: P71; Crosswords: P45; TV: P71; TABform P59; Lottery (7627): P46.   TeleClassifieds 02 9288 2000

Boxed in: the incorrect caption that ignited business hostility to Fels' use of the media.

Delivering the State Chamber of Commerce
Common Good Annual Address, August 2002.

Isabella, Allan, Isabel and Teresa at Government House, Victoria, in 2002 when Allan received the Order of Australia.

Getting tough on internet scams, 2002.

Allan Fels and Brian Cassidy giving evidence to the Senate Inquiry into Media Ownership.

The big picture: keeping abreast of world news.

In the interests of good health. Giving evidence on the AMA.

Educating the next generation at the Australian National University in Canberra, May 2003.

The new face of the ACCC, Graeme Samuel.

about the electronic future of multi-channel television in the household.

Even so, Telstra had to agree that Foxtel, still a loss-maker, would absorb hundreds of millions in Optus costs in order for the merger to go ahead. How long would it be before some of the Telstra hard-heads began to ask why they were underwriting the future of Optus as their major telephony competitor?

After initially declaring the content merger anti-competitive, Ross Jones then negotiated significant concessions from Foxtel enabling competing pay-TV providers to access the Foxtel cable network and telephony rivals to use the Foxtel channels in their own 'bundling' offers of telephone and pay-TV services. But Foxtel refused to 'slice and dice', that is, enable competitors to take only movies or sports. They had to take a package, although competitors could negotiate separate arrangements with movie suppliers.

Although accepting the merger for analogue pay-TV services, Jones and Fels would later have another bite at the electronic future in a separate report to Communications Minister Richard Alston on digital television and the future broadcasting market. Alston had requested the report, but clearly did not like what he received some 15 months later. Jones and Fels urged a new landscape in future communications, pay-TV and broadcasting. Telstra should divest both Foxtel and its fibre cable network, they urged. As well, Alston should bring forward the 2006 moratorium on the issuing of new commercial TV licences.

Telstra's dominance and the lack of new TV channels were seen as locking out competitors from the multi-channel future, with its promise of interactive television services such as email, internet and video-on-demand. But Telstra was 'in a position to largely dictate the type of services that consumers will be able to access and the time at which these services become available', the report said. Alston took only a few days to reject the recommendations about Telstra and new TV channels.

Some in the media industry saw this as Fels' last hurrah, a farewell from a competition regulator who had to stand on the sidelines and watch an industry gain protection through its direct lobbying of politicians. The combination of cross media rules, foreign ownership restrictions and other protectionist measures such as a ban on new commercial television channels had largely kept Fels out of the business of the media. In one way, this was a godsend. It enabled him to develop excellent relations with journalists without what he might or might not be doing about their bosses getting in the way. (One exception was a sustained dressing down from News Limited publications after the ACCC rejected the Foxtel/Australis merger.)

Fels did occasionally run across the media magnates, however. In 1995, after an ABC *7.30 Report* appearance in which he referred to 'Packer's company', Fels received a note from the man himself. If you're referring to the company it should be PBL not Packer's, he said. What's more, if Fels really wanted to discuss a few matters, why not come over and have a cup of tea?

As it happened, Fels was in Sydney that day, and when he called to accept the offer for tea, he was immediately invited over. The two talked over several cups of tea for three hours, with young James Packer present. 'Kerry Packer talked pretty much non-stop, giving me his views on protection, competition, the role of the media, the current state of Australian politics, all in a very colourful and persuasive manner', says Fels.

There was only one problem. Fels had a prior arrangement to do an ABC radio appearance, and had to use a telephone in Packer's outer office to do the interview. If only the ABC had known, it would have had a minor media scoop on its hands — competition regulator's social afternoon in Kerry Packer's office!

Fels' brushes with Rupert Murdoch did not entail cups of tea. The ACCC pinged Murdoch's Sydney *Daily Telegraph* over a misleading statement on a mobile telephone promotion, and also forced the Brisbane *Courier-Mail* to drop its ban against allowing internet advertising in the newspaper's classified section. Newspapers, of course, regard the internet as a threat to classified advertising.

Although media policy has been a step removed from the ACCC, Fels has watched its twists and turns with disbelief. The root of the problem, he believes, is that politicians rather than an independent agency always set the media rules. 'The longer history of media policy has been of poor decision making marred by excessive concern with the interests of the media moguls and lack of concern for competition', he reflects.

Fels has a point. From the long battle for FM radio, to a 10-year moratorium on pay-TV, to locking up digital spectrum with under-utilised high-definition television (HDTV), the emphasis has been on producer rather than consumer interests. Fels was particularly disappointed with the HDTV decision. From his perspective, the Commonwealth was lecturing the states on the need to introduce competition reforms via the Hilmer process on the one hand, and on the other hand ignoring competitive principles in its own area of media by locking away digital spectrum from competition.

The Foxtel–Optus content merger demonstrated to Fels that the ACCC was the one government agency with the authority to deal with the media moguls. Any broadcasting authority given the job would get rolled by the political power of the moguls. 'We've got the power and authority in my view', says Fels. 'Whereas we couldn't maybe 10 years ago, somehow the rise of the ACCC meant that if a government gave it a job to do in regulating media for the public benefit, it would do that properly.'

Over the years, as successive governments have wrestled with media merger rules, Fels has often suggested empowering the ACCC with some media-specific rules plus a public interest test that would likely include the aim of maximising media diversity. Now that the ACCC's true media competitive colours are out in the open with the report to Alston, it is unlikely to ever happen. Politicians understand the power imperative of keeping control of the media levers. Media moguls might not be able to swing elections these days, but they still own very influential voices to the electorate.

Fels had singled out media reform as one of the issues on his future competitive agenda when he addressed the National Press Club after his appointment in 1991. Twelve years later, appearing at the Press Club on the eve of his departure, he could only lament that there had been little progress. 'Substantial deregulation is needed', he said. There is little sign of it, despite occasional Howard Government attempts to remove cross-ownership restrictions, which would likely only increase concentration of ownership. The media talks a lot about the need for competition in Australian industry — but not in the media, please!

CHAPTER 10

'DON'T MESS WITH ME OVER THE MEDICAL PROFESSION'

Over the years Fels became accustomed to summonses from ministers. But the call to see Health Minister Michael Wooldridge in 2000 set him back a few paces — it amounted to a heavy-handed attempt to derail ACCC inquiries into anti-competitive practices by doctors. Wooldridge had invited Fels to his Parliament House office after the ACCC began an inquiry into training of surgeons. Fels took Sitesh Bhojani with him, the commissioner responsible for all dealings with the professions.

There were no direct orders at the meeting, but the message was clear to both Fels and Bhojani: 'Don't mess with me over the medical profession'. Fels recalls the conversation: 'He more or less just told us not to interfere … It was going to get in his way, and there was hardly any more important policy for the government than dealing with health issues. We were seen, in his view, as obstructing that'.

Wooldridge adopted a stern countenance and politician's language to deliver an 'I'm the Minister for Health' message. But he also took it one step further, implying that he had the backing of the Prime Minister and Cabinet. This was so important for the government, Wooldridge said, that he would have strong support. 'What he really meant was if we took him on, the government would take his side not ours', says Fels.

The meeting puzzled the two ACCC commissioners. What was Wooldridge really on about? Wooldridge was then having one of his regular spats with the prickly Dr Kerryn Phelps, head of the Australian Medical Association (AMA). At the same time, the ACCC was starting to inquire into selection and training by the Royal Australasian College of Surgeons to determine if it was a closed club, or met community demands for surgeons. Was Wooldridge trying to win brownie points among other doctors in his stoush with the AMA by showing that he could warn off the competition regulator?

A more likely explanation emerged later. The Howard Government feared that if Fels' ACCC opened the floodgates by breaking down the barriers imposed by the Royal Colleges there could be thousands of new specialists, creating demand for their services. This would blow out the government's already ballooning health costs. Maybe it was a case, says Fels, of the government fearing that supply would create demand.

Wooldridge has something of a different interpretation. Certainly he was telling the ACCC to 'sod off' but for a good reason. Wooldridge regarded the government, and particularly himself as health minister, as in charge of health policy, not any outside body. Cabinet and the prime minister had discussed it, and there was a strong view that it was the prerogative of government to make policy. A potential blow-out in costs may have been part of the issue, but he was not trying to get the ACCC to 'lay off' the royal colleges of medicine. In fact, he considers that the ACCC's report on the colleges was outstanding. 'Health is an extremely difficult portfolio, and I had no intention of having people outside making it harder still', he says. 'I just wanted to put my point of view to them.'

Whatever the reason for Wooldridge's ministerial foot-stamping, Fels decided to ignore him. With the GST coming in, he reasoned that the ACCC was more important to the government than Wooldridge's attempt to protect his turf. Moreover, Fels' own minister, Treasurer Peter Costello, would likely back him in any Cabinet punch-up as he was usually a strong supporter of vigorous application of the *Trade Practices Act*, notwithstanding his personal intervention over newsagents.

The upshot was that Fels heard no more of Wooldridge's threats. But Wooldridge was not the only one wanting the ACCC off medical backs; most of the profession also did. Yet when the profession got what it wanted — an inquiry into how the ACCC was supposedly ruining rural medical practices — the report was as critical of the AMA as it was of the ACCC.

The professions are a relatively new brief for the ACCC. Lionel Murphy's 1974 legislation left them somewhat in limbo. Although it included 'work of a professional nature', in practice they continued to be largely excluded from ACCC regulation. The problem was that many professionals practised either in partnership or in other non-corporate forms not covered by the trade practices legislation. Professional practices that did not operate across state borders were also exempt. The states handled most of the regulation of professions, providing in some cases specific exemptions from competition.

The Hilmer review in 1993 swept all that away. It recommended, and everyone agreed, that competitive conduct rules be extended to include all non-incorporated businesses and that provisions permitting state exemptions be repealed. Some were nervous, however. The Australian Council of Professions wanted continuing freedom for professions to set and enforce entry requirements and practice standards, although not fees. The Australian Medical Association argued for transitional arrangements, while the Victorian Bar Council claimed that application of the Act was unnecessary as it did not engage in any anti-competitive conduct.

That was not necessarily how the Trade Practices Commission saw it. Although the Victorian Bar was theoretically ahead of some of its state colleagues in allowing a 'fused' profession in which barristers and solicitors could practice, the state's legal profession still operated under numerous restrictions. Indeed, the 'fused' profession was more a theory than a practice. These days, every state operates a fused profession except Queensland, and the National Competition Council says it is expected to follow suit soon.

A competition regulator takes a unique view of professions. It is not primarily focused on their standards or ethics. Rather, it looks beyond these to the barriers to competition. Fels sees these competitive barriers falling into two categories: structural barriers and conduct barriers. The structural side covers the way entry into the market is regulated including educational standards, licensing and restriction on foreign professionals, as well as the separation of the market functionally into discrete professional activities. On the conduct side, the professions set fee limits and ethical rules, and prohibit certain kinds of advertising.

(Fels has tried to lighten discussions of this topic with a scorecard joke. Contributing to a forum on 'Economics or Law — the Second Oldest Profession' in the Canberra Bulletin of Public Administration in March 2000, Fels awarded the medical profession 10 out of 10. The key to professional economic success, he said tongue in cheek, was to create a monopoly, reserving an area of work for yourself, and then ensure that as few people as possible were allowed to enter.

So, over the years, the medical profession gained a monopoly and restricted entry, 'with some success'. Lawyers deserved only 5 out of 10. They had reserved a large area of work for themselves, indeed a monopoly, but allowed a fairly free flow into the profession, driving down average incomes. Economists scored nil out of 10: they had not created a monopoly or restricted entry in any way.)

While some professional regulation is necessary to protect the public, various inquiries have pointed to a complex web of regulatory barriers around many Australian professions. These include entry qualifications, registration requirements, reservation of titles, reservation of practice, disciplinary processes, conduct of business and business licensing.

In Australia, the usual method of health regulation is to define the area of practice as widely as possible, authorise the relevant profession to work in that area, and bar everyone else. Such 'reservation of practice' covers doctors, nurses, dentists, optometrists, physiotherapists, pharmacists, chiropractors and psychologists. Some states even subdivide these reserved areas further into optical and dental paraprofessionals, chiropodists, osteopaths, occupational therapists, radiographers and aboriginal health workers. The tendency has been for professions like dentistry to create new subcategories like dental therapists and dental hygienists who then try to rival dentists.

Canada's Ontario province takes a different approach. Rather than reserve an entire area of practice, it reserves 'controlled acts'. These are the more skilled and dangerous procedures like surgery only to be performed by trained and licensed professionals. Less risky acts are not regarded as controlled and can be performed by others.

Competition analysis of the usually sacrosanct professions dates back to Adam Smith, the 18th century author of *The Wealth of Nations*. Smith, regarded as the founder of modern economics and competition, penned some acerbic words on the worth of degrees and the titles they conveyed. The title 'doctor', he said, 'gives some credit and authority to the man upon whom it is bestowed; it extends his practice, and consequently his field for doing mischief; it is not improbable too that it may increase his presumption, and consequently his disposition to do mischief'. More recently, the American Economists Milton Friedman and Simon Kuznets gave the professions a dose of Chicago school market economics in their 1945 book *Income from Independent Professional Practice*, which sets much of the groundwork for modern study. Friedman goes all the way, advocating a completely open market for medicine with no licensing at all for doctors.

In Australia, it was not until the states all passed Hilmer legislation mirroring the Commonwealth's new universal application of trade practice law, in the mid-1990s, that the way was open for Fels' ACCC to bring the professions into the competitive fold. It was not an easy task. The long-standing exemptions had allowed the professions to see themselves as above the law.

The competition regulator had already made an initial foray into the area with studies on architects and accountancy. Both professions received a good report card.

It was a different story for lawyers. In March 1994, after a draft report and submissions from interested parties, the TPC recommended nothing short of a revolution in the legal profession. Governments should open up the supply of non-legal services, such as conveyancing, to outsiders. Licensing arrangements dividing the work of barristers and solicitors should be abolished, as should rules restricting the ownership of legal practices. Fees and charges should be deregulated, with contingency fees allowed. Lawyers should be allowed to attract clients with advertising, particularly of fees. The states should drop the traditional system of selecting Queen's Counsels, as well as rules distinguishing QCs from junior barristers.

The judgement of restrictions in the legal profession was harsh. The Commission concluded that many of the profession's regulations could not be justified on grounds of public interest, and recommended reforms to expose legal practitioners to competition. Regulations in the legal profession, it said, went 'far beyond' those applied in other sections of business and professions. The legal world's raft of traditional regulations discouraged innovation and inhibited competition. 'These inefficiencies will be reflected in the costing and pricing of legal services', the report found.

This was not the only finding that the costs of professional services were driven up by excessive regulation. An Industry Commission Inquiry into Hilmer found that control of supply of services by surgeons was reflected in their high remuneration.

Not surprisingly, the Commission's report on the legal profession sparked an uproar. But John Fahey, the Liberal New South Wales Premier, was a supporter and introduced substantial reforms. Among these, Fahey removed the legal profession's monopoly on conveyancing, price scheduling and advertising restrictions. The National Competition Council later reported that conveyancing costs in New South Wales dropped 17 per cent between 1994 and 1996.

A decade later, the reform process remains a work in progress. After years of trawling state restrictions on the professions, the National Competition Council in 2002 found that reforms remain to be implemented in pharmacy, architecture and the legal profession. Among the last-mentioned, it listed some problems with eerie echoes of a decade earlier, including reserved areas of practice, advertising restrictions, legal practice ownership restrictions and the monopoly provision of professional indemnity insurance for solicitors.

In New South Wales, the reform process has even slipped into reverse. In a bid to curb the blow-out in insurance premiums, the Carr Labor Government in early 2003 introduced restrictions on legal service advertising to people who suffer personal injuries. The aim was to cut damages awards, but it angered lawyers, consumers and the ACCC.

Although given new competition powers over Australia's 200 000 professionals by Hilmer, Fels and his fellow ACCC commissioners knew the reform route would be a long battle. The professions are powerful lobbies, with umbilical cords to colleagues who move into politics and up the political chain into Cabinet.

Fels decided to first use the education route rather than straight-up enforcement of competition law to the professions. Fels and Bhojani embarked on a hectic schedule of briefings for professional groups, flagging the new culture of competition after Hilmer. One of the first of these was an April 1997 set-piece conference in Perth provocatively titled 'Can the professions survive under a national competition policy?' The consensus was that the professions would survive, but professionalism — the character, spirit and methods of a professional — might not. There was also doubt about whether the future of the professions should be solely determined by economic policy.

These issues have been an undercurrent when putting the professions under the competition microscope. At the 1997 conference, Attorney-General Daryl Williams cited the contrasting views of High Court judges on professionalism. Sir Anthony Mason had written: 'The professional ideal is not the pursuit of wealth but of public service. That is the vital difference between professionalism and commercialism'. Noble sentiments, observed Williams, contrasting the views of Sir Daryl Dawson, who said in a paper at the 29th Legal Convention:

> It is the free play of market forces, not the voluntary maintenance of professional standards, in which we now place our faith and in this regard there is little distinction to be drawn between the practice of a profession and any other form of commercial activity. Since the professions are no longer seen as having a special responsibility to serve the community rather than themselves, they no longer speak with the authority which they used to command. They are seen as not significantly different from any other commercial activity driven by market forces.

Dr John Southwick, President of the Australian Council of Professions, laid it on the line at the Perth conference. Professionalism, he said, contained a tradition of sharing knowledge, research and new techniques. 'Professionalism may be at risk under competition policy', he warned. Williams injected the economic dominance dilemma in viewing the professions. The balance, he maintained, was between the competition policy principle of more efficiency in the delivery of professional services, and the public interest that such services not suffer any lack of quality. 'Enormous responsibility is placed on the ACCC to get the balance right', he said. 'If it doesn't, then ultimately it will be the Australian community that will be the poorer for it.'

Fels was alert to the dangers that competition policy could be tagged with destroying professionalism. That could lead to pressure to ease up on the application of competition law to a large section of Australian business. Professionals may regard themselves as 'different', but they also operate small businesses, a hard reality that many find difficult to accept. At the core of the professionalism argument is the issue of 'relationship of trust', or fiduciary relationship, between a professional and client. Opponents argued this was not taken into account in competition law.

'What is it about the fiduciary relationship between a professional (doctor or lawyer) and his or her patient or client that requires the professional to engage in price fixing with his or her competitors?' Fels asked rhetorically in a bid to defuse the argument. 'What is it about the fiduciary relationship between a professional and his or her patient or client that requires the professional to engage in a misuse of market power? What is it about the fiduciary relationship between a professional and his or her patient or client that requires the professional to engage in exclusive dealing, or resale price maintenance, or other conduct prohibited by the [Trade Practices] Act? The ACCC response to those questions is, "Probably nothing".'

However, if there were anti-competitive practices that benefited the patient or client, Fels pointed to the obvious solution — authorisation. If professions could demonstrate the public benefit of any anti-competitive conduct they could receive immunity.

This would be a consistent ACCC line as its inquiries into the professions started to draw strong reactions, particularly from doctors. Opponents argued that authorisation might be available, but it was time-consuming and expensive.

One development after the landmark Perth conference somewhat shocked the ACCC, accustomed even as it was to dealing with all sorts of commercial intrigues. At the conference, Dr David Roberts, President of the Australian Medical Association (WA), while indicating that the medical market was different and that doctors wanted to be able to negotiate in groups, said: 'The AMA is committed to working with the ACCC and other authorities as this new era of competition unfolds'. Later Dr Roberts was fined $10 000 for involvement in price fixing and primary boycotts in breach of the Act that occurred about the same time as the conference!

The price fixing in Western Australia involving Dr Roberts was one of five major cases that would push the ACCC into a bitter and increasingly personal conflict with doctors, and particularly the AMA.

Why did the ACCC decide to marshal its firepower on the medical profession rather than on the lawyers? For starters, the new National Competition Council would review much of the legal profession's regulatory restrictions, which were based on state legislation. Also, the ACCC was receiving complaints about the medical profession. There was also a somewhat cynical but probably realistic internal view that the ACCC stood little chance of winning cases against the legal profession on its home turf, the courts.

The first medical case was virtually textbook cartel conduct. In October 1999 the ACCC alleged in Federal Court proceedings that anaesthetists at St George, Kareena and Greenoaks private hospitals in Sydney had reached an unlawful agreement to charge a $25 per hour on-call fee for emergencies and after hours, even though they were not on site at the hospitals. A boycott of one hospital was proposed unless the on-call fee was agreed to. Just to top this off, the 'on-call' payment scheme was part of a strategy by the New South Wales section of the Australian Society of Anaesthetists.

Normally such clear boycotts and price fixing are hard to prove. Fortunately the anaesthetists seem to have been partaking of their own drugs — they were so relaxed about the matter it was put in their official minutes. The ACCC quickly sussed these out. The anaesthetists owned up, giving undertakings to the court they would not engage in such conduct again. They also paid $60 000 towards the ACCC's costs.

It was embarrassing for the medical profession, and Fels used it to mock claims that the ACCC was damaging professional values. The anaesthetists, he said, had wanted $25 an hour while sitting around at home or 'in their yachts'. As for the boycott, the anaesthetists were telling hospitals they were welcome to get on with their operations 'but the patients might have to stay awake during them because there would be no anaesthetists present'. This, said Fels, had nothing to do with quality of service, ethics or doctor–patient relationships. 'It was the naked use of market power to increase the income of a powerful monopoly at the expense of consumers, governments and others', he said.

The second case set a precedent, as it was the first time that an Australian court imposed penalties on a professional association for price fixing and boycotts. The culprit was the Western Australian AMA. The ACCC initiated legal action over deals allegedly struck between the AMA and Mayne Nickless Ltd as it moved to establish a health 'campus' at Joondalup, an outer-Perth suburb, after acquiring the hospital from the state government. The ACCC said this was an important case as Joondalup was the first health 'campus' in the state, offering both public and private services on the one site. It offered an opportunity for the hospital operator to individually negotiate fees with doctors to provide services to public patients.

In court, the AMA (WA) admitted it informed Mayne Nickless in negotiations that the doctors had agreed to take 'whatever action necessary to conclude the negotiations' and that it had advised them to withdraw services and discharge patients from Joondalup unless a deal was reached. Justice Carr fined the AMA (WA) $240 000 for price fixing and primary boycotts. Justice Carr also found that two AMA officials, Executive Director Paul Boyatzis and former President Dr David Roberts were knowingly concerned in the AMA (WA)'s contraventions, fining them each $10 000.

The spin both sides put on the outcome showed how relations between the ACCC and AMA were deteriorating despite earlier assurances of cooperation. Fels, not surprisingly, again pointed out that the case was not about ethics, standards or quality of treatment. 'The issues are about the collective use of market power to increase doctors' income or shield them from competitive forces', he said.

The AMA, again not surprisingly, took a different view. Federal Vice-President Dr Trevor Mudge said the decision would deter doctors going to 'areas of need' in rural and outer-suburban locations. The Joondalup case, he said, was all about attracting the best possible medical services to the area. 'The AMA (WA) was acting in the best interests of the patients of that community', he said. Just how the best interests of patients squared with them possibly being tipped into the street in a boycott was left unexplained.

Negotiations to take a settlement to court over the Joondalup case lasted for more than a year. Fels and Bhojani dug in at a fine of just over $250 000, while the AMA made counter offers. At its final meeting on the issue the ACCC also had to agree on a recommended level of penalty for the Maritime Union of Australia over its secondary boycotts to try to win the business of cleaning ship holds. The maximum penalty for such behaviour by a union is $750 000, while the maximum penalty for price fixing in the AMA case is $10 million. After a day of weighing the cases of the two 'unions' the MUA got a $200 000 fine while the AMA got $250 000. Fels has an after-dinner speech routine in which he pretends to get the two confused. Which 'union' deserves the bigger fine for a boycott ... the doctors or the wharfies? It always draws a laugh.

In the Joondalup case AMA flagged arguments about rural services that would come to the fore in the next confrontation with the competition regulator — obstetric services in Rockhampton. The case encapsulated the two headline grievances of the AMA, the effects of the *Trade Practices Act* on rural doctors, and on medical rosters. In April 2002 the ACCC instituted Federal Court proceedings alleging that Rockhampton's three obstetricians, Dr Mark Leyden, Dr Stephen Robson and Dr Paul Khoo, had boycotted 'no-gap' billing arrangements offered by private health insurance funds.

One of the trio, Dr Robson, had charged no-gap fees, in which the doctor accepts the health fund benefit as the full payment rather than the patient paying the usual gap between the fund benefit and the higher doctor's fee. No-gap insurance boomed in Australia after AXA Health Fund pioneered its Ezyclaim system. Doctors bill the fund directly for an agreed fee, usually in excess of the so-called scheduled fee, leaving the patient no gap between the fund benefit and the doctor's bill. But many doctors remained strongly opposed, arguing that the no-gap system would lead to US-style managed care in Australia by bolstering the muscle of the health insurance funds.

After unsuccessfully trying to negotiate a roster for emergency coverage of his patients with his two obstetric colleagues, Dr Robson wrote to his patients: 'Until January, 2001, I was able to offer "no-gap" billing for management of labour and delivery. Unfortunately, other obstetricians in Rockhampton now refuse to treat my patients if I participate in "no-gap" schemes in any way. This would have meant that, if I was unavailable and you went into labour or had an unexpected emergency, you would have to be transferred to the Base Hospital as a public patient. To make sure this does not happen, I have had to abandon "no-gap" billing in all forms'.

Following complaints from patients, the ACCC took all three to court, alleging a boycott. The effect of the boycott, it said, was that some 200 patients were required to pay a gap fee for their hospital expenses for childbirth that they would not otherwise have paid. Correspondence in the case shows the ACCC plays hardball when it comes down to finding evidence. In a tough letter to the three doctors, the ACCC spelt out the hefty penalties the *Trade Practices Act* provided for, then held out the prospect of leniency for 'full cooperation', including provision of details on meetings, arrangements and communications. 'The Commission seeks your in-principle agreement to cooperate on the abovementioned basis', the letter said in bold type. 'The Commission also seeks your acknowledgment that you will not contact any party (except for your legal representative) in relation to this matter or discuss in any way, the issues raised in this letter or the Commission's investigation with any such parties. Should you be contacted by anyone, including other obstetricians, in relation to this matter you should immediately provide the Commission with full details of these communications.'

Patients were also asked for information, the letters noting that any loss or damage suffered as a result of the boycott could be recovered. The Federal Court accepted consent orders from the three obstetricians, requiring them to repay almost $97 000 to affected patients.

'This case highlights that medical practitioners are not beyond the reach of the competition laws', said Commissioner Bhojani. 'The current shortage of medical practitioners in rural and regional Australia is not an excuse to act illegally by breaching competition laws which are intended to enhance the welfare of all Australians.' The AMA's press release claimed simply: 'ACCC bludgeons doctors out of country towns'.

There was no such press release when the ACCC claimed its fourth medical 'scalp' on the issue of boycotts. In March 2003 the Federal Court found that a Melbourne doctor had attempted to induce a boycott of both bulk billing and after-hours services by other doctors seeking to practise at a Berwick Springs medical centre. The ACCC had instituted proceedings against Dr Abraham Freund and his company, alleging they had tried to incorporate rules into leases in the medical centre which required doctors not to bulk bill except for pensioners, health care card holders and immediate family members. As well, no medical services should be provided after 8 pm Monday to Saturday and after 1 pm on Sundays.

Fels said the case showed the lengths some doctors would go to shield themselves from competition.

While the AMA avoided media releases after the Berwick Springs case, the combination of the Joondalup fine and the Rockhampton obstetricians case brought the powerful medical lobby onto a full war footing against Fels and the ACCC. Through 2001 — an election year — it pushed for an inquiry into the application of competition regulation to doctors, with the hope that this would deliver a special deal, perhaps even exemption.

The AMA's strategy was to link the *Trade Practices Act* to the decline in doctors in the bush, and generally to the wider economic malaise in rural Australia. The tactic was to highlight the issue of rosters to cover patient needs. 'Virtually every conceivable business arrangement between country doctors may be subject to scrutiny by the ACCC', warned AMA President Dr Kerryn Phelps, when launching a joint campaign with the Rural Doctors' Association in February 2001 for a government review of the Act.

Rosters between doctors covering emergencies are part of the medical fabric, and the AMA knew it was pressing a popular button. Fels and Bhojani rejected the AMA's claims as misleading and mischievous. 'Genuine' rosters ensuring the availability of medical services were not a problem under the *Trade Practices Act*, said Fels. But 'sham rosters', agreements involving boycotts or price fixing, were.

The AMA, however, sought legal advice, which dismissed the ACCC's draft guidelines to doctors as 'unhelpful' and even 'dangerous' by not pointing out that arrangements to avoid breaching the *Trade Practices Act* could themselves be breaches.

The AMA's language began to verge on the intemperate. It accused Fels and the ACCC of everything from 'fear tactics' to 'persecution', as well as of being 'extremely hostile'. Phelps said the actions of the ACCC against country doctors could be described in two ways — 'a vendetta against doctors or bureaucracy gone mad'.

The AMA's campaign also turned personal. Its May 2001 *Medicine* journal published a cartoon of then Health Minister Michael Wooldridge climbing into a double bed with Fels. At the time, the AMA had both in its sights, and the message was about collusion over country doctors. It might have been just a political cartoon, but the poor taste was obvious. With its own president a celebrity lesbian, the AMA would have been rightly outraged if opponents had depicted her getting into bed with a man.

The AMA's real threat, however, was political. It wanted an inquiry to get the ACCC off doctors' backs, and was prepared to link the ACCC with the Hansonite fear of declining rural services while emphasising its own muscle in marginal electorates. Phelps was quite open about the political pitch. 'We have the support of the Deputy Prime Minister, the empathy of the Prime Minister, and undivided attention of MPs who hold seats in marginal regional electorates', she said in May 2001. 'I have no doubt that the general public — the punters — are with us as well. People are sick of losing services from their communities. They've lost the banks and the post offices and government agencies and the rest. If they lose doctors or some medical services as a consequence of the possibility of breaches of the TPA it will be the last straw.'

By August, with an election only a few months away, Howard gave the AMA its inquiry. All politicians are aware of the potential for doctors, chemists and newsagents to influence the stream of voters they come into contact with daily. Phelps' use of the word 'punters' — the political parlance for voters — and quaking marginal Coalition MPs left no doubt about the dangers.

The inquiry, chaired by Warwick Wilkinson, a consultant with a long career in professional standards, turned out to be somewhat of a disaster for the AMA. Wilkinson took both the professional groups and the ACCC to task. That might not be surprising to any objective observer, but the AMA had no hesitation in immediately declaring the report had 'failed' to meet the 'rural health crisis'.

Wilkinson's report, in effect, drew a commonsense line between the warring parties. On the key issues of rosters and fee-setting, it rejected the AMA's alarmist claims. After taking independent legal advice, it concluded that the *Trade Practices Act* did not threaten the ability of doctors to arrange rosters or after-hours arrangements. Uncertainty among doctors over the issue 'has been generated by the public debate'.

Wilkinson also rejected the AMA's claim that doctors entering rosters also needed to set fees, hence breaching the Act. The inquiry agreed with an Australian Consumers' Association submission that rostering could proceed without the need for fee collusion. It also rejected the AMA argument that authorisations for any potentially anti-competitive conduct were time-consuming or costly. Tellingly, it observed that no research pointed to the *Trade Practices Act* as creating the problem of rural doctor shortages.

Wilkinson tried to put the debate into perspective. 'While recognising the professional values and high level of ethical commitment that doctors have, the Committee concludes that medical practitioners, including those practising in rural and regional Australia, essentially are practising to earn a living and, in doing so, are subject to the norms of commerce', it said. Wilkinson told both the ACCC and AMA to end the acrimony through new mechanisms such as a recommended Health Services Advisory Panel as a liaison forum.

The report was also cutting to the ACCC, stating that its use of the media and the high profile of the cases it had taken up 'appears to have served to intimidate doctors rather than educate them, particularly in the case of rostering arrangements'. The ACCC obviously had an image problem with doctors. Wilkinson said that in private consultations the ACCC had been described as 'intimidating', 'threatening' and 'aggressive'. However, the report also found that medical professional groups had 'exploited' this fear of the ACCC. Wilkinson urged these medical lobbies to adopt a more collaborative approach. 'This lack of communication has needlessly complicated relationships, and promoted fear and distrust', it said.

It will take both sides some time to accept this formal slap on the wrist. Both sides briefly engaged in a post-Wilkinson public spat. Some months afterward Phelps said the Wilkinson report had found there needed to be a 'significant culture change' in the ACCC, and there was 'no sign of that yet'. She omitted to mentioned Wilkinson's findings about the AMA, perhaps indicating there was no sign of any culture shift at the AMA either.

'It is time for the AMA to accept the act and encourage doctors to live with it', Bhojani said in an article in *The Australian Financial Review*. 'It has spread enough misinformation around the bush.' The ACCC was spreading nonsense, verballing the AMA and Wilkinson, Phelps shot back. Stop spreading mischief, responded Bhojani, accusing Phelps of misleading Prime Minister Howard by informing him the ACCC had prosecuted doctors over rosters.

This last claim resulted in a sharp exchange of legal letters, which fortunately were copied to the editor of the *Financial Review*. The AMA said Bhojani's claim that Phelps had misled the Prime Minister was defamatory, and demanded an apology. Prosecutions over rostering arrangements was exactly what had happened in the Rockhampton obstetricians case, it claimed. The ACCC reply was cutting. The prosecution in Rockhampton had been about boycotts of no-gap billing. The ACCC had never launched a prosecution over rostering. The only other case of ACCC prosecutions against doctors which also involved rostering was the anaesthetists. But again, this prosecution was about price fixing and boycotts, not the actual rostering. If Dr Phelps had informed the Prime Minister that the ACCC had taken action over rosters she had misled him. Game, set and match. No further letters from the AMA on this subject hit the *Financial Review*'s desk.

Amidst all the grapeshot, the doctors have one reasonable point. The profession does have an unusually heavy reliance on collaboration, by necessity, as doctors need to refer patients on to specialists and arrange for rosters to cover emergency needs. Yet this was lost in the AMA's colourful campaign, with the profession failing to convince independent arbitrators like Wilkinson of its claims. By its clumsy campaign for exemptions from the Act and its 'vendetta' claims, the case for some simpler authorisation process for doctors and their rosters was damaged.

Another medical lobby, the Royal Australian College of General Practitioners, seemed to have no problems with the issues that the AMA found so confronting: it sought, and gained, authorisation from the ACCC for GPs in group practices to agree on fees charged to patients. Interestingly, the later Dawson inquiry which was inspired by business opposition to Fels offered another possibility. It recommended collective bargaining rights for small businesses, including doctors.

With the doctors on hold while the government considered the Wilkinson report, Fels and Bhojani's next battleground with the professions became the medical specialists, or Royal Colleges as many are known. After an initial look at allegations that the Royal Australasian College of Surgeons (RACS) processes restricted entry to advanced medical training, the Commission took the view that the College did indeed breach the Act.

Australian surgeons are not trained or qualified in universities, but in public hospitals by Royal College fellows. Surgical trainees, in effect, are apprenticed to College fellows. The RACS selects the trainees and sets the selection criteria. It also determines the number of surgeons to be trained, by accrediting the number of hospital training posts (surgical training must take place in hospitals). The system has given rise to claims that the RACS has kept fees up by keeping professional numbers down.

After the initial thumbs down, the RACS applied for formal authorisation of its training process on the grounds of public benefit. Following a lengthy inquiry, the Commission found there was indeed 'significant public benefit'. The RACS ensured that surgical training was of high quality, which contributed to a low rate of adverse surgical outcomes and reduced patient time in hospital. As well, College fellow surgeons provided significant pro bono work by training new surgeons, probably valued at about $20 to 25 million a year after taking into account some state payments for training.

However, the Commission also reported 'significant concerns' that the RACS' training process was also used to restrict the number of surgeons. Some examples: the Australian Orthopaedic Association simply ignored an increased target set by the Australian Medical Workforce Advisory Committee for the number of orthopaedic surgical trainees. In addition, the College erected 'invisible barriers' to overseas-trained surgeons, delaying and prevaricating about their qualifications. Also, many complainants about the College were unwilling to 'go public' for fear of being targeted.

The Commission's inquiry into the Royal College produced an extraordinary example of regulatory capture by a profession of the very agency that is supposed to be its regulator. Inviting the views of state health departments on the College's application, the West Australian Department of Health in a one-page response supported the College 'maintaining its current role', and indicating no concerns about the training system.

A month later, the West Australian Health Minister, Bob Kucera, dropped a remarkable letter into the Commission, stating that his view 'had precedence' over any views received from his department. Kucera wanted reform of the system, unlike his department. Another incident that shocked Fels and Bhojani was the discovery that the Australian Medical Workforce Advisory Committee, which sets surgeon numbers, merely aimed to keep numbers stable rather than assessing numbers based on need.

In the upshot, the ACCC gave the Royal College interim authorisation provided that its training process was vetted by an independent committee with appointees from the College and the various governments which, after all, fund the process in hospitals. In effect, the Commission wanted more sunlight to ensure the training system was not run to protect a 'club' of surgeons. The ACCC had commissioned independent research showing that Australia faced surgical shortages, particularly in general surgery and orthopaedics.

It was a difficult call. The ACCC was approving the specialists playing God with their future numbers — subject to more oversight — largely because governments did not want to tackle it. The earlier Wooldridge incident indicated government fears that opening up the number of specialists could create a boom in demand for their services that would be very costly for government budgets.

The decision received short shrift in the tabloid press. Sydney's *Daily Telegraph* editorialised, a trifle unfairly, that the ACCC's decisions did nothing to address the shortage of surgeons. 'The sooner responsibility for training positions and surgeon numbers are ripped from this old boys' club the better', it said.

In its final authorisation of the surgeons' training scheme issued on 30 June 2003, the day Fels departed, the ACCC certainly agreed with *The Daily Telegraph's* sentiments, but seemed a touch torn about whether the 'closed shop' was the fault of the Royal College or of governments failing to take responsibility for the cost of training extra surgeons. Noting that both government surgical workforce planning and the College played a role in restricting entry, the ACCC said that if its reforms eased concerns about the role of the College 'the spotlight will fall squarely on government if shortages of surgeons continue'.

It is not the only dilemma over regulation of the professions which confronts Fels' successor. The ACCC's landmark authorisation of the training practices of the Royal Australasian College of Surgeons opens the way for other colleges such as the psychiatrists, radiologists and orthopaedics to seek similar approval. That will put the future ACCC at the centre of determining specialist numbers in Australia — and whether any shortages are the fault of medical 'clubs' or parsimonious governments concerned about the cost of training specialists and the potential blow-out of their use.

❧

Ironically, Fels' long-running confrontation with the medical profession may have saved his life. At least, it saved him from a serious illness. Fels has had the same GP for 30 years. But one weekend Fels became quite ill, and as his GP was unavailable his wife Isabel called a locum. Fels thought he had a bad dose of flu and the locum confirmed this, handing him a prescription. However, the young doctor also recognised Fels as the ACCC head, and started to tell him his own tale of woe. He felt there was insufficient competition among doctors and this was the cause of his poor salary. He spent about 10 minutes telling a spluttering and coughing Fels that the ACCC should do more. Suddenly he stopped, and said, 'Hey, I've just been noticing how badly you've been coughing. I think you might actually have pneumonia'. More intensive treatment was quickly arranged. The illness put Fels out of action for two weeks, but as a result of his high profile he was saved from any more serious effects.

❧

If the ACCC had deliberately set out down the medical path in its quest to bring the professions under the competition umbrella, it did not forget lawyers. Legal professional privilege is another area that has come under ACCC scrutiny. Professional privilege is part of the inner sanctum of the legal club: advice to clients and the documentation on which that advice is prepared are protected from scrutiny. But what else is buried from scrutiny under the cloak of legal professional privilege?

The ACCC has an interest in this issue. Its accessorial powers mean that professional advisers such as lawyers and advertising agents can face prosecution for advising clients to breach competition laws.

Fels and Bhojani took the issue head-on in 2002 when they challenged legal professional privilege in what became known as the Daniels case. The ACCC had been investigating bid-rigging in the health maintenance industry when Daniels Corporation claimed legal professional privilege for documentation. The Full Court of the Federal Court allowed access to the documents, sending a collective shiver across the legal world. Retailers Coles Myer and Woolworths, in particular, were in the process of fighting an ACCC bid in liquor trading cases it was pursuing for documents claimed to have professional privilege. The decision also had huge implications for the Tax Office and other regulators.

Fels maintained that the ACCC was not interested in overriding legal professional privilege as such. It just sought to maintain its belief that its Section 155 search orders allowed access to such documents. It was a fine point. When the High Court upheld an appeal by Daniels in November 2002 it also found that legal professional privilege did not apply to documents drawn up with the purpose of breaching the law, including competition laws.

The dilemma the ACCC now faces is determining what evidence it needs to produce to get access to documents that are part of a breach of laws. It is a catch-22. The ACCC cannot say the documents are part of a breach of the law without seeing them, and they cannot get access to determine that.

CHAPTER 11

'UNEASY LIES THE HEAD THAT WEARS A CROWN'

Shakespeare's quote from Henry IV is a favourite of Fels. Henry, tired, ill and confronting rebellion, was bemoaning the fact that he could get no sleep. Fels did not have a sleep problem, but he had good reason to be wary of plotting against him.

For years Fels jousted with some of the most powerful business-people and politicians in Australia. His aggressive, publicity-conscious ACCC not only rubbed many vested interests the wrong way, it garnered powers that made it the gateway of government dealings with business.

One incident epitomised this new role. In 2001, as the clouds gathered around Ansett Airlines, Fels was on Hayman Island speaking at a conference. Geoff Dixon, the Qantas chief executive, telephoned from Singapore while Fels was watching the evening news. Ansett was going into liquidation, possibly at 6 am the next day. 'Allan, I would like to have a very good look at Ansett to decide whether or not to take it over', said Dixon. 'I would not look at it if you didn't tell me it was OK to do so.'

Fels responded that nothing stopped Dixon looking, but he could not agree to anything as the competition regulator. 'If you ask me to agree, I cannot agree', he said. Fels also told Dixon that if the situation was so serious he would have heard from Ansett or its parent company,

Air New Zealand. Fels said he would talk to colleagues and ring Dixon back.

At 10 that night Gary Toomey, Air New Zealand's chief executive rang. Ansett would be closed the next morning. Toomey asked if Qantas could take it over, implying the end of the airline unless Fels acted. Fels had experienced this tactic before: a last-minute appeal that unless he gave an immediate approval for a merger a business would close.

'I cannot agree on the telephone', Fels again said, and outlined the necessity of the Commission making a decision. The next morning, Fels took a call from the Prime Minister. Howard was in Washington, attending a garden party for the Bush Administration at the Australian embassy. Howard said he had heard that Fels objected to Qantas even taking a look at Ansett. This was not quite accurate, but also not a total misrepresentation. Surely you don't mind Qantas taking a look? asked Howard, adding that there would be no transaction. Fels said that was fine, and rang Dixon to tell him.

Fels agonised that the Commission would be immediately faced with a decision on whether to oppose Qantas's acquisition (resulting in Ansett then going under), or whether to agree, with the obvious implications for competition. In the upshot, the Qantas board walked away from the deal. Dixon reportedly took to the board a proposal to buy Ansett for a nominal amount, assuming the large debt of the struggling airline. Whether it was the intervening terrorist attack of September 11 or the woeful state of Ansett itself, the board rejected it. Qantas chairman Margaret Jackson said that both the federal government and the ACCC had been supportive, but the board felt the acquisition would be 'negative' for Qantas.

From merger approvals to prices in regulated utilities, market power cases and consumer protection, all business roads led to the ACCC. A decision on the seventh floor of the ACCC headquarters on Canberra's Northbourne Avenue could make or break business fortunes. In many ways, Fels' agency had replaced the old Tariff Board as the centre of business lobbying for favours and fortunes.

The difference, of course, was that Fels was prepared to wage battle in the open, take on high-profile issues, disrupt cosy market arrangements, and use the media to make life uncomfortable. Many of those stung by Fels took their complaints to senior politicians. 'When I first became Treasurer in 1996 practically every business in Australia wanted me to sack him', says Costello.

Some confronted Fels directly. 'You're f___d', one business leader told Fels to his face in the lead-up to the 1993 election, when John Hewson was expected to lead a Liberal victory. In this era Fels was regarded by some — including many in the Liberal Party — as an ACTU plant, and a Liberal win would have ensured a new chairman at the Commission. Hewson lost.

Fels was always aware that his high-wire act needed some form of political safety net. In the Labor era he was protected by his ACTU connection. Despite a nervous start with the Coalition Government in 1996 and direct Cabinet intervention on newsagents, the GST success gave him renewed political comfort to push the competition envelope. 'I was always conscious of the power situation and most of the time I felt that we were safe pushing things', he says. 'But it was on my mind quite a lot.'

It was certainly on his mind in the wake of the GST. Confrontations with some business sectors about the new tax may have been bruising, but the ACCC had lifted its profile enormously. Surveys showed that among consumers those who knew a 'little' or a 'fair amount' about the competition regulator rose from 40 to 56 per cent. Among business, the 'little' and 'fair amount' recognition had risen from 52 to 69 per cent.

Despite this higher recognition the ACCC was anxious not to lose any momentum after the GST, and consciously decided to press the consumer pedal. Reports swept the business community of a Commission meeting at which Fels lamented that the ACCC was 'losing traction' after the GST.

'We had this idea in mind, "Well, look, it's really important that we don't fade from the public mind after GST" and that we also keep doing our job, we don't just sort of put our feet up', says Fels. The ACCC felt that its role in embedding the GST gave it a new level of political protection.

The banks loomed as a target. A joint study by the ACCC and Reserve Bank, published in October 2000, revealed that interchange fees charged by the banks for credit cards were excessive. In some cases banks were earning revenues of 64 per cent above costs. Separately, the Commission instituted proceedings against the National Australia Bank for price fixing of credit card fees. The ACCC had told all the banks that their interchange fee setting process breached the *Trade Practices Act*. The banks wanted only a limited review of these fee processes, but agreed to the ACCC's terms once the Commission took action against NAB.

The NAB case was discontinued in April 2001 when the Reserve Bank 'designated' credit card schemes, giving the Reserve the authority to set fees and reform the system. However, a few months later the ACCC caught NAB on an unconscionable conduct prosecution, involving guarantees given by the wife of an incapacitated company director that resulted in the forced sale of their Hobart home.

Fels' belief that the Commission's GST performance would protect it was soon shattered. As it happened, the first blow came not from business opponents but his supposed protector — the government. Fels' five-year contract was up towards the end of 2000, and he had an appointment with Peter Costello to discuss his future.

The Howard Government had lived up to expectations on the success of the GST introduction, with the ACCC gaining a 28 per cent budget increase. Although this was after a review by the Finance Department, many in the Commission believed the government had given the department the nod to 'see what could be done for the Commission'.

Given this unusual largesse, and positive comments by ministers about the Commission's GST role, Fels saw no looming difficulty in the Costello meeting. His own idea was to serve another five-year term to 2005, and then likely retire, when he would be 63. Costello, however, had other ideas. 'I'd like to offer you until June 2004', said Costello, a new term of three years and eight months.

Fels was taken aback. Even more startling was Costello's rationale. The ACCC and Fels, explained Costello, had become 'very, very powerful'. With an election due at the end of 2001, the new government — whichever party might be in power — should have the opportunity during its lifetime of deciding Fels' future. Costello said he had deliberately set the reappointment to June 2004, which would be just before the next election, given the normal three years' cycle of federal elections.

'I'd prefer five', responded Fels. 'But 3.8 will do since you say so.' The standard ACCC commissioner's term is five years, although shorter terms are not unusual. The *Trade Practices Act* calls for appointments 'not exceeding five years', consistent with the concept that an 'independent' Commission should have life beyond the government of the day.

Costello, in effect, was sending Fels a message: 'You've become very powerful, and we want to keep a rein on you. If you behave, you might get a further term'. Any idea that Costello was acting out of a democratic belief that an incoming Labor Government after the 2001 election should have an opportunity to consider Fels' future is laughable. Australian politics is very tribal. Ministers are more likely to worry about their agency appointments surviving changes of government. If the Treasurer really believed Fels was the right person for the ACCC chairmanship he could have given him a term stretching out beyond the first term of any incoming Labor government in 2001.

The fact that he did not, and preceded his remarks by saying that Fels and the ACCC had become 'very, very powerful', demonstrated political nervousness about popular, high-profile regulators. Fels had carved out his own brand. Far from being just a reflection of a minister or government, Fels had given the ACCC its own distinct identity. Any minister would see this as threatening: Fels' public image as the consumers' friend was such that it might become impossible for a minister to influence him.

Within government there was a growing feeling that Fels had outgrown the ACCC. Some ministers even believed it was Fels, not the ACCC, that epitomised consumer protection in the public mind. So, though he had done a great job on the GST, the consensus appears to have been that Fels needed a touch of political discipline. The three-year offer filled that bill.

For all his willingness to confront business leaders and seemingly shrug off stinging criticism, there is a hint of insecurity about Fels. Politicians see it in his relief when they come to his defence. It is also reflected in his pleasure in relaying to ACCC colleagues pieces of praise he might pick up in airport conversations with ministers when the Commission is under fire from business. Costello might not have known, but he was massaging that streak with the three-year term.

Costello puts his remarks about Fels' growing power in the following context: 'I think people can remain in statutory appointments too long. You know, J Edgar Hoover is the classic example. In the end he'd been there so long they couldn't get rid of him'. Costello says Fels had become the ACCC in the public eye. 'I just thought — and I said this to him — that when I'd come in he'd been on a five-year term and I had not had the chance in my first term to make an appointment here', he says. 'I did not think I should lock this up against successive government terms. I think I said that at the time.'

Anti-Fels pressure on Costello, from both business and government, was strong. But dismissal had not been an option when the Coalition came to power in 1996 — Fels was on a five-year fixed contract — and still wasn't in late 2000 because of the amazingly successful introduction of the GST. That did not stop rumbling against Fels within Cabinet. 'I was essentially his greatest defender in the Cabinet and in the government, I was', says Costello. 'That's because I believe in competition, which makes me unpopular in some circles.' Costello appears to have somewhat of a chameleon quality when it comes to competition, supporting tough enforcement yet not fully backing the regulator. It is a dilemma of many believers in free markets — they need regulators.

Business read the curtailed reappointment as a compromise. The Howard Government believed it 'owed' Fels on the GST and so would not sack him outright, but was putting him on a tighter leash.

Fels did not need reminding that disgruntled business leaders were whispering in Costello's ear. Shortly after his truncated reappointment, Fels received a stark appraisal of how the accumulation of ACCC activities and its role in the GST had scarred relations with business. After its huge burst of GST publicity died down, the Commission decided to survey current perceptions of the ACCC among both business and ACCC staff, to develop a new communications strategy.

The results were less than flattering. Good Information Co. Pty Ltd, who conducted the survey, found that the Commission had no clear communications focus, leading to disparate messages. Moreover, big business and industry associations had a poor image of ACCC processes, questioning the value of what they saw as threatening and unfair tactics, and particularly 'execution by media release'. ACCC decision-making was mysterious to many groups, who saw the Commission as a 'black box'. There was also widespread confusion on the split personality of the Commission as both a competition and consumer agency.

For Fels and his fellow commissioners there was nothing particularly new in the findings. Charges of 'powerful, threatening and academic', as contained in the report, had been ringing in their ears for some time. Yet the research did lay it all on the table, including a view from within government that the ACCC might be good at the big stick but not so good at conveying the 'we're here to help' message. It also underlined a new reality: the GST had added focus to the tensions already existing between Fels and business, galvanising business sentiment against him.

There is a curious dichotomy among business over competition regulation. Business is generally in favour, recognising that competitive markets lower costs from suppliers. Yet support is half-hearted, and business usually argues for a weak regulator. Australian business has never grasped the Thatcherite argument that a fully competitive economy provides opportunities for entrepreneurs to move into new markets.

The ACCC moved to improve its communications strategy after the report, but it could only go so far. It is a bit like Fels' luncheon speech joke about all the bright-eyed MBA graduates who come through the ACCC's doors looking for jobs, with grandiose plans to reshape the world, usually involving schemes to ensure 'satisfied customers'. As Fels points out, many of the ACCC's 'customers' have actually broken the law. For many in the ACCC, the take-out of the research was that if business was whingeing the ACCC must be doing its job.

Business, in fact, was doing more than whingeing. The post-GST era saw the emergence of an unprecedented campaign to 'do something' about Allan Fels. Business leaders increasingly saw Fels as on a crusade to characterise business as 'bad'.

Howard ministers fielded regular telephone complaints. One minister recalls a particular business leader being on the telephone every three weeks or so. 'Business hated him and they were prepared to do anything to stop him', says the politician.

The GST brought home to business just how far the balance of power in their relationship with Fels had swung to the publicity-conscious regulator. From the change in the merger test to 'substantial lessening of competition', to Hilmer opening up professions and utility regulation, to new unconscionable conduct provisions, heavier fines and the power to negotiate court-enforceable undertakings, the competition regulator under Fels was a completely different animal than under his predecessors.

It was not just the power, either. Business began to agitate at the way that power was exercised. Publicity, hair-trigger press releases and an aggressive legal stance all led business to believe that not only had the game changed, but the rules of play as well. 'Natural justice' became a catchphrase around business discussions, with the Video Ezy case giving it a specific edge. 'Natural justice' — fairness in being given a hearing and lack of bias by a tribunal — is a public euphemism for what the Business Council of Australia (BCA) privately calls 'blackmail'.

Business press critiques of Fels began to pick up as its PR flacks tried to beat Fels at his own game. Justice Finn's remarks in a 1999 electricity case, questioning Fels' media tactics while also labelling them as 'public theatre' were passed around the business world, with journalists copied in.

Still, at this point there was not much direct public criticism of Fels. Business recognised that attacking the consumer watchdog was a loser's game. Don Argus, the former NAB chief executive who had moved on to become the chair of BHP and Brambles, epitomised the caution when he said: 'I have no problem with the *Trade Practices Act*, [only with] the way it is being interpreted'.

Behind the scenes it was a different story. Meetings of the Business Council of Australia, the peak body of big business, became gripe sessions for ACCC horror stories. The GST was just the latest incident. Retailers seemed in constant battle with the regulator over issues ranging from acquisitions to advertising. Target accused the ACCC of a 'sue now, talk later' approach. The oil companies were angry over franchising problems, the failure of their ambitious refining mergers — although the Mobil/Shell merger was called off by global corporate pressures — and the ACCC's forced divestiture of independents in the Caltex/Ampol merger. The banks were furious over credit card reforms. Big companies like Pioneer had had serious confrontations with the ACCC (and now its managing director, John Schubert, was President of the BCA). Apart from a big fine for its involvement in the concrete cartel, Pioneer had also been fined $5 million for an illegal takeover of competitors in the south Queensland concrete masonry market, A Class Blocks and Q Blox. This was the first fine for a breach of the merger law, with Pioneer pledging that it would not attempt further acquisitions without notifying the ACCC.

'The resentment was palpable', said one BCA member who attended meetings at this time. Business leaders also grumbled privately to Prime Minister Howard at dinners at The Lodge, or on any occasion they could grab the ear of a minister.

Pointedly, Howard praised the GST performance of Fels and Tax Commissioner Michael Carmody at the annual dinner of the Australian Chamber of Commerce and Industry in November 2000. While Fels' GST role was then fading from business consciousness, Carmody was in corporate gunsights over the cumbersome quarterly Business Activity Statements for the GST. However, Howard also gave Fels a few backhanders on other occasions. Fels 'had a view on everything', Howard told one radio interviewer.

In early 2001 the cases on business lips were Video Ezy, on the 'natural justice' issue, and failed mergers such as Australis/Foxtel, the Stock Exchange and the Futures Exchange, AAPT/Optus, Taubmans/Wattyl in the paints market, and the plans for halving the number of petroleum refiners from four to two. When *Business Review Weekly* magazine trotted out these list of failed mergers to Fels, he replied: 'I have no regrets on any of them'.

It was the merger issue that enabled the BCA to develop an entirely new line of attack on the ACCC — that its actions would create a branch office economy. The worry that in a globalising world Australia might be reduced to a branch office economy had been around for some years. It was usually expressed as a concern about the possibility of global headquarters of multinational companies setting policies for their Australian offshoots. The BCA claimed, in a new twist, that if they were denied 'scale' locally by tough merger and tax laws, moving offshore might become attractive to Australian companies. 'Corporate emigration' became the buzzphrase.

'Fear of branch-office nation', shouted the front-page headline of *The Weekend Australian* on 10 February 2001. 'Business leaders are about to confront the Howard Government with the ultimate issue for corporate Australia: how our best companies can stay onshore so the nation can avoid becoming a New Zealand style branch-office economy', wrote Paul Kelly, the paper's international editor.

The Kelly article was no accident. The BCA had briefed him before the upcoming annual retreat of its council, due to be held at Coolum in Queensland. Kelly listed the four priorities for the BCA at Coolum

— the ACCC, tax, population and domestic capital markets. The four, and particularly the ACCC, were all wrapped up in the branch office economy parcel. 'I think this is now the biggest single [issue] facing major Australian companies', Kelly quoted Stan Wallis, the AMP chairman and former BCA president who had chaired the 1997 inquiry into Australia's financial system. 'In the next five to ten years there will be scores of companies moving offshore', said Wallis. 'The government needs to address this issue now, because it will happen much faster than our politicians begin to understand.'

David Buckingham, the BCA's chief executive, was quoted as demanding that the branch office economy issue should command 'attention now at the top of the national agenda'. Kelly listed Lend Lease, BHP, AMP, Pioneer, Brambles and the National Australia Bank as major groups which had either moved their headquarters or were considering listing on foreign exchanges.

The branch office economy was suddenly headline material. It was a clever BCA tactic, used not in a narrow sense to raise concern about companies moving offshore, but rather to focus on shoring up the domestic base. And that meant corralling Allan Fels and his ACCC. To avoid decamping for foreign parts, the argument went, Australian companies needed 'scale' to grow locally and enable them to compete on the global stage. Domestic mergers, perhaps even 'national champions' might be necessary to compete against global majors. It was a re-run of the merger test argument — dominance versus substantial lessening of competition — that business had lost to Fels almost a decade before.

The branch office economy argument, however, was somewhat of an artifice. Certainly, big business was concerned about international tax comparisons and other inhibitions to expansion. Some even believed the merger test could be rolled back, but not many. The argument was mainly aimed at fixing something big business was really concerned about — Allan Fels and his aggressive style of operations. The branch office economy story laid some of the blame for Australia's departing companies on Fels.

For the BCA, it was a convenient platform for its members to use to publicly zero in on Fels and the ACCC without being accused of conflict of interest. President John Schubert, for example, could hardly sail into Fels without the media questioning whether he was motivated by Pioneer's disastrous history with the competition regulator. But the branch office economy story gave him and other BCA members a nobler motive than narrow commercial interest: Australia's corporate future was at stake.

At Coolum on 20 February the BCA announced its new agenda, headlined in its media release 'Let's make Australia great'. After detailing a need for e-transformation, education and training, greenhouse emissions, removal of tax disincentives for Australian headquartered firms to expand overseas, and 'a regulatory system which is consistent with international trends', the BCA said: 'The Forum recognised that the existing *Trade Practices Act*, which was enacted in the early 1970s in very different circumstances, had failed to take account of international trends and needed to be modernised to ensure Australian companies are able to compete'.

This was the first public sign that the BCA was now campaigning for a review of Fels and his *Trade Practices Act*, although Fels was not mentioned, of course. If the BCA believed its new strategy to make Australia 'great' would be seen in the wider context of taxation, education and e-transformation, the media quickly honed in on what it saw as the real agenda — merger law and the ACCC. On Channel Nine's *Business Sunday* a few days after Coolum, Schubert faced some hard questions from interviewer Ali Moore on the need for merger law change to avert the branch office threat.

> *Moore:* Where is the evidence, if we look at competition law, that competition decisions, or ACCC decisions, are forcing Australian companies offshore?
> *Schubert:* I think it's, in many cases, the evidence isn't public. I think in many cases it's the possible mergers, or possible acquisitions that don't take place, didn't reach

the light of day, because it was determined that the process was one, too long, and then, secondly, too uncertain.

Moore: But, at the same time in recent years, the ACCC has given the nod to the carve-up of the steel industry, they've said yes to NAB's purchase of MLC, Rio Tinto's North takeover, something like just 25 of the 500 deals they've looked at over the last three years have been blocked.

Schubert: That's true. And there's a number which have gone ahead, there's a number which, you know, haven't come to the light of day or perhaps haven't gone ahead.

Schubert went on to detail other factors such as the need for companies to be large in order to be 'on the radar screen' of the large global funds. Without such blocks of investment, the share price of these companies would be lower. But Moore wanted to return to the main game.

Moore: But you did say that there is evidence, often not in the public view, that competition law is forcing Australian companies offshore?

Schubert: I think it's one of those things that tends to work against it. And I think Australia, with our size and with our geographic location, must have anything we possibly can, helping companies to stay in Australia and be as muscular as possible in the Australian marketplace.

Moore: Where's the public interest in watering down today's merger laws?

Schubert: Well, I think there's clearly a balance that has to be made. And it's a balance between having very rigorous competition laws, which is good, and the need to have, you know, large Australian companies that can punch above their weight in the Australian marketplace — and beyond the Australian marketplace, importantly.*

---

* Reproduced with permission of *Business Sunday*, Nine Network Australia

Moore then tackled Fels in a back-to-back interview following Schubert. Is big business targeting you personally? she asked perceptively. 'Oh, there's a bit of playing the man and not the ball, but it doesn't really affect things', he replied. 'It's usually a sign that they haven't got a very good argument.' Fels went on to list some of the big mergers the ACCC had approved, a common tactic of his as the attack intensified. The ACCC had opposed only 13 of 1108 mergers and acquisitions considered in the previous five years. A further 28 had been resolved by undertakings from the parties.

Importantly, the Commission had not opposed any mergers in the last decade where import competition or potential import competition was significant, he told a Sydney Institute conference on globalisation in April 2001. Fels cited BHP's acquisition of NZ Steel and later Tubemakers, Amcor's acquisition of APPM (later split up by Amcor), Email's of Southcorp and Rio Tinto's of North. Of the top 10 mergers in 2001 by dollar value, the ACCC had opposed none, including Commonwealth Bank's bid for Colonial and Rio's bid for Comalco. Treasurer Costello, however, stopped Shell's bid for Woodside on separate national interest grounds.

In line with his style of never taking a backward step, Fels took the argument right up to the BCA. 'The virulence and persistence of the attacks on the Commission raises the question of motive', he told the Sydney Institute audience. 'Do the attackers want the unfettered right to establish monopolies so they can dominate the market and, by raising prices, earn greater profits? This may bring cheers from shareholders but not necessarily from consumers or other companies that buy inputs from the monopolies.'

Fels also had a real crack at the BCA. 'If our most persistent critic, the Business Council of Australia, were serious about promoting large internationally competitive Australian companies it would acknowledge the benefits of competition. Would Australia's big companies be internationally competitive if they had to secure their raw materials from a monopoly supplier, export through a monopoly transport company or raise finance from a monopoly bank? And what about consumers? If we had no merger law in Australia, consumers could shop at Woolcoles supermarket, buy petrol at Moshell and get beer from Carlion. Such monopolies would surely mean no competition.'

The BCA saw this as another sign that Fels' taking on the business community was a crusade. Privately, some business leaders tried to reassure Fels that while there might be a case for a review of the ACCC, it was nothing personal.

An interesting footnote on the branch office economy debate occurred a year later. In a little-noticed report in February 2002, the Productivity Commission surveyed Australian firms on their offshore investments. Only four of the 201 firms surveyed had relocated key headquarters functions offshore, while a further four were considering doing so. (These eight were relatively large, however, employing some 35 000 people in Australia.) The firms reported that international market access was the single most important factor determining headquarters location decisions. Proximity to shareholders and new investors ranked second. Of factors subject to government control, the Australian tax regime and the foreign tax environment (that is, lower tax) were the most important, but neither ranked as highly as international market access. The Productivity Commission reported that Australian taxes carried most weight of all commercial and government-related factors for the four considering shifting headquarters abroad.

Turning to the issue of domestic growth, the Productivity Commission said respondents cited taxation and labour market policies as the two regulatory aspects inhibiting them. 'Australian merger law was not considered a particularly important impediment to domestic growth by respondents as a whole', it found. 'However, firms active in relocating their headquarters regarded it as the leading regulatory factor constraining their domestic growth, just ahead of taxation and labour market policies. Mergers regulation was also considered to be a more important constraint on domestic growth by firms active in offshore investment than by other firms.'

Such independent analysis of the real factors behind fear of a branch office syndrome — proximity to markets and investors — was not known or probably wanted when the BCA dropped in on Canberra a few weeks after Coolum to deliver its new strategy for a 'great' Australia to Prime Minister Howard and Opposition Leader Kim Beazley. Such briefings of political leaders are not uncommon, but 2001 was an election year, and the BCA was anxious to push with Howard its aim of securing a 'review' of the *Trade Practices Act*.

Strangely, the BCA's meeting with Howard has fallen through the cracks of formal recording of government–business dialogue. The PM's office says it has no record of any such meeting, although Howard himself remembers it. The BCA only confirmed it after initially saying that it also could find no records. One reason could be that the meeting was arranged by telephone, but as one BCA member says, the Council does not like to advertise its pipelines to the Canberra power structure.

John Schubert and David Buckingham, the BCA chief executive, met Howard and his chief of staff Arthur Sinodinos, as well as other officials, in the Cabinet annex immediately across from Howard's Parliament House suite. When you've got the Prime Minister's ear, it pays to be direct. Reports of the meeting that later circulated around the top echelons of the BCA said Schubert and Buckingham took the branch office economy argument as a premise and then focused specifically on the agenda of Fels' ACCC. Reportedly, the duo spilled out business anger on 'natural justice' and the way Video Ezy and David Jones had been 'targeted' during the GST.

The BCA, said Schubert and Buckingham, wanted a review of the ACCC and the *Trade Practices Act* to deal with the Commission's attitude, as they saw it, on mergers. Scale was the problem, and the two gave Howard case studies. The petroleum industry was mentioned. The BP/Caltex refining merger had failed after a similar proposal by Shell and Mobil was withdrawn following pressure from their global owners. The inability to gain quick decisions was highlighted, with the two BCA executives saying that the authorisation route of gaining merger approval by citing public benefits that offset anti-competitive effects was costly and time-consuming.

While they complained about the ACCC's processes, the two were careful not to specifically target Fels. However, when it comes down to some of the nitty-gritty of the Commission's methodology, and the perceived lack of 'natural justice' it can become personalised.

Reports fed back to BCA members said Howard actually gave a commitment that, as a matter of urgency, he would look at a review of the administrative performance of the ACCC. If correct, this was a bold promise by Howard considering that the minister in charge of the ACCC, Treasurer Peter Costello, was not present and apparently had not been consulted. Still, Howard is the Prime Minister.

The BCA went away expecting some form of quick in-house government inquiry. But it heard nothing. The months dragged by. Then, in the lead-up to the October election, the BCA was stunned by a policy statement from the Coalition promising a review of the trade practices legislation 'and its administration'. Stunned because some of the language of the proposed review even seemed almost identical to the BCA's discussion with Howard some six months earlier.

The Dawson inquiry, said the pre-election announcement, would look at whether the ACCC's Act and administration 'continue to encourage an environment where Australia can grow and compete internationally'. This was the BCA's scale argument: the ACCC was stopping domestic mergers that enabled firms to gain size to compete globally. The BCA interpreted the policy pledge of an ACCC inquiry as a clear message from Howard: 'I heard what you said and I'm giving you what you were looking for'.

The means of delivering that message, wrapped in a 'protecting small business' package, stunned others as well, namely small business. 'Small business representatives have argued that a wider review of the competition provisions is now needed', said the Coalition election policy pledge. They certainly had. The National Association of Retail Grocers of Australia — the small guys — had been pressing hard along with the Council of Small Business of

Australia for reviews. But the small business lobby wanted two main things: an examination of Section 46, which deals with abuse of market power, and new provisions to stop creeping acquisitions of smaller competitors, which NARGA claimed were how Coles and Woolworths were slowly dominating the retail industry.

Any idea that small business was pressing to ensure that firms could 'grow and compete internationally' was absurd. On the contrary, small business wanted mergers reined in, particularly in the retail trade. Yet here was a review, aimed at ensuring scale for international competitiveness, but stuck in the middle of a small business package. For the Coalition, however, supporting small business was politically popular. It would be folly to be seen agreeing to pressure from the big end of town against the consumer champion.

Howard's review gave the BCA and other anti-Fels business lobbyists another win, too. The inquiry was empowered to ensure the ACCC and its administration 'deal fairly with affairs of individual companies'. But there *was* a small business kicker in the package which would not have pleased the BCA — the inquiry would look at providing 'adequate protection for the balance of power between small and large businesses'. This addressed the heart of small business worries that market power and merger provisions of the *Trade Practices Act* were not strong enough to combat big business predators.

The Howard Government made much play of the 'win' by small business in gaining the inquiry. It emphasised the appointment of Curt Rendell as one of the three members of the inquiry, to be chaired by former High Court judge Sir Daryl Dawson. Rendell has a long history in the small business sector, and the government said he was the only appointee clearly from one of the business sectors. The third member was Jillian Segal, then deputy chair of the Australian Securities and Investments Commission. Fels also had a small win. The terms of reference precluded the inquiry from rehashing the merits of past cases. This meant that sensitive GST cases like Video Ezy were dead and buried.

As Howard was unveiling the Dawson inquiry, Fels and the ACCC were taking flak from another direction — the federal parliament. The House of Representatives Standing Committee on Economics, Finance and Public Administration, chaired by Victorian Liberal David Hawker, usually took a straight up and down look at the performance of the ACCC in its annual review of the competition regulator. The review went from positive in 1997 to being very critical in 2001. In 1997, for instance, it recorded the view of consumer advocate Louise Sylvan that the ACCC had been 'extraordinarily efficient', and that 'One of the important features of the ACCC is that it's willing not to fire shots over the bow. It is prepared to start proceedings and tell industry, "You'll lift your game, and you'll do it fast". The ACCC gets results.'

Then, in 1998 it highlighted two contentious issues: the Gilbert & Tobin fee arrangement in the failed Foxtel/Australis merger, and criticism by gas company Santos of its many run-ins with Fels and the ACCC. 'A recurring pattern of criticism pervading many of the ACCC's activities appears to be developing', it reported that year. 'As well, friction appears to be increasing as the number of sectors in which the ACCC operates expands — a fact that is acknowledged by the ACCC itself. These concerns are particularly prevalent regarding the ACCC's activities in the mergers area.' The Hawker Committee also listed some of the grievances it was picking up, including that the ACCC 'had a tendency to transform markets to accord with its views of the best competitive outcome'. The ACCC as industry policy-setter was another of the business grumbles doing the rounds. Other complaints echoed the growing chorus about the ACCC's use of publicity 'which [lacked] objectivity and which may overstate or distort official policy', and an unwillingness to admit that its actions or information were wrong.

In September 2001, the Hawker Committee came out with its most serious critique of the ACCC, in a review entitled 'Competing Interests: Is There Balance?' The Committee's answer to that question was itself a picture of balance. On one hand, it found that the ACCC was 'an effective regulatory body', as evidenced by its role in the GST. But on the other hand, it found the ACCC was under increasing fire over its tactics and allegations of heavy-handedness. 'It has also exhibited a dismissive attitude towards criticism of its actions', it concluded.

Rebalancing itself again, the Hawker Committee endorsed Fels' calls for jail terms for participants in what he termed 'hard-core cartels'. Yet it also issued government with a warning on giving the ACCC any new powers. The Committee was broaching issues that were sensitive territory for Fels' ACCC: was it now prosecutor, judge and jury, and facing conflicts of interests in its many roles? Should future competition and industry regulatory functions be handed to a possibly stretched ACCC or to new agencies?

The Hawker Committee's balancing stretch reflected the growing question marks about the ACCC and Fels that surfaced in 2001, and were to run through the Dawson inquiry and government thinking. Had the ACCC gone too far? Had it accumulated too many possibly conflicting powers as price setter as well as competition enforcer along with consumer policeman?

Business, however, was not prepared to publicly criticise Fels or the ACCC, the Hawker Committee discovered. So it was impressed by the thoughts of Warren Pengilley, the Professor of Commercial Law at the University of Newcastle. Pengilley was a foundation commissioner of the old Trade Practices Commission from 1975 to 1982, and later the trade practices managing partner of the law firm Deacons.

He is probably the toughest academic critic of the ACCC. Pengilley took the Hawker Committee through much of the material in his 55-page study in 2001 *Competition Regulation in Australia: a Discussion of a Spider Web and its Weaving*, which, as the title suggests, blasts the tactics of Fels' Commission. While stating his own involvement in several ACCC cases, one the failed Taubmans/Wattyl paints merger, Pengilley takes a stick to the ACCC's accretion of powers, its regulatory 'arm twisting', talking up of penalties, misrepresentation of its views as 'the law', and use of publicity.

Detailing the ACCC's growth beyond its traditional competition and consumer protection to arbitration and price setting in many utilities and its (temporary) GST powers, Pengilley said: 'In many areas, the ACCC has the multiple functions of prosecutor, judge and jury and, many believe, of executioner as well. It sits like a spider at the centre of the competition web, much of which it has been responsible for weaving'.

The Hawker Committee took up some of Pengilley's accusations with Fels and the ACCC. Were the criticisms fair? The ACCC replied, reported the Committee, that the criticism had no real basis. The Committee responded that some trade practice lawyers 'found no fault' with Pengilley's attack. The ACCC claimed these were lawyers who represented big business.

It was at this time, too, that Fels 'congratulated' Pengilley about his discovery of the ACCC's slip in issuing a GST press release saying it could impose penalties of up to $10 million for failure to pass on tax savings. The ACCC of course cannot impose any penalties. It must go to the courts for these. Fels responded: 'I cannot recall any time in the last 10 years that anyone from the Commission has ever said that we can fine people, with the one exception of the statement that Pengilley — who spends his life fault-finding with the ACCC — has managed to uncover. So I congratulate him on this discovery of his. It should not have been said.'

Fels might have chosen his words more carefully, as the Hawker Committee said when accepting this as an inadvertent and uncharacteristic error by the Commission. 'The reaction of the Chairman suggests an intolerance for criticism, even where it is well-founded', it noted. 'The committee is concerned that other justified questions about the ACCC's performance are being similarly dismissed.'

⌐

By late 2001 business critics appeared to have lost any inhibitions they might have had. The combination of the GST, the Dawson inquiry and continuing activism by the ACCC (with occasional heavy-handedness as in the Caltex raid) made the Commission — and Fels — open game.

Dick Warburton, chairman of Caltex and David Jones, labelled Fels' methods of regulation 'unfair, unjust and immoral'. Commonwealth Bank chief executive David Murray said the ACCC was guilty of 'false and misleading behaviour'. Qantas chief executive Geoff Dixon accused Fels of a 'well-honed knack' of ensuring his comments about alleged improprieties of business were widely circulated. Woolworths' chief executive Roger Corbett said the ACCC 'really doesn't have any line of accountability at all'.

Run a line through these critics and a common theme emerges: they all had run-ins with the ACCC. The ACCC had forced Caltex, upon its merger with Ampol, to divest service stations to keep independents in the market. The Commonwealth Bank faced credit card reforms and an ACCC prosecution alleging unconscionable conduct on a Gold Coast unit loan. Qantas had been in and out of rucks with the ACCC, with the regulator opposing its bid to buy Hazleton Airlines. Qantas also faced proceedings for allegedly misusing its market power on the Adelaide route against new entrant Virgin. Woolworths had been in the GST wars, and also faced ACCC probing over liquor marketing.

Whether or not this diminished their credibility as critics, the press lapped it up. The ever-vocal Gerry Harvey provided particularly colourful copy, with his references to Nazi Germany and hatred. The issue — which also provoked an extraordinarily savage attack by Harvey as Fels left the job in 2003 — was an investigation by the ACCC of alleged bait advertising by Harvey Norman. The case was unusual in that this time it was Harvey Norman that publicly revealed the inquiry. It took court action against the ACCC investigation, but then withdrew. With the investigation in the open, Fels was able to point to a possible motive behind Harvey's media campaign. 'The public will (now) have a better understanding of the context of his criticism of the ACCC', he said. (Harvey versus Fels took on a savage personal twist just as Fels left office, with newspapers carrying articles about Fels' family spending in Harvey group stores. The details of this spending could only have come from Harvey records, inviting questions about invasion of privacy.)

The other Fels line of response, to both the Dawson inquiry and business criticism, was to welcome it as proof that the ACCC was doing its job. He would also applaud the fact that it brought criticism out into the public domain from the backrooms of politics. Fels had been completely unaware of the BCA lobbying of Howard.

In this welter of criticism Fels' political masters again appeared caught between defending him and siding with his critics. Costello, for instance, can swing between calling Fels and his successor Graeme Samuel his only supporters on competition policy — 'there wasn't much political support outside of that group' — to siding with business over Fels' use of publicity.

Prime Minister Howard also adopted a subtle combination of praise for Fels and condemnation that he also made mistakes and went 'too far'. In August 2002, as the business campaign hit a crescendo in the wake of the bungled Caltex raid, Howard had the following 'defence' of Fels in an interview with Neil Mitchell on Radio 3AW.

> *Mitchell:* [Allan Fels is] getting a bit of a hard time at the moment isn't he?
> *Howard:* Yeah, that's understandable but I think fundamentally he acts in the public interest.
> *Mitchell:* He's got your support?
> *Howard:* Of course he has. We reappointed him.
> *Mitchell:* Why are they all going after him?
> *Howard:* Well that's fair enough. He can look after himself. I mean people go after me all the time and I think … I mean it's right and he's a big boy and he can look after himself, and maybe from time to time he makes mistakes and goes too far but fundamentally I think he's doing a good job.

> *Mitchell:* Can you think of those times when he's made mistakes?
>
> *Howard:* Well [before I] said anything about that I'd speak to him first.*

Fels had now gone full circle with the Coalition. When Howard came to office in 1996 Fels was regarded with suspicion as a Labor plant. In Opposition, Costello had said Fels had to prove he was not a 'captive' of the unions. On coming into office, Costello recalls many business leaders wanting him to get rid of Fels. Curiously, even one of the senior Labor ministers gave Costello a piece of advice as he left office: 'sack Fels'.

Fels' star had certainly risen with the Coalition during the GST. Now it was on the wane again. Not that the ACCC was seen as unnecessary. Competition regulators are always handy repositories of complaints: 'Thanks for raising that, I'll refer it to Fels and the ACCC'. More importantly, the ACCC had become a key part of the government's continuing micro-reform agenda. From a primary role as a cartel-buster in the early 1990s, the ACCC had become a player in transport, energy and communications reform. In that sense, the need of government for an ACCC agency is probably stronger than ever.

But that will be an ACCC without Fels. As Costello had indicated when truncating Fels' reappointment, the government was concerned about his growing power. So there were no pleas to reconsider when, in mid-2002, Fels informed Costello of his decision to accept a new post as the inaugural dean of the Australia and New Zealand School of Government, a joint project of 10 universities and five governments.

Fels had been offered the post some time before. Attending a performance of Richard III in Melbourne with Isabel one night in early 2002, Fels chatted with Terry Moran, secretary of the Victorian Department of Premiers and Cabinet. Moran told him of the new school, and asked if he would be interested in running it. The idea

---

* 3AW, Southern Cross Radio Pty Ltd

appealed, and to Isabel as well, who says it has been a dream of hers for Allan to return to academia. Ironically, he would not have been available for the job if Costello had reappointed him for five years. That would have seen him locked in at the ACCC until 2005, when at aged 63 he probably would have retired. Now a 'last hurrah' had opened up for him in academia.

The new career opportunity came when Fels was quite susceptible to interesting new offers. Publicly, he brushed aside the rising tide of business criticism. The only critic that ever hurt him, he joked, was Sir Donald Bradman. In 1974 the famous cricketer, then a stockbroker, had ticked off Fels' Prices Justification Tribunal. 'I was slightly distressed that my name had come to his attention as a regulator when I was hoping all my life it would come to his attention as a very good junior cricket player.' However, public bravado aside, the criticism weighed on Fels. 'I wasn't feeling threatened by the big business assault because I felt I was in a really powerful position with public opinion', he says. 'If big business is attacking you the public basically thinks well of you.' But he regretted that his relationship with business had deteriorated to such an extent.

As well, internally, the workload was increasing. Costello had not appointed a new deputy chairman to replace Allan Asher, who had left in 2000. Initially Fels had not been worried about this, but as the months and years rolled by with no replacement he began to realise how much his workload had increased as a result. The chairman or deputy signs a lot of paperwork around the Commission, and it all needs to be read.

Potential candidates were endlessly turned over, but with no success. Costello was not keen on an overtly consumerist replacement for Asher, even though the Act requires at least one commissioner with consumer experience. Asher's zeal had left a bitter aftertaste with politicians and business, although not with consumers. Privately, too, Costello began to worry that Fels' high profile might be frightening off candidates, who would see themselves as very much in the chairman's shadow.

Costello did appoint two new commissioners: Jennifer McNeill, a partner with law firm Blake Dawson Waldron, and Ed Willett, former Executive Director of the National Competition Council. But still there was no deputy chairman. Costello appeared content to have just one consumer person on the Commission — Fels.

With the job more exhausting, and the two to three days a week in Canberra requiring continual absences from his family, Fels found the idea of a Melbourne-based academic career enticing. At the time, his daughter Isabella was experiencing one of her periodic bouts of illness due to schizophrenia, another factor contributing to Fels' concerns about his family responsibilities.

At least Fels had no need to worry that Costello would fall on his knees and ask him to stay. Costello took the departure news without any obvious reaction. He asked a few questions about timing and possible conflicts of interest, and said he would think about it.

The Howard Cabinet's uneasiness about Fels' growing power was resolved. Fels had achieved unique distinction for a regulator: his energy and integrity in enforcing competition laws had cost him support from both sides of politics. In the waterfront and later in the GST he had lost Labor and trade union support. Then, after a spell in the GST sunshine under the Coalition, he had become dispensable to them too.

Little wonder that in his decade as the competition czar, Henry IV's musing 'uneasy lies the head that wears a crown' kept recurring in his mind. It was probably only Fels' public profile — the thing politicians and business feared — that had protected him over the years.

CHAPTER 12

'WHAT DO WE DO NOW?'

Be careful what you ask for because you might get it. Such a thought may well have been running through business minds as they contemplated the new inquiry into the *Trade Practices Act* business had sought in early 2001, and had been granted in Howard election promises later that year. The Dawson inquiry started as an opportunity for business to turn the tables on Fels after a decade of watching his growing powers and media skills. But as it progressed, and news of Fels' early departure trickled out, it became more of a challenge to ensure a Fels 'culture' did not permeate the ACCC after his departure.

The initial problem for Costello, however, was to find someone to run the inquiry. After scratching around, Treasury asked Fels, who suggested John Lockhart, a former Federal Court judge who had also served as president of the Australian Competition Tribunal between 1982 and 1999. The Tribunal, as it is known around competition circles, reviews the decisions of the ACCC.

Lockhart was approached, and accepted. But at a late stage in the process complications arose because of an overseas judicial role, and he had to withdraw. The Productivity Commission was also a possibility, but Treasury considered it a bit too fundamentalist in its approach.

The Productivity Commission and the ACCC enjoy some friendly rivalry. Essentially their goals are the same, to improve regulatory and market efficiency, but they jockey for the government's ear occasionally over solutions. The Productivity Commission believes the ACCC should be lighter on the regulatory side sometimes, to encourage investment. There have been wins and losses on either side, with Productivity winning on the regulation of airports and harbour towage and Fels on the *Prices Surveillance Act*. However, Fels believes that the rivalry, though amicable, has diminished both, as industries play them off against each other.

The Lockhart episode heightened interest in having a judge. After all, the government had promised the review would be independent. Fels' choices, in order, were Sir Anthony Mason, the former Chief Justice of the High Court, and Sir Daryl Dawson, a former High Court judge. Dawson had just completed a royal commission into the Longford gas explosion in Victoria, and was available. Curt Rendell, an accountant with a small business background, and Jillian Segal, a lawyer with business and regulatory experience, were also appointed to the inquiry.

Announcing the three, Treasurer Costello pointed to their balance of legal, business and public policy expertise. Quite so. But where was the consumer representative? As the ACCC's very name says, it is both the competition and consumer commission. Here was its Act being reviewed without a consumer voice being heard.

The government, in fact, had specifically ruled out a consumer member. Not required. Ms Segal was billed as providing 'regulatory experience in consumer protection', and that was seen as sufficient.

The Dawson inquiry's terms of reference also took a few turns before arriving at their final form. An original aim to review competition provisions to ensure they 'support the growth of businesses in regional Australia' took a back seat. In the event, the Dawson inquiry made no recommendations specifically on regional business.

As Dawson got down to business, all the players began polishing their claims. The stakes were high: Dawson could endorse the thrust of Fels' activist ACCC, or cut it down. Either way, the future power balance between business and the competition regulator was up for grabs. Just a few tweaks to merger policy or the problem-prone Section 46, which governs misuse of market power by firms, could dictate the future structure of industries as well as the profits — and losses — of its participants. Small business in particular saw Section 46 changes as a way to at last stop some of the predatory behaviour of big business, especially in retailing.

Fels had already set the hares running. In a speech to an Australian law reform conference before the Dawson inquiry was promised, he raised the prospect of jail terms for hard-core cartel activity. With Dawson looming, he pressed the case harder. 'It seemed to me it would be very, very hard to defeat this key argument and, sure, it put big business on the back foot in relation to the whole inquiry', he says. He was worried that there would be such an outcry against executives going to jail that the government would immediately rule it out. But by 2002 there was a growing backlash against corporate excess, and his fears were unfounded. Still, to ease the amendment's acceptance Fels proposed that jail terms should be confined to big business members of cartels, not small business. This was not well thought out, as small business could be just as guilty of price fixing. The qualification was later dropped.

Fels raised the bar, however, in other directions. He resurrected the idea of an effects test for Section 46, and proposed that the ACCC be given 'cease and desist' powers as an interim measure to stop market abuses until a court could decide on the issue. Fels also wanted collective bargaining rights for small business in their dealing with big companies.

The effects test idea was a bid by Fels to clean up the troublesome Section 46, the key but underutilised control on abuse of market power. The section says a corporation that has a 'substantial degree' of market power shall not 'take advantage' of that power for 'the purpose' of eliminating or damaging competitors, preventing others entering the market, or deterring competitive conduct. So, the ACCC faces three hurdles to win a prosecution that a company has damaged competitors. First, it must prove a corporation has 'a substantial degree of market power'. Second, it must show how it has 'taken advantage' of that power. But third, it must prove 'purpose' in the exercise of that power. 'Purpose' can be difficult to prove. Clearly it would be easier to show that the 'effect' of that exercise of power eliminated a competitor, rather than trying to prove elimination was the company's purpose.

The argument for an effects test had swirled around for 25 years or so, ever since the Fraser Government, responding to big business pressure, weakened the *Trade Practices Act* in 1977 by introducing a dominance test for mergers and inserting the purpose test into Section 46.

The idea of an effects test horrified big business — it would give the ACCC power to prosecute all manner of market power cases. As it was, the ACCC had lucked out over Section 46. Despite some big wins, such as the privately run Queensland Wire case against BHP's refusal to supply a competitor, there had been years of doubt at the ACCC that it could surmount the hurdles for a successful case.

When it did try to litigate using Section 46, it largely failed. The ACCC lost cases against Boral, Rural Press and Safeway, all testing various 'limbs' of Section 46. (The ACCC won an appeal on the Safeway case in June 2003, but the case could end up in the High Court.) The Federal Court found that Universal and Warner Music had engaged in misuse of market power, but the finding was subject to appeal. The frustration at the ACCC about the difficult hurdles to securing a market power conviction was evident. As Justice Northrop said in one case:

> A contravention [of Section 46] may take many forms and in many cases a wink, a look or a nod may be more effective than the written or expressed word. Proof of those aspects may be difficult to obtain.

He was dead right. Yet Section 46 is supposedly about fair dealing. It goes to the heart — or should go to the heart — of claims by small independent traders that their market share is being eroded through fair means and foul by the big supermarket chains. 'If the law does not even prohibit large firms with substantial market power from taking advantage of it with the effect of damaging competition — by virtue of such actions as an anti-competitive refusal to supply, predatory behaviour, leveraging of market power in one market to damage competition in another market — the law is not only deficient as a matter of economic policy, but deficient in relation to (these) objectives', the ACCC would later tell Dawson.

In arguing for an effects test as well as cease and desist orders, Fels was trying to set Dawson's agenda, throwing up some big contentious bones for all parties to chew over. But as the inquiry progressed, Fels in turn was pressed on his most sensitive issue, the use of publicity. In the end, he gave ground.

Meanwhile, at the Business Council the initial quandary was, 'What do we do now we've got the inquiry?' The BCA had campaigned hard on the merger side, arguing that Australian companies were handicapped in achieving 'scale' to compete abroad by the difficulties of the ACCC's merger and authorisation processes. The realisation quickly dawned that continuing down this road would only mean pushing for a return to the old dominance test — which would be fruitless. Many BCA members argued they had had no problem with the current test, acknowledging Fels' argument that the ACCC only blocks a few mergers. Substantial lessening of competition was not a serious barrier to mergers, as the approval rate demonstrated.

Did business having nothing else to say? The BCA decided to focus more on the way Fels' ACCC administered the whole process. This would swing the spotlight onto authorisation, the cumbersome and little-used system under which the ACCC can approve a deal that has a public benefit even though it lessens competition.

How long did ACCC merger or authorisation processes take? How did the ACCC decide on attaching conditions to a deal? How were the issues played out in the media? All these questions assisted the BCA in shifting the focus onto what was essentially its main beef — Fels' style and his canny use of the media.

Some in business wanted the BCA to take a strong stand arguing for a separation of the ACCC's competition and consumer functions. They worried that Fels was becoming almost doctrinal in his pursuit of consumer interests, damaging business in the process. Separation, however, was judged too radical a step. When the BCA drafted its initial submission to Dawson the number one 'ask' became 'strengthening governance and accountability of the ACCC'. In other words, corralling Fels.

Mergers, the original public justification, came second. Nevertheless, the BCA did a lot of homework on mergers. While big business complains about Fels' publicity, it is actually the ACCC's process and mergers that generate much of the hostility — 'They might have got us, but they bullied us'. Apart from arguing to Dawson that the ACCC should give more extensive reasons for a merger rejection, the BCA also proposed a new route for merger parties — straight to the Australian Competition Tribunal. This, it argued, would be speedier.

As for Fels' push for an effects test in Section 46, the BCA was scornful. It would catch 'innocent, competitive behaviour', the BCA argued, opening a line of attack that would dog the ACCC as the Section 46 debate grew. Fels' ACCC, claimed the BCA, seemed more interested in protecting specific competitors rather than competition itself. 'There is a risk that, if Section 46 is cast to protect competitors, it will result in inefficient or less competitive players being protected from robust competition, resulting in a decrease in competition overall', it claimed.

The argument is that 'robust' competition might wound some players, but consumers benefit. If an effects test protects inefficient players, consumers and the economy lose. The ACCC responds that 'robust' competition might benefit consumers initially, but if small players are then driven out of the market prices will go back up again. The trick, of course, is to ensure 'robust' competition is not predatory.

The BCA gave Dawson some examples of how an effects test would wound competition. Say Pharmacorp, a hypothetical company with strong market share, develops a revolutionary new treatment called Wonderdrug, which becomes a top seller. A smaller competitor, Medico, has been working on a similar treatment, but abandons the launch as Pharmacorp's Wonderdrug now dominates the market. With an effects test, Pharmacorp could face charges of anti-competitive conduct, whereas in reality it had increased consumer choice.

Surprisingly, the BCA agreed, or half agreed, to Fels' idea of jail terms for business executives engaging in hard-core price fixing cartels. It was a close run decision. Business could not be seen to be against sending serious offenders to jail. Further, if business opposed jail terms it would play into Fels' hands and focus attention on price fixing. Better to ensure that the debate was not distracted. The BCA hoped, too, that business' backing of jail terms might generate community support for wider pro-business changes to the *Trade Practices Act*. That would never happen if business was seen to be defending cartel behaviour. So, cautiously, the BCA put up its hand, saying it would support criminal sanctions 'if the Review Committee considers that greater deterrence is needed'.

In its first submission to Dawson, the BCA stated that it supported jail terms provided they applied to all executives regardless of the size of the business. Some months later, in a final submission, it stepped back a bit. Other business groups, such as the Australian Chamber of Commerce and Industry, were opposed, and the BCA's initial support was finely balanced internally. While repeating that the idea had its support if Dawson believed jail a necessary sanction, this later submission also said the BCA now had 'serious reservations' about Fels' idea. It would need to be accompanied by a test that the executive had a deliberate intent to either act dishonestly, known in law as *mens rea*, or was recklessly indifferent to the harmful consequences.

After attempting to neutralise Fels' criminal sanctions idea, the BCA got to its main game: neutralising Fels himself. The wording was very careful, but pointed nevertheless. After citing a list of ACCC 'sins', including conflicts of interest and duty, conflicts of regulatory philosophy between competition and consumer protection, bias, and lack of objectivity, the BCA said:

> The Business Council does not believe that the current questions over the operation of the ACCC stem just from the style of the current Chairman. While it is true that certain issues, particularly relating to the use of the media, may be linked to a particular personal style, the majority of the concerns raised in the Business Council's submissions relate to cultural and administrative problems with the ACCC, and not just the public persona of its Chairman. The Business Council is therefore strongly of the view that governance and accountability remain issues, regardless of the tenure of the current Chairman.

There it was. A decade of watching the Asher/Fels duo beef up the ACCC's enforcement regime while also winning the media debate had convinced business that the ACCC's culture was beyond redemption whoever led it. The ACCC needed wholesale reform.

Interestingly, this business view that the ACCC required root and branch reform was not in the BCA's opening submission to Dawson, but in its October 2002 supplementary. The timing of the addition may not have been accidental. Only just over a month earlier the ABC's *Australian Story* had lifted the veil on Fels' family life, dramatically ending the program with Fels' revelation that he would not seek renewal of his term as chairman, due to expire in June 2004.

Given the circumstances of Fels' shortened 2000 reappointment, it is doubtful that he would have been offered a new term in 2004. Business, however, did not know that. Fels' surprise announcement, made against a background of still-secret deliberations about leaving even earlier and taking up the new job with the Australia and New

Zealand School of Government, suddenly changed the whole Dawson debate.

The *Australian Story* program showed Fels' mastery of the media, once again. When approached by the ABC he knew that the program would be sympathetic to his daughter Isabella's schizophrenia. Both Fels and his wife Isabel believed the show was a good opportunity to finally bring Isabella's illness out into the open. Fels also wanted an opportunity to make the point that if he did jump to a new life in academia there were major family pressures involved in the decision. Any suggestion that the business campaign had finally 'got him' was to be precluded.

Australian Story did indeed handle the Felses' family life and Isabella's illness very sensitively. Younger daughter Teresa revealed the closeness of the family, and the fact that Fels had raised the two girls on a steady diet of jokes. Humour also runs on the Cid side. As Fels and Isabel are filmed watching television, with business commentator Terry McCrann calling Fels a 'media tart', Isabel asks Fels deadpan, 'Do you think he's competing with you?' Isabella talked of her father's dilemma in dealing with his busy life and her illness. 'He really drops everything to help me', she says. 'If I have a problem, sometimes he stops a meeting so he can come to my rescue.' Isabel had perhaps the most poignant moment in the program, describing how Isabella in her schizophrenic episodes believes her belongings will be taken away, or she will lose a limb.

The program built to a point at which Fels lamented that the burden fell more on his wife. 'In my own personal world I've had a pretty strong tendency to spend too much time thinking about work and letting my own inner, emotional, personal life get neglected.' Isabel followed that up by saying her 'dream' was for her husband to go 'full circle' back to academia: 'I don't know whether it is possible', she said, seemingly hinting that it might be.

Fels had struck a deal with the show's producers. After this comment by his wife they would shoot a final sequence showing him strolling through the campus of Monash University (where he held the title of honorary professor of economics and business) dressed in coat and cap, and then stop to say this:

> After much reflection I've decided that I will not seek renewal of my position as chairman of the Commission. I find that it is quite difficult for the family, my absences. I would like to return to the academic world. Before I retire I'd like to come back and impart some of that knowledge to a new generation and to, perhaps, future leaders in the public service.

Fels then had final say on whether or not the ABC could use this to conclude the program. At the last minute, he said 'go'.

The end credits of the show then said: 'This announcement means Allan Fels will leave the ACCC at the end of his current term. Isabella is still in hospital.'

Fels was extracting himself from the ACCC on his own terms. When Fels' appointment to the new school of government was later announced, few commentators read into it that the business community had 'got him'. That's not to say that the shortened reappointment from Costello, which Fels regarded as an insult, and the business campaign did not impact his thinking. But Fels wanted no suggestion in the media that either had.

While most of the media looked no further than the family problems — and they were genuine — *The Australian Financial Review*, perhaps because of its business orientation, raised wider issues. Under the headline 'Why Fels Jumped' Colleen Ryan said a friend had warned Fels before the 2001 election: 'Allan, you've got a big train heading for you. Keep your head down'. Ryan listed the public business campaign against Fels led by David Murray of Commonwealth Bank, Roger Corbett of Woolworths, Geoff Dixon of Qantas, Dick Warburton of Caltex and David Jones (who was also a member of the Reserve Bank board) and John Schubert of the BCA. 'Each of these heavies has had a round or two with Fels', she said, listing their runs-ins with the ACCC.

The Review's Chanticleer columnist, John Durie, went a step further. 'The fact that he tied his daughter's tragic plight to the decision not to seek another term (when one wasn't being offered) is unlikely to win much sympathy for the mere reason that she was dragged into the spotlight', he said. However, Isabella actually benefited from the 'spotlight', as indeed did public understanding of schizophrenia. Isabella's story generated a media debate on treatment of the disease. Fels and Isabella later launched a campaign for better care for the mentally ill outside of institutions.

If sections of the media were critical, the letters to the editor columns told a different story. 'Not since the retirement of Sir William Deane have I felt such sadness as when Allan Fels announced his retirement last Monday evening', Judith Spooner of Foxground wrote to *The Sydney Morning Herald* — a representative response. 'He joins the ranks of true Australians who served his country and his family well as he protected our rights against big and little business. Enjoy your retirement. The only plus is that the stockmarket will probably react strong tomorrow as the "big end of town" rejoices.'

Others were contemplating Fels' retirement in a less charitable fashion. Gerry Harvey sarcastically wished him well, adding that he was going to buy the retirement home Fels went to. 'That way I can treat him the way he's treated me', he said.

More serious heads around business were trying to lay down markers for a future ACCC sans Allan Fels. The Business Council's model, as proposed to Dawson, involved three tiers of added checks and balances. First, there would be a charter to provide a 'clear framework' for the administration of competition regulation. Second, a Board of Competition would be created to 'monitor' the ACCC's performance against the principles in the charter. Third, an 'inspector-general' would be appointed to 'examine and advise on systemic issues with the administration of the TPA [*Trade Practices Act*]', including the use of the media.

This Orwellian array seemed to trouble even the BCA, which devoted a section of its submission to refuting claims that they constituted just 'more bureaucracy'. Within the BCA there were still deeper criticisms of these proposals. Even though ideas like the 'inspector-general' ended up in the BCA submission they were never a matter of serious promotion. 'It was fiddling at the margins', says one business strategist. 'The real driver ultimately was the desire to get a handle on the Commission and, they hate to say it, they see that meaning getting a handle on Fels.'

Surprisingly, the BCA tiptoed around a central issue of its entire campaign — Fels' use of the media. Other business lobby groups, while endorsing various ideas for a board of governance around the ACCC, went in much harder on media. Australian Industry Group, for instance, wanted a set of 'dynamic procedural guidelines' to cover use of publicity. The Australian Chamber of Commerce and Industry was toughest of all. 'The aggressive and calculated manner in which the ACCC uses the media in ways that is directly intended to damage the reputation of firms must end', it declared, urging a separate code of media conduct for the Commission.

The Dawson inquiry slowly ground its way through the 212 submissions it received, including 14 confidential ones. The inquiry encouraged quite a few 'confidential' supplementary submissions from various groups, so that outsiders — including presumably the media — could not read which way it was heading. The ACCC, surprisingly given its usual media open house, responded to these requests, lodging a host of confidential submissions.

In one, listed as 7B, it is apparent Fels *could* see the 'train' coming his way that a friend had reportedly warned him about, and he was prepared to get off the rail lines. In 7B, Fels laid down a more rigorous ACCC media policy. The Commission would only announce an investigation in 'special circumstances', including cases where the media had already found out or where the Commission had been called on to make an inquiry, where public confidence needed to be maintained, or where it wanted witnesses to come forward. Press releases on legal proceedings would be 'moderately worded and factual', while those on court outcomes would be more expansive, detailing not only the result but Commission views about it and the lessons for business and consumers. In private exchanges between the Commission and Dawson staff there was some talk of a 'media code', but this was dropped. The ACCC was surprised to find it resurface in Dawson's actual report.

When the inquiry's report was finally released — Costello sat on it for three months — Dawson proved to be the competition version of the curate's egg, with good and bad parts for all the players. For openers, it rejected all the pleading for additional regulation to stop market concentration in particular areas. Small retailers, for instance, had sought provisions to stop so-called creeping acquisitions by the big supermarkets.

'Whilst it is appropriate for the ACCC to scrutinise conduct in such areas carefully, the Committee considers that competition measures which are specific to particular industries should be avoided', it said. 'The competition provisions should protect the competitive process rather than particular competitors. They should not be seen as a means of achieving social outcomes unrelated to the encouragement of competition or as a means of preserving corporations that are not able to withstand competitive forces. Competition regulation should be distinguished from industry policy.'

Small business fumed over what were seen as insulting comments about companies 'not able to withstand competitive forces' being abandoned by competition policy. What about all those companies protected by tariffs, anti-dumping measures, foreign investment controls, government largesse or rural assistance schemes?

Dawson was right in pointing to the need to separate competition and industry policies. But governments are notoriously susceptible to bending competition rules for special interests. While the Howard Government ticked Dawson's view, it will be interesting to watch Cabinet's reaction when, say, newsagents or special deals for the oil companies to merge refinery businesses are next on the agenda. Dawson's guiding principle should also be sobering when Cabinet considers ideas for special regulators for an industry, rather than having it all under an ACCC less open to industry capture.

Dawson also rejected any change in the merger test. Substantial lessening of competition stays, and now appears permanently locked in. But the ACCC will be required to provide reasons when making decisions under its informal clearance process. As well, a new parallel formal voluntary merger process is proposed, providing a 40-day decision-making limit with a right of review to the Australian Competition Tribunal.

If this was not a sufficient win for the business lobby, Dawson tacked on a surprise. Merger parties fearing they may breach the substantial lessening of competition test could go direct to the Tribunal to argue their case for authorisation because of other public benefits.

This may not be so good for consumers. If mergers lessen competition, consumers have a big interest in seeing that they provide offsetting benefits before authorisation. The Tribunal, however, is a more legalistic body than the ACCC. Consumers and small business may come off second-best.

Merger authorisations are, in effect, licences to create monopolies. The new route direct to the Tribunal allows for no appeal process, whereas the ACCC route does. It seems odd that this should have got past both Dawson and the government without being questioned. The multi-merger tracks will create a lot of legal game-playing around the future ACCC.

Big business had yet another win when it came to market power. Dawson said 'no' to an effects test for Section 46 as sought by Fels, as well as rejecting powers for the ACCC to issue cease and desist orders until a case could come before the courts.

It did not go all business' way on market power provisions, however. Dawson recommended that small business be allowed to collectively bargain with big business. The provision is limited to transactions up to $3 million, and so should benefit groups such as shopkeepers and doctors. But the ACCC quickly cautioned small business that collective bargaining did not extend to collective boycotts.

To balance business 'wins', Dawson ticked Fels' scheme for jail terms in hard-core cartel cases. Well, sort of. Gossip around the competition 'mafia' of lawyers and regulators had the Dawson committee split 2-to-1 in favour of criminal sanctions. The two junior members, Curt Rendall and Jillian Segal, apparently tipped the balance against Dawson. Certainly the language endorsing criminal sanctions is lukewarm. While the committee said it was 'persuaded' that criminal sanctions deterred cartel behaviour, it wanted further work on defining 'serious cartel behaviour' and a workable way of combining criminal sanctions with a leniency policy that provides amnesty for the first member of a cartel who blows the whistle. Dawson did, however, urge stiffer civil penalties. Fines in future could be the greater of $10 million, three times the gain, or 10 per cent of a corporation's turnover. With the turnover of big corporations stretching into many billions of dollars, this should be sobering.

The government's response showed it was also nervous about criminal penalties. In addition to the solutions that had to be found to the problems identified by Dawson, 'any new criminal penalty must be applied broadly and must not impose significant additional uncertainty and complexity for business', it said. With a further study planned, criminal sanctions could well slip between the cracks of these various difficulties, endangering the package of reforms.

Curiously, Dawson also rolled out a major change to the *Trade Practices Act* with little justification. The current Act bars certain forms of market conduct such as price fixing, bid-rigging and market sharing — as in one party taking the south side of the river and the other the north. These are 'per se' offences regardless of whether or not they lessen competition. In a huge softening of the law against bid-rigging and market sharing, Dawson proposed — and the government accepted — that exclusionary conduct such as bid-rigging be subject to a substantial lessening of competition test rather than an outright ban.

The ACCC was horrified. 'This will have a serious impact on the ACCC's ability to combat agreements between competitors to rig bids, collude in tendering or share markets, all of which are directed at the buyer rather than competing suppliers', said Fels.

There is a respectable case to be made out for softening the current outright bans, as indeed the Law Council of Australia made in its submission to Dawson. The world has moved on since the outright bans were laid down in 1974, and these days, joint ventures could be unfairly caught. Discounts offered by supermarkets to buy petrol could also be caught by prohibited third line forcing, which bars the practice of a company selling one good provided the purchaser acquired goods or services from a third party.

The ACCC itself was willing to see a softening, provided some prohibitions were maintained. But Dawson opted for a lifting of all exclusionary dealing prohibitions, to be replaced by a substantial lessening of competition test. The ACCC will now have its work cut out to put bid-rigging and market sharing cases through this test.

Fels fears the end of exclusionary prohibitions and the new direct route for anti-competitive mergers to the Tribunal will haunt the future ACCC and governments. He is most concerned about the new opportunities for bid-rigging and market sharing, and the lack of explanation in Dawson. 'My conclusion is that if the authors make a comprehensive policy change and do not mention it, they are unaware of it', he says.

It was not long before the trade practices 'mafia' began to hack apart Dawson recommendations. Henry Ergas, managing director of Network Economics Consulting and also chairman of the government's Intellectual Property Review Committee, claimed that some Dawson recommendations could do more harm than good. Ergas also cited the relaxed rules for dealing with market sharing and bid-rigging. Dawson, he said, recognised in one part of the report that these are capable of such harm as to warrant being sanctioned by criminal penalties. Yet the report then says an outright ban should not continue. This, said Ergas, 'is very difficult to understand'.

Ergas also raised questions against Dawson's recommendation to relax some of the per se price fixing bans for dual-listed corporations

— structures in which firms create a single entity while maintaining dual stock exchange listing. The Dawson report, Ergas stated, acknowledged these could amount to mergers yet recommended exemptions from the *Trade Practices Act*. This could drive a 'potentially large hole' in the current merger regime, in his view.

If the government is forced to backtrack on these debatable decisions it will raise questions about Dawson's processes. Contrary to standard practice, Treasury did not seek Fels' or the ACCC's comments before drawing up the government's response. This can avoid embarrassment that recommendations of a review are impractical. As well, the Dawson inquiry did not include a consumer representative, and there were no trade practice specialists on its staff.

If some of Dawson's recommendations raised doubts, there was no misunderstanding when it came to future administration of the ACCC and its media profile. Dawson walked away from ideas for a charter of competition, supervisory board or inspector-general of competition as suggested by various business lobbies. Instead, it opted for oversight by a new joint committee of parliament as well as a more formal consultative committee than the ACCC now has. The consultative committee would report to parliament in a dedicated section of the ACCC's own annual report.

'The ACCC's use of the media was one of the issues most frequently raised with the Committee', Dawson said. It cited complaints about prior publicity of investigations and prosecutions as well as media statements that lacked balance and objectivity. Dawson's solution was to pick up on the suggestion of many, including Fels, for a tighter media policy at the ACCC. But Dawson's media code was much stricter than that proposed by Fels. It suggests that the ACCC should not comment on investigations, and issue a formal press release only at the commencement of any prosecution, and that that should be confined to the facts. As well, ACCC reporting of the outcome of prosecutions should be accurate and balanced.

The Dawson code contains some fascinating nuances. It is intended to cover both formal and informal comment by the ACCC, meaning that the Commission and Fels' successor would be hobbled in giving background material to the media. Other parties, of course, would not be so constrained. And there is a pre-electronic age feel to the limitations on announcements of court proceedings. These are to be only a 'formal media release confined to stating the facts', appearing to rule out any television appearances.

Apart from media, Dawson also recommended that the ACCC's formidable powers to issue Section 155 notices to obtain information, require people to appear before the Commission, and raid premises, be curtailed. Noting that the use of Section 155s had grown of recent years, it recommended that the ACCC be required to seek a warrant from a Federal Court judge before it actually raided premises.

In the big picture, Dawson makes the ACCC process more legalistic, with its proposals for formal authorisation procedures and a direct route to the Competition Tribunal. Privately, Fels sees that business had a 'win' on merger policy, but that the ACCC had 'struck back' on criminal sanctions. On the new media policy, Fels regards this as a 'slap on the wrist'. If he had been staying around 'I'd have to be more careful, but it's not a massive style change'.

Costello hardly had time to digest the Dawson report when the High Court moved the ground from under him. The court's decision in the Boral case opened new ground in the long debate over Section 46, the crucial market power provisions of the *Trade Practices Act*, saying that predatory or below-cost pricing was not a misuse of market power.

This appears to remove the Section 46 safety net from under small business, which believed it was always there to protect them. Section 46 will now be the touchstone of any reforms to the *Trade Practices Act* as recommended by Dawson. A formidable cross-party coalition is building in the Senate, demanding changes to Section 46 to accommodate small business fears in any passage of Dawson proposals.

The Boral case raises the classic trade practice policy conundrum discussed in chapter 1: is the Act there to protect competition, or to protect competitors in the shape of small business? Those who believe the former say protecting competition benefits consumers. Supporters of the latter say there will be no competition benefit for consumers without competitors. Ranging between the two are those who want to protect small business for social or ideological reasons, often using the illustration of the predatory behaviour of the big supermarket chains.

The issue that brought all this to a head, and forced the High Court's first decision on predatory pricing, was the humble concrete building brick. In February 1994 C&M Brick Pty Ltd opened a state-of-the-art plant in Bendigo to produce concrete bricks and pavers, using a new Hess machine. A price war was already under way for concrete bricks on major Victorian building projects, but the new entrant really brought out the price razors. Boral Besser Masonry Limited, part of the wider Boral group, aggressively priced bids, as did Pioneer. Two other competitors, Rocla and Budget, fell by the wayside.

Boral decided not only to cut prices, but to upgrade its own new plant and increase production. The High Court judgement recited various Boral documents about 'crushing' or 'wiping out' competitors. In March 1998, the ACCC instituted proceedings against Boral alleging its predatory pricing was a misuse of market power.

The case then bounced around courts for the next five years. The Federal Court found no contravention of Section 46. The Full Federal Court unanimously overturned this on appeal, finding Boral had a substantial degree of power in the Melbourne concrete masonry market and — crucially — had taken advantage of that power to deter new entrants and drive out competitors.

By a 6-to-1 vote, the High Court then overturned this. It found that if Boral's aim was to wipe out C&M it had not succeeded, and that despite price cutting Boral's share of the market in 1996 was about the same as it had been in 1994, around 30 per cent. Boral therefore did not have a substantial degree of market power, a key test under Section 46. As Justice McHugh noted, predatory pricing without a substantial degree of market power cannot result in a breach of Section 46. What had failed to be demonstrated was that Boral had the necessary market power to set prices as it saw fit without concern about competitors.

As Frank Zumbo (the senior lecturer in law at the University of New South Wales) stated, however, only a monopolist could set prices indiscriminately of the market. Section 46 would now be of little use in markets of two or more players. 'For the small, medium enterprise competing with larger, more powerful entities, the High Court's finding means it will ordinarily have no recourse under Section 46 for allegations of predatory pricing by those entities', he said. 'It also means that Section 46 may not be — if it ever was — the right vehicle for dealing with allegations of predatory pricing.'

The Boral decision immediately sparked a political furore on whether, and how, small business should be protected. 'Section 46, which aims to prevent abuse of market power by large corporations, is as good as dead and buried', declared the National's Senator Ron Boswell, a vigorous defender of small retailers. Queensland Liberal Senator George Brandis, a barrister with extensive trade practice experience, pointed to parliament's intention over Section 46. Labor Attorney-General Lionel Bowen, introducing amendments in 1986, had made it clear action was being taken … 'To ensure that small businesses are given a measure of protection from the predatory actions of powerful competitors.'

Not surprisingly, Small Business Minister Joe Hockey immediately took it up with Costello, who is in charge of the *Trade Practices Act*. 'Small business readily and properly expects that the *Trade Practices Act* would provide them with some protection from what might be seen as predatory activity', he said.

Fels took the issue right up to Costello as well, publicly warning him that the High Court judgement had undermined the ability of the *Trade Practices Act* to prevent the targeting of small business and efficient new entrants. Realising the emerging political issue, Costello promptly fired his then-unreleased copy of the Dawson report back to its authors, asking them to again review Section 46.

Dawson had already urged no change in Section 46, and equally promptly told Costello there was no reason to change this recommendation. Let judicial interpretation work it out, said Dawson, perhaps not surprisingly in view of the fact that he is a former High Court judge. Section 46 cases currently before the Federal and High courts — Boral, Safeway, Rural Press and Universal Music — should provide 'great practical guidance in the application of Section 46', Dawson said, also noting that fundamental change that risked uncertainty was to be avoided.

Boral, however, injected new uncertainty. While the small business lobby was in full flight, others saw it differently. Bill Reid, a partner in Blake Dawson Waldron, the lawyers that acted for Boral, picked up on the potentially pro-consumer side of the decision. Boral had clarified just how vigorously businesses could now respond to competition. In the previous uncertainty, Reid said, many businesses had actually been advised to be more cautious in their pricing response to competition, to the detriment of consumers.

While cynics might mutter 'he would say that wouldn't he', Reid was not the only one taking a different line. Russell Miller, a partner in Minter Ellison and author of *Miller's Annotated Trade Practices Act*, the industry 'bible', saw the decision as a victory for competition and common sense. Law firm Allens Arthur Robinson noted how the court had used the US recoupment test to determine whether predatory pricing meant the predator had market power. Under this test, predatory pricing is not illegal unless the predator has the ability of recouping the losses by later charging supra-competitive pricing.

The High Court ruling that 'deep pockets' do not necessarily mean market power puts the issue of whether small business needs protection from predatory pricing squarely on the future political agenda. The Howard Government will not have to push its Dawson reform package through a cross-party alliance in the Senate that threatens to rewrite Section 46 unless the government itself proposes reform. Should Section 46 be stiffened with predatory pricing powers, or should these be in another section of the Act? Should other

Section 46 tests on 'substantial degree of market power' or 'taking advantage' be better defined to catch abuses?

There is no magic bullet answer. Fels, however, is in the camp that says something needs to be done. He points to the string of unsuccessful cases mounted by the ACCC, an otherwise usually winning litigator. 'The result is that only once in the last 12 years has the ACCC been able to find that a firm with substantial market power took advantage of it to harm competition', he notes incredulously.

Political answers may take time. The government might want to wait for court appeals on the Rural Press, Safeway and Universal/Warner cases to see how further jurisprudence changes Section 46. That could take the issue into mid-2004 or later, meaning Parliament is unlikely to deal with Dawson and Section 46 for some time despite pressure to act from small business lobbies. In June 2003 the Full Federal Court gave the ACCC a partial win in the Safeway case, unanimously finding the retailer had engaged in price fixing on bread. But only a majority of the court agreed on the key misuse of market power tests. Similar Federal Court disagreements were evident in Boral, opening the possibility of a High Court appeal on Safeway as well. The Safeway 'win' was only the ACCC's second on Section 46.

If the Howard Government thought Dawson would relieve it of pressures over the *Trade Practices Act* and Allan Fels it was clearly mistaken. In political terms, Dawson misread the balance between the conflicting forces — the ACCC, big and small business. The ACCC got its criminal sanctions wish, and not much extra governance. Big business got a string of wins, including new merger paths, removal of outright bans on some anti-competitive conduct, court oversight of ACCC raiding powers and greater controls on ACCC's use of media. Small business, the government's public justification for acceding to the BCA's call for the inquiry, got only collective bargaining rights, and will face difficulty trying to exercise this extra muscle by collective boycotts. Stiff ACCC opposition will diminish the small business 'win'.

The High Court's Boral decision set a political fire under Dawson's avoidance of market power issues, including Section 46, concentration of market power and creeping acquisitions. Small business mounted a vigorous lobbying effort for predatory pricing protection, including claims that big players be forced to prove their innocence. Costello was faced with the sensitive political issue of whether, and how, to change Section 46 to make the Dawson package saleable. Will he come down to protect competitors (small business), or competition? And whatever he proposes, would the Senate make it even more favourable to small business?

The business sector is rightly wary of any rewriting of Section 46 market power abuse sections to help small business. So wary in fact that in late June 2003 it told both Costello and Howard that it would rather forgo any of the benefits of the Dawson package than be forced to accept changes to Section 46 to reverse the Boral decision which seemingly permitted predatory pricing. Wrapping herself in a consumer flag, Katie Lahey, the BCA's chief executive, said any restrictions on 'competitive pricing' would lead to consumers paying higher prices. It is on the difference between 'competitive' and 'predatory' pricing that the politics will now swing.

This was an extraordinary admission by the BCA. Forget the whole Dawson exercise, it was effectively saying. The benefits of keeping the High Court's liberal interpretation of predatory pricing are greater for the BCA than all the new merger processes and nooses around the ACCC recommended by Dawson. The prospect of the Senate, under small business pressure, rewriting Section 46 was just too horrendous for the BCA. *The Financial Review*'s headline summed it up: 'BCA says it prefers to be predatory'.

The BCA campaign which set out to limit Fels' powers wound its way via political lobbying through an inquiry and was then sidetracked into a High Court decision that in turn threatened a powerful Senate backlash. The result was a focus, not on Fels, but on the ACCC's ability to deal with big business abuse of market power.

Be careful what you ask for ...

CHAPTER 13

'You'd need rocks in your head to follow him'

A llan Fels spent 12 years building up the competition regulator's patch, with Treasurer Peter Costello even comparing his empire building to that of the legendary Sir Humphrey Appleby. Yet his departure seemed to herald an era of great uncertainty for the regulator. Much of this centred on its future leadership. The process for appointing Commission members and the chairman is cumbersome anyway, but in the case of Fels' replacement it degenerated into political farce.

In October 2002, a month after Fels used the *Australian Story* program to flag that he would be leaving the Commission in 2004, Treasurer Peter Costello wrote to all the states nominating both a new deputy chairman and a new commissioner: National Competition Council president Graeme Samuel and his executive director Ed Willett.

In many ways Graeme Samuel was an ideal choice for deputy chairman. A lawyer-turned-merchant-banker, he had made a pile in the market and was now committed to a career of public service. Moreover, Samuel had been a foundation member of the small coterie of lawyers, judges, academics and regulators who had nurtured the *Trade Practices Act* from its inception in 1974.

Samuel, in fact, was the inaugural chairman of the real inner circle of this group, the trade practice committee within the business law section of the Law Council of Australia. Whether it was a fine point of the law — for instance, the difference between a 'substantial' and a 'significant' lessening of competition — or the natural tensions between the legal and economic side of competition law, it would be thrashed out at this group's annual workshop.

Such is the power of the group that Senator George Brandis, a member through his former work as a trade practice barrister, penned a poem about it cheekily titled 'The Cartel'. After listing some of the judges, lawyers and 'high priest' Allan Fels in attendance, the poem, composed for an after-dinner speech at the 2000 workshop, concluded:

> A self-anointed kinship
> Of the brightest and the best
> Cabalistic, close, exclusive —
> A cartel by any test.*

Like Fels, Samuel gained a lot of enemies by sticking his nose into cartels and many other cosy, anti-competitive market sharing arrangements. But Samuel's competition regulator's beat was quite different to Fels. As head of the National Competition Council (the NCC), his constituency was confined to state premiers and treasurers: policing their progress in meeting targets in eliminating state regulations inhibiting competition, and handing them cheques as reward. Fels, on the other hand, had a wider business and consumer constituency.

The NCC was a child of the Hilmer reforms of the mid-1990s, which, among other initiatives, agreed to a review of all government regulatory restrictions on competition. The Industry Commission (later the Productivity Commission) estimated in March 1995 that Hilmer reforms could add 5.5 per cent, or $23 billion, to Australia's gross domestic product per year. But the Commonwealth stood to gain more in revenues than the states — $5.9 billion a year as

---

* © Senator George Brandis

opposed to only $3 billion. Led by Victoria's Jeff Kennett, the states argued for a bigger share of the reform pie. Prime Minister Paul Keating agreed.

So the NCC was handed the tough task of policing state reforms in sensitive areas like shopping hours; dairy, electricity and taxi deregulation; water reforms; and agricultural marketing, and providing financial rewards for compliance. This pushed the so-called national competition policy into the very bowels of small business. The gains of reform might be great, but the political pain was enormous for state governments.

Samuel began at the NCC in a publicly upbeat manner, but stoushes with states on sensitive issues like electricity market reform and shopping hours created some very negative publicity. Pauline Hanson's One Nation made national competition policy a lightning rod for popular anger about deregulation. While Samuel could point to falling consumer prices across milk and electricity, growing retail sales due to easier shopping hours and a national lift in productivity, the process was also accompanied by some job losses and industry dislocation. Wounded industries can be loud and powerful lobbyists; happy consumers are quiet.

Not surprisingly, market research in the late 1990s showed the Council of Australian Governments (COAG) — the formal mechanism of state and federal meetings — that national competition policy was very much on the nose. Samuel asked a senior officials meeting of COAG for a budget to 'sell' the reforms. He got only $200 000, which failed to dampen the screams of pain from affected industries.

Right up to the Queensland and West Australian elections in early 2001, in which national competition policy was derided as 'out of control', Samuel was handing it back to the politicians. 'Those [politicians] who pursue political opportunism, deliberately calculated to misinform and mislead, when their communities need honesty and leadership, deserve disdain', he wrote in *The Australian*.

Shortly after the elections, however, Samuel had a long session with Howard and Costello about his future style. Howard gave him two pieces of advice. 'First of all, Graeme, this is a very tough policy', Howard told him. 'You've got to take it one step at a time. You're on a rocky road and if you run you'll fall over and break your leg.' Howard was telling Samuel to ease up on the publicity. But he had another message, as well: 'Don't lecture governments publicly, it doesn't work'.

Samuel and the two politicians decided to 'punch out the lights' of national competition policy — Samuel would go into his 'merchant banker mould' of achieving results by negotiation rather than public confrontations. 'I'm here to get an outcome by going around things and working out problems', he would tell premiers. Samuel even advised one premier not to hold a public review on the super-sensitive small business issue of trading hour deregulation. 'You know what the outcome will be', he told the premier. 'Let's see if we can work our way through to an end.'

A classic example of Samuel's merchant banker 'let's do a deal' style occurred in grain deregulation. Samuel met the agriculture minister of a state holding out against reform in a private meeting room at Melbourne Airport. 'I'm telling you now that we are not going to do it', said the state minister as he entered. An hour and a half later the two signed an agreement.

Inevitably, Samuel also had some private brawls with state premiers and treasurers. States often accused him of 'taking away' their payments under competition reform. 'I'm not taking it away, you're not earning it', Samuel would respond. 'If you don't earn it you're not entitled to get it.' Some premiers privately warned Samuel that they intended to use him as a whipping boy in state elections, adding that he should not take it personally.

'Punching out the lights' may have worked in the sense of results, but it left many scars on Samuel's relations with state treasurers. It also ensured a very low public profile for Samuel. Around the NCC headquarters in Melbourne there is some frustration that Fels is rated the third most powerful person in Australia for his stoushes with big business while Samuel hardly makes the score sheet for his brawls with the states.

Yet his competition reforms are substantial. As Samuel left the NCC in mid-2003 the major 'competition reforms' of restructured government business, competitive neutrality with the private sector and a national electricity market were virtually in place. A few sectoral reforms such as shopping hours, water reform, taxis and agricultural marketing remained incomplete. Some states will suffer withheld payments over these, but fortunately for Samuel he will not be there to administer the harsh medicine.

Costello and Samuel mix among Melbourne's unique political, business and football tribes. Samuel is the consummate insider who over the years has held a string of corporate directorships as well as being involved in sports, arts and Jewish organisations. National competition policy, however, made him a firm ally of Costello. 'The states who had to accomplish these things took no responsibility but told all the industry lobbyists it was the evil Commonwealth, and in particular the Treasurer', says Costello. 'There was no great support [for national competition policy] in either the Liberal or especially the National Party, or the Labor Party for that matter. I think Samuel was very brave in that period [the late 1990s]. I think he kept it going.'

Samuel's business, competition and Liberal Party credentials — he had also been president of the Australian Chamber of Commerce and Industry and Victorian Treasurer of the Liberal Party — were so appealing to Costello that he bypassed the agreed formula with the states to nominate him for deputy chairman as Fels signalled he would not be seeking a further term beyond 2004.

Appointment of chairmen, deputy chairmen and Commission members of the ACCC is a clumsy process devised in the Hilmer aftermath to get the states to sign up to national competition policy. In effect, Canberra nominates and the states vote. In a two-step process the states are initially given 35 days to suggest candidates, and then a further 35 days to vote on the candidate actually proposed by the Commonwealth to go forward to the Governor-General.

As a frustrated Costello would later say, Canberra pays all the bills of the ACCC but has no vote in who runs it. The states had a veto, but paid nothing towards the ACCC's budget. 'All power and no responsibility', he says, inviting memories of Rudyard Kipling's famous added line about media baron Beaverbrook, 'the prerogative of the harlot throughout the ages'.

Costello's frustration over Samuel's appointment was set in train by his own impulsiveness. He ignored the state consultation of stage one, and went straight to stage two of nominating Samuel and Willett. Do it properly, cried the states, initially citing objections to the process rather than Samuel himself. Costello pointed to earlier requests for nominations from the states which had led to nothing, but it did not wash. As the state and territory responses came in, five indicated they opposed Samuel, while seven approved Willett, who was then appointed to the ACCC as a commissioner.

Costello swallowed his pride, announcing in November 2002 that he would go back to square one of the formula and ask the states for candidates. But by then the ground was changing. The news spread that Fels was actually going much earlier, by June 2003 in fact, to become foundation dean of the new Australia and New Zealand School of Government. The Samuel imbroglio had now become a vote for chairman, not deputy.

The states began to look harder at Samuel. Victoria, his home state and with a Labor government, supported him, but New South Wales, another Labor state, led the opposition. Samuel's cause was not helped by a tall, imperious Costello patting the shorter New South Wales Treasurer Michael Egan on the head during a televised Canberra news conference. Needless to say, Egan was not impressed.

The vote was being conducted among the very people Samuel had head-butted for years. 'Too close to the big end of town', some states muttered about Samuel. Some claimed to have been penalised regarding competition reform payments by Samuel's NCC on political grounds, and may have opposed him for that reason.

Enemies of Samuel tried to influence the vote. Fax machines around the offices of state treasurers churned out anonymously sent copies of an old magazine article claiming Samuel, in his merchant banker days, supported insider trading, a surprising view for someone about to be anointed for a top market regulatory job. A misquote, Samuel responded to this accusation.

Fels supported the Samuel nomination, but could now see it slipping away. Samuel, he felt, was strong on competition policy though as yet untested on enforcement. His main 'problem', however, was lack of consumer balance. Fels and Samuel accordingly cooked up a ticket to overcome this, proposing that Louise Sylvan, the articulate, no-nonsense chief executive of the Australian Consumers' Association, be Samuel's future deputy chairman.

Sylvan had earlier taken it upon herself to run a consumer eye over the possible contenders for the ACCC chair mentioned in the press, including Samuel, Jillian Segal (the Dawson inquiry member) and Tom Parry, the New South Wales prices regulator. 'Is this a job interview?' Samuel asked when the two sat down for a chat. Sylvan left the meeting feeling, like Fels, that while Samuel's understanding of competition issues was first rate, he lacked the consumer affairs balance.

Nonetheless, Sylvan lobbied for Samuel around the states. She was therefore amenable when Fels — at the urging of both Samuel and Costello — rang with the idea that she agree to let her name go forward as deputy chair. For Sylvan it was not a personal move. The consumer movement was keen to protect its lock, established by Allan Asher, on the deputy's position.

This 'dream ticket' — a business-savvy chairman and a consumer deputy — seemed to hit the spot. At least, one state which had earlier opposed Samuel, Western Australia, came over. Western Australia's letter, when it arrived, caused a lot of chuckling. Samuel was apparently unsuited as a deputy chairman, but entirely suitable as chairman! Such are the exigencies of federal–state politics.

But the remaining opponents dug in, forming a 'coalition of the unwilling', as they termed it. New South Wales, Queensland, the ACT and South Australia held a telephone hook-up, and then locked in their stance with a public announcement. They even tried to involve Prime Minister Howard, just to ram home the politics of their claim that Costello had botched the appointment process. Costello fought back. Reports circulated of Commonwealth lobbying of South Australia and the ACT, which were regarded as the weak links in the coalition of the unwilling.

The coalition stuck. When the proposals came in four nominated Samuel (Victoria, Tasmania, Western Australia and the Northern Territory), New South Wales wanted its prices regulator, Rod Parry, the ACT wanted Rod Sims, chairman of the New South Wales Rail Infrastructure Corporation, while South Australia and Queensland were simply negative about Samuel. As the Commonwealth has no vote it was a 4-to-4 deadlock, at least on the first round. Samuel needed just one more vote.

Costello ruminated on this from Christmas 2002 through the first half of 2003, privately prodding various members of the coalition of the unwilling to test their resolve. Rumours circulated that the ACT, needing cash after its January 2002 bushfire disaster, might be amenable to federal offers. But the Labor government there held firm. One South Australian minister told his colleagues that various deals were on offer from Canberra if the state shifted its vote. Again, no deal.

Presumably Costello was waiting to prise away one vote from the coalition of the willing before formally nominating Samuel in the required second round of voting. At one point Costello appeared to suspend the 'Sylvan as deputy chair' idea, saying he wanted to first pursue Samuel's appointment. He never did it. The curious part of the entire exercise was that Graeme Samuel was never formally put forward by the Commonwealth for voting by the states. Costello read the writing on the wall from the nomination stage, and never put his candidate to the test of a vote.

In late May, with only a few weeks to Fels' departure, Costello took the high road, appointing Samuel as acting chairman for up to 12 months, as the legislation says he can do. At some point through the next year, said Costello, he would formally propose the Samuel and Sylvan ticket. It was one in the eye for the recalcitrant states, but it may also be one in the eye for the future

ACCC as it shifts the Commission from the certainty of the Fels era to ongoing leadership uncertainty.

Samuel will inject a totally different stride into the ACCC from Fels. 'You know, Allan, the real problem is that 50 per cent of the constituency want me to do things exactly the same way you've done them, and there's another 50 per cent that would want it to be done exactly the opposite', he told Fels in one of their chats during the protracted process of his appointment. 'One way or another everyone's going to be unhappy in the end.'

Fels will indeed be a tough act to follow. Samuel himself jokes with friends that 'you'd need rocks in your head to follow him'. The biggest initial jump for Samuel will be dealing with the private sector and consumers rather than governments as he did at the NCC. That means raising his profile from the deliberate low key used by the NCC. Still, while Samuel will be more publicity-conscious at the ACCC, he has said he will not 'do a Fels'. 'I'll have a different approach', he tells acquaintances. Essentially he plans to be more cautious about publicity. In his first few days at the ACCC office in Canberra he told staff the Commission, as a policy-reforming body, needed to deal more privately with governments rather than through the media.

Samuel's philosophical beliefs about competition may also take the ACCC in different directions. For instance, he is more concerned with protecting competition than competitors. In an Ansett situation he would be more inclined to let Ansett go under rather than try to prop up two struggling competitors against Qantas. This allies Samuel more with the forces who claim that Fels' ACCC has been too concerned with propping up small competitors at the expense of the wider benefits of competition for consumers.

That should not be read as Samuel being more slanted to big business, however. In some respects Samuel will be a shock for business. He believes, for instance, that corporate leaders found guilty of trade practices offences should not only face fines but be barred from holding positions on boards.

It is enforcement, however, that could starkly highlight the difference between the Fels and the looming Samuel era. Consistent with his merchant banker background, Samuel is more inclined to the negotiated out-of-court settlement than Fels' harder line on prosecutions. Samuel sees the Fels-era ACCC as having a kick them in the head, take no prisoners style, punishing companies in the media and the courts. Not that he plans to go soft. It's just that he believes sitting down and negotiating can also change corporate behaviour.

Samuel may not find much sympathy for this view in the ACCC culture. Enforcement has been a pillar of the Fels style, not just to catch wrongdoers but to drive home to business that the ACCC is a serious player. Enforcement style was the one area where Samuel and Fels differed in their talks leading up to Samuel's appointment. Samuel told Fels he would think about it more, but remains inclined to the 'merchant banker' negotiated settlement approach. Of course, that could change after Samuel sits through a few of the ACCC's Friday enforcement committee meetings.

Indeed, in his early days in office Samuel appeared to have swung more to the enforcement side, saying that some cases required penalties, not 'backroom deals'. Samuel was referring to the Safeway case, where the retailer had been found guilty of price fixing on bread. Responding to a television interviewer's question on criticisms by business chiefs such as Roger Corbett (Woolworths and Safeway), Geoff Dixon (Qantas) and Gerry Harvey (Harvey Norman), Samuel discounted these as attempts to 'put pressure on the ACCC in the way it carries out its duties'. Samuel may have started in the merchant banker mould, but he was soon sounding more like Fels.

One area of enforcement policy that will test the Samuel style is the power of the big two supermarket chains, Coles and Woolworths. Fels' ACCC has wrestled with the problem for years, as the big two consolidated their position in groceries with some 70 per cent of the market, and are now extending their tentacles into petrol and liquor. It poses a quandary for the competition regulator. The duopoly can offer some good prices for consumers. But the spreading power of the two across new markets is a worry. On his last day in office, Fels launched actions against the two for anti-competitive behaviour in liquor marketing. Small business pressure is mounting to insert creeping acquisition laws in the *Trade Practices Act* to combat the big two, an issue that will be on Samuel's plate when the Dawson reform package reaches the Parliament.

Aside from style and publicity, the manner of Samuel's appointment could also cause real tremors at the ACCC. While Costello has the power under one provision of the legislation to appoint an acting chairman, another provision says that all 'members' of the Commission must have the approval of the states. Is an acting chairman a 'member', also requiring state approval? It is a moot point, with legal opinions flying on the eve of Samuel's arrival at the ACCC.

The danger for the ACCC in the immediate future is if an unhappy party in, say, a merger, challenges the legality of Samuel's appointment. If the challenge is successful, it would not only overturn the decision at issue but all other decisions made by a Samuel-led ACCC. With Samuel disqualified, and no deputy chairman, the ACCC simply could not operate. Of course, the federal government would quickly move to appoint a new interim chairman from within, but the resulting uncertainty and upheaval is something any competition regulator could do without.

The continuing vacancy in the deputy chair's office is a real weakness for the ongoing ACCC. Apart from a court case disqualification, ACCC staff, examining Samuel's impressive CV of previous corporate appointments, also worry about possible conflicts of interest in the hundreds of cases and issues that the Commission regularly addresses. Samuel would have to excuse himself from Commission deliberations. In that event, the government would have to appoint another acting chairman, a messy exercise which opponents would use to push their anti-Samuel line.

The circumstances of the acting chairman appointment place Graeme Samuel in a tricky position. Some see him as now having to 'audition' to the states for a permanent job. Others see him beholden to Treasurer Costello to proceed with a permanent nomination. Samuel himself is adamant that his acting appointment will not involve any compromises of his principles to gain permanency. Any such compromises on his part would invite states voting on his future to see him as 'damaged'.

Far from 'auditioning' for a permanent job, Samuel's plan, as outlined to supporters, is to act as if he was already there for the long term, 'with the possibility of being foreshortened'. Samuel is fortunate in one aspect: he will not be at the NCC to wear future opprobrium when it hands penalty notices to the states for failure to complete competition reforms. He will be at the ACCC, where he can act on much more popular consumer protection issues. The trick for Costello will be to judge when Samuel's image has started to turn among the four refusenik states, and then put up the promised Samuel/Sylvan package for a vote. Graeme Samuel's future at the ACCC is all a matter of timing.

Costello may have overridden state objections to push Samuel into an acting position, but he left the other half of the 'dream ticket', Louise Sylvan, waiting on the outside. The consumer movement is deeply protective of its commissioner spot on the ACCC and the recent hold of that commissioner on the deputy chairmanship. But the deputy slot has remained vacant since late 2000 when Asher departed, with no attempt to fill it with a new consumer representative. When the Samuel battle erupted consumers initially saw further stalling on the consumer member. There was talk of cutting all cooperation with the ACCC, talk that was stilled when Costello announced he would formally propose Samuel and Sylvan at some time in the future. Costello needs to be careful that he does not open a new political wound for the ACCC.

Despite Fels' energy and tireless promotion of competition, the end of his era left the ACCC vulnerable: no deputy chairman or consumer member; an acting chairman facing a political battle for appointment; imminent changes in the publicity style; doubts over the future of the tough enforcement stance; and threats to the future reach of the competition regulator, particularly in energy.

Around the ACCC there was a feeling of trepidation. Graeme Samuel's qualifications aside, many lamented the departure of the man who had created their 'brand' of vigorous competition regulation. Faced with leadership uncertainty, a continuing deputy chair vacancy, High Court erosion of controls over abuse of market power, and the looming future carve-away of powers in energy regulation, the feeling in the Commission at the end of the Fels era was very much that the wolves were at the door.

CHAPTER 14

ONE FELS SWOOP

There is nothing set in stone on the future of competition policy in Australia. The *Trade Practices Act* certainly offers legislative hope, laying down rules for competitive conduct and a commission to police that conduct. The mission statement is clear: competition should enhance the broad welfare of the nation.

To be effective, however, the Act requires commitment from government (that is, politicians) to provide funds for an independent commission and appoint competent commissioners — not always a sure thing. The outstanding example of failure in this regard was the Interstate Commission, formed just after Federation to regulate trade and commerce. Despite being enshrined in the Australian Constitution, it enjoyed only a brief life. More recently, Henry Bosch's National Companies and Securities Commission withered on the vine in 1990 as the federal government replaced it with the Australian Securities Commission.

This is not to say that the ACCC and competition policy will go the way of either of those examples. However, the sweep of its comparatively short 40-year life in Australia bodes ill for its future. The hallmarks so far have been a largely symbolic political commitment combined with political and vested interest interference, usually behind closed doors.

From our convict roots, a competitive culture has never been the Australian way. Australia was almost unique among comparable countries in having no effective trade practice (antitrust) legislation until the mid-1960s. Then, when Attorney-General Garfield Barwick proposed trade practice law to end the web of restrictive agreements hobbling the economy, big business successfully lobbied the Menzies Government to water it down. Lionel Murphy's subsequent *Trade Practices Act* of 1974, based on the tougher US Sherman Act, almost did not last the arrival of the Fraser Government a year later. It survived, but not without alterations — a lower merger barrier as well as insertion of a 'purpose' test for misuse of market power that dogs competition enforcement to this day.

The initial Trade Practices Commission was a marginalised agency, hampered by lack of funding. Bob Baxt, Fels' predecessor, even complained publicly about the lack of resources, which pretty much cost him his job. Despite the Fels brand of wings that opened up the agency's brief in the 1990s, it was not until the GST exercise in 2000 that the Commission was properly resourced with a legal fighting fund for its enforcement role.

It was not just lack of money. Canberra did not take competition law very seriously. Until the early 1990s, when Treasury grasped the importance of competition in the micro-reform agenda aimed at making Australia grow faster, the Commission was something of a sideshow. The first three TPC chairmen, Ron Bannerman, Bob McComas and Bob Baxt, were essentially limited to a holding pattern, all trying to consolidate the new agency. Political interference was rife. Support for competition policy in that era carried a strong whiff of the symbolic. The existence of the regulator demonstrated a government commitment to competition, but the agency was not supposed to do too much. Interestingly, such political symbolism was very much the brief the Howard Government gave Fels for the GST — bark, but don't bite too much.

Allan Fels was Australia's competition watershed. His legacy will be that he embedded a competitive culture in the nation for the first time. Fels' achievements were twofold: he electrified business into taking competition law seriously, and he showed how a regulator should operate to be effective. Nobody likes the bureaucracy of regulation. Yet, as the HIH and One.Tel collapses showed, there can be a lot of pain if regulators are asleep at the wheel.

Fels' methods went to the heart of the criticisms about his style — a heavy reliance on both publicity and talking up of the powers of the ACCC. Yet more was required for Fels to have survived for as long as he did. He was canny in his use of political patronage, first under Labor, and then Coalition governments. Fels used this to gain enhanced powers for the ACCC, particularly the tougher merger test. And Fels was also lucky. He arrived at the Commission just as competition policy was coming into vogue. And he was blessed with strong support, initially from Allan Asher and Hank Spier, and more recently from Ross Jones and Sitesh Bhojani.

The publicity obsession was crucial. In effect this became the shield for Fels' ACCC, creating an aura of power and public support that protected the agency from attacks by politicians and business. In retrospect, it is amazing that Fels survived as long as he did, considering the vested interests that hoped to topple him. The big business campaign against him started before he even came into office in 1991. Fels, then chairman of the Prices Surveillance Authority, was canvassed in the press to also become head of the Trade Practices Commission. The Business Council wrote to Prime Minister Bob Hawke pointing out that the TPC was already 'heavily weighted in favour of academic and economic backgrounds'. Hugh Morgan, then chairman of the BCA's law and regulatory panel, told Hawke that this had been the source of friction between the business community and the Commission. Morgan urged appointment of a chairman with practical commercial law experience: 'We would therefore urge the Government to delay the appointment until a practical commercial lawyer or a businessperson of wide experience can be found', he wrote.

Business might have lost this one, but it was successful a decade later in winning the Dawson review of both Fels and his Act. Business, of course, has every right to put its case. Unions and other pressure groups do the same. But if the *Trade Practices Act* is all about the 'national welfare', it is hard to see how that is advanced when vested interests are successful in private lobbying for favours. If the national interest is served lobbying should be out in the open. It rarely is. One reason why Fels' open style created such opposition is that it is so threatening to Canberra's closed-door style of business. 'In the past we got knocked off by behind-the-scenes lobbying by powerful interest groups with politicians', Fels told a television interview on his departure. 'Now, it's not quite so easy, if everyone knows all about the Act and its importance, to get the business concessions that used to be made in the past.'

Fels was certainly expected to be sacked when the 1996 election brought the Howard Government to power. Apart from business antipathy, many in the new government regarded him as a Labor plant because of his association with the ACTU. An early Howard Cabinet meeting discussed the future of the many Labor appointees running statutory agencies, including Fels. One version of the discussion is that the new Cabinet wanted Fels and some others sacked. The new government had already dispensed with some permanent heads of departments. Max Moore-Wilton, the new head of Howard's Department, reportedly advised, however, that this was impossible because the statutory agency chiefs were on fixed appointments. Another version is that the Cabinet meeting was more philosophical, discussing the inherent opposition of the new conservative government to creating such bureaucracies in the first place.

Fels survived. But his departure in 2003 was accompanied by signs that the competition 'house' he had built against the odds was in danger of being dismantled. A foundation of that house was the policy of both Labor and Coalition governments after the Hilmer report to have one major competition regulator, not industry-specific regulators prone to capture by the industries they supposedly monitor.

Fels had been assiduous in protecting this policy, never letting government drop its guard in response to pleas for more pliable individual regulators. One episode demonstrated how easily the policy can slip. The Parer report in 2002 recommended a sector-specific national energy regulator to replace the patchwork of state agencies, and their overlap with the ACCC. Fels took up the issue with Industry Minister Ian MacFarlane, who agreed that the new energy commission should come under the umbrella of the ACCC while operating as sector-specific. 'My understanding is that Professor Fels sees this as a more realistic model than perhaps the one put forward by Parer', MacFarlane told the *Financial Review*, which headlined the change: 'ACCC wins in energy shake-up'.

Not so. If MacFarlane thought this a more realistic model, some of the states did not. When crucial negotiations began MacFarlane was ill and acting Industry Minister Joe Hockey faced a heavy campaign from the states to retain control of national electricity and gas regulation, despite the emergence of a national market. Some states, New South Wales in particular, cross-subsidise their electricity market, and were keen to slow any reforms that could threaten these subsidies. A deal was struck: the states would nominate two commissioners to a new independent regulator, while one would come from the ACCC. In one hit, the ACCC had lost powers to control energy prices and the rules of access to facilities in the emerging national market. As Fels left office there was a rearguard action for the ACCC to operate the secretariat for the new national energy agency. For Fels, this demonstrated a disturbing retreat from commitment to a national competition regulator. 'It is alarming if, as it seems, it (the new regulator) is to be controlled by a majority of the states', Fels said on his departure.

Could it be a harbinger? Fels has always worried that communications could also be shifted out of the ACCC and combined with the Australian Broadcasting Authority (ABA) and Australian Communications Authority (ACA) into an Australian version of the US Federal Communications Commission. Given the so-called 'convergence' of communications and media there has been pressure to do so. On 30 June 2003, the day Fels departed Canberra,

Communications Minister Richard Alston announced a study to merge the ABA and ACA. Inevitably, it will raise questions about the ACCC's competition powers in communications.

The energy retreat was a clear sign that political patronage for the competition regulator — or at least for the Fels style of regulatory activism — was waning. Such patronage (or at least lack of opposition) played a significant role in Fels' unique position in Australia's contemporary economy. He had neatly walked between Labor and Coalition governments. Both had needed him, but for different reasons. Both had been lobbied to sack him.

Fels always relied on his 'comfort blanket' of political protection, whether it was the ACTU link under Labor or the GST handling under the Coalition. In cases where he plunged ahead regardless, such as when Health Minister Michael Wooldridge tried to warn him off the medical patch, Fels felt his GST success aura would see off the threat. He was right.

Occasionally, political reality told him to accept the inevitable. In the long newsagents battle the determination of the Howard Cabinet to protect the industry from competition forced Fels to trim his deregulation plans. When Cabinet threatens an override of powers, the wise regulator retreats.

Along with political patronage, another lever of government control, the power of appointments, can also exert enormous influence on regulators. The ACCC may be called independent, but government can hardwire it by appointment of commissioners. Governments of both persuasion have sought to 'control' the ABC by appointing political cronies. Labor probably believed it had hardwired the ACCC by appointing Fels.

Like the commitment to a single competition regulator, Fels' departure appeared to open the way for radical change across the ACCC's executive structure. Costello's controversial imposition of an acting chairman over the objection of some states (leaving aside Samuel's qualifications) showed a determination for top-down change. Only a few days before Fels' departure Costello moved again. Ross

Jones, the ACCC's respected mergers commissioner, was informed by Treasury that Costello would like to appoint him as deputy chairman of the rejigged Australian Prudential Regulatory Authority.

In terms of regulatory pecking order it was a step sideways, although deputy chairmanships are not to be sneezed at. Jones had to weigh the options. Costello wanted him to take the job. As well, there was no guarantee that when his ACCC appointment came up for renewal in 2004 Costello would offer him a new term. Jones, who had been seen by many as the ideal compromise candidate for ACCC chairman in the Samuel imbroglio, took the job.

Costello, in fact, has the opportunity for a clean sweep of new commissioners under Graeme Samuel. The terms of two other commissioners who might be seen as the last remnants of the Fels era — Sitesh Bhojani, who looks after the professions and runs the enforcement committee, and John Martin, who handles small business — expire before the expected 2004 election date.

Fels' own truncated reappointment shows that the supposed independence of commissioners, in terms of their length of appointment, is a weakness of the *Trade Practices Act*. One test of independence is fixed terms, long enough to survive a change of government. In the US, commissioners of the Federal Trade Commission, which is responsible for antitrust, are appointed for seven-year staggered terms. In Europe, the standard is usually five years. In Australia, however, the Act loosely stipulates terms 'not exceeding five years', enabling politicians to juggle exits to their own timetables, as evident with Fels.

Unfortunately, there appears little chance of altering this. Any change would require state approval, unlikely in the stand-off over Samuel's appointment. Indeed, some states see the Samuel appointment as a 'declaration of war'. Combined with the state grab for energy regulation, the concern must be that the Hilmer era of enlightened federal–state cooperation to use competition to lift national productivity unfortunately might have been just a brief period of sunshine.

Samuel, of course, will have considerable freedom in the way he runs the ACCC. Government powers to direct the Commission are pretty much limited to its consumer protection functions, and even there any direction must be published. Government cannot direct the ACCC on its crucial oversight of mergers and market power abuses. This leaves Samuel with a free hand to run the enforcement side of the ACCC. It will be the acid test of whether a Fels culture remains at the ACCC, or whether Samuel injects a merchant-banker negotiating style with offenders.

The political fireworks about Fels' use of publicity, culminating in the disastrous Caltex raid, have overshadowed his equal dedication to enforcement. The ACCC carries a big stick, and for Fels it was the combination of enforcement and publicity that galvanised business to take notice and campaign against him. Fels ratcheted up litigation, launching 271 cases from 1991 to late 2002, and winning 94 per cent of those eventually decided by a court. The big stick can have a powerful effect on behaviour if business believes it will be used, which, in the Fels era, was a reasonable assumption.

On his departure, Fels seemed to have a queasy feeling that the competition chess pieces were moving against the ACCC. 'You need us', he told government in an obvious attempt to put some steel into political backbones. Effective enforcement of the *Trade Practices Act* was as important as ever for Australia to maintain a competitive, efficient economy. 'The political challenge is to handle serious interest-group pressures, each one of which wants an exemption or soft treatment for itself', he wrote on his departure day. 'Reconciling these conflicting goals requires a strong, continuing commitment to competition law by government.'

⤺

Fels' own perspective on his 12-year performance confirms that regulators must keep a weather eye on the political landscape. He had come into the competition regulator's chair in 1991 with the general thought that if he lifted the profile of the commission 'things will happen'.

Just what, he wasn't certain. But the two previous outsiders brought in as chairman had both been lawyers who, in Fels' view, 'saw their space' in the legal world. Fels was the first economist, and he saw a bigger space for interacting with the public and government, and seeing how competition fitted the economy.

Fels' 12 years of 'aggressive regulation' — his term — combined with minimal blunders and periods of political patronage more than filled a space. 'On the whole, the aggressive tactics were well managed', he reflects. 'There were not many blunders. The only substantial one was the Caltex raid and that was unfortunately timed and excessive in execution, exposing us to the critics. I regret it. In general, however, the publicity and enforcement style worked. The negative reactions from the Business Council could be countered by saying, "Well, that's inevitable if we're doing our job properly".'

While Fels believes there is consumer and small business support for continued aggressive enforcement, he accepts that the political winds are changing. 'There isn't the unqualified support of the past', he says. What would have happened had he stayed? 'That might have required some adaption, some running on the spot for a while, perhaps identifying areas where it would be safe to move ahead.'

The newsagents episode is implanted in Fels' mind as an example of the stop–go sequence for competition regulators when it comes to political intervention. The ACCC had just been ringing up some big wins against cartels when the Howard Cabinet threatened override powers, not just on newsagents but possibly across the regulator's wider powers.

'This seemed so dangerous to me that it was worth pausing and accepting that we just couldn't achieve what we would have liked to in newsagents', he says. 'Then we got back on full bore for the rest of our activities, with the view that maybe we could get back to newsagents a bit later. On the whole, we were careful. But things may have slipped a little bit in recent times. The power bases are a little different from my point of view. In the past I had certain government support and just fearlessly charged on.'

This was the art of the Fels style: pushing the envelope as far as possible, pulling back when necessary, and then pushing ahead again, all the time watching the political barometer. 'My view is that, while I agree there have been some problems towards the end of my period, we've made 10 steps forward and then two back, so we're still a long way ahead', he says. 'I don't see the ACCC and competition policy rolling all the way back down to the bottom of the hill. But, who knows? There have been quite a few threats to the Commission over the years. We were worried about the waterfront dispute, the GST, even a little worried about Hilmer. Then there was Dawson. In the end, we've generally come through. But, I grant you, there have been a few worries lately.'

Fels is sanguine that no government these days would walk away from a 'fairly strong' *Trade Practices Act*. 'They may fiddle with it, they may marginally weaken it', he says. 'There are very, very big economic interests involved in ACCC decisions, and it is inevitable there will be heavy pressure on politicians at times. I believe, however, that in the immediate future consumer and small business pressure for strong competition law will remain. It will be hard for politicians to ignore that and have any kind of return to the weaker policies of the '80s.'

Certainly there will be no diminution in cartel activity, says Fels. The Microsoft case showed that the new information economy did not eliminate the need for trade practice law. In echoes of Adam Smith's much-quoted phrase more than two centuries ago that merchants would always conspire to fix prices, Fels believes trade practice law will be around for as long as human nature — 'forever'.

A future ACCC, however, may be a different animal. Much will depend on the nature of government support. A hostile government could split the Commission, hiving off consumer protection or sectoral areas like communications, leaving only mergers and policing of anti-competitive market conduct. Big business would applaud that. A future

Labor Government might again hive off policing of union secondary boycotts to softer industrial courts. Unions would applaud that.

On the other hand, a sympathetic government could expand the ACCC's horizons. A full merger with its New Zealand counterpart is possible. Areas like health and education, where the Howard Government is deregulating, could become new territory for a competition regulator. Fels has always cast covetous eyes on media regulation, but politicians are too alert to the power sensitivities to hand this over. A regulator with the ACCC's strong views on competition could cut too much of a swathe through the media club.

Trade could be another new area, however. As global trade barriers fall, domestic barriers that restrict markets will become more important to trade negotiators. The Organisation for Economic Cooperation and Development (OECD), for instance, has been taking a serious look at the overuse of anti-dumping actions as possibly disguised protectionism. Should they be controlled by competition regulators? Other trade quotas and tariffs can also harm consumers. Is trade policy just competition policy gone wrong?

Another concept for the future of competition policy comes from Michael Porter, the influential author of *The Competitive Advantage of Nations* and the man who provided Fels with valuable ammunition about the need for domestic competition in his 1992 battle on raising the merger barrier. Porter's latest thesis is that antitrust (trade practice) regulation relies too heavily on narrowly based consumer welfare theory, and overlooks some of the main benefits of competition for society. His argument is that productivity growth should be the basic goal of future antitrust policy. In other words, instead of many of the current competition tests such as substantial lessening of competition there should be a new criterion — whether or not anti-competitive behaviour lifts a nation's economic performance. Interestingly, that is not far removed from the thrust of the Keating/Hilmer reforms of the mid-1990s, although they are now sadly in retreat.

Whatever new fields the ACCC may enter, Fels left the competition regulator much stronger than when he entered the doors. Universal application of competition law, a stronger merger test, and increased fines — with the looming possibility of criminal sanctions — are in place. Intellectual property is on the agenda, as is unconscionable conduct. There may be some backward slides by politicians over energy regulation in particular, but it is off a much higher power base.

Australia's improved competitive culture also gains ticks from foreign commentators. IMD, the Swiss-based management research group, publishes an annual World Competitiveness yearbook which ranks national performances. In 2003 Australia was ranked as the second most competitive economy in the world for nations above 20 million people, behind only the US. More importantly for the ACCC, Australia ranked first for having a legal framework that encouraged competitive enterprise.

Has the Fels brand of vigorous enforcement coupled with publicity that stood behind these international ratings left a lasting imprint in Australia? Ironically, it was starting to really catch on just as Fels departed. ASIC and APRA, the financial market regulators, both lifted their game in the wake of collapses such as HIH and the clear public demand for greater enforcement of corporate governance standards. The Cole Royal Commission recommended the ACCC as the model for a new construction industry commission to stamp out corruption. Even the Therapeutic Goods Administration took on a dash of the Fels upfront regulatory style when in 2003 it moved on Pan Pharmaceuticals, recalling many products.

'I think we showed other regulators that you could do this and be successful', says Fels. And draw a lot of opponents? 'Yes, but we survived a long time. It shows that it doesn't necessarily lead to early termination of your career as a regulator.'

Did the business lobby get him in the end, however? 'Yes', says Fels, although he sees it as a complicated issue. 'Much of the criticism made me more popular and harder to remove. The major attacks through 2001 by people like Warburton (Caltex/DJs) and Dixon (Qantas) I thought didn't have much effect. But I suspect the big business lobbying over the years had some impact on the decision to only reappoint me for three years and eight months. Yes, big business had an influence on the government's decision. But it took 12 years to get me.'

For Fels, the competition regulator's dilemma was always whether to do too much or too little. 'On the whole, however, if you don't do much the public feels let down', he says. His aim was to do a lot, accepting there would be mistakes along the way, but hoping these would be cancelled out by the volume of successes. Fels sees an unrecognised trap in the ACCC's high level of activity, however. Did it let things through it should have stopped? The thrust of the Dawson inquiry was about what the ACCC had blocked. Perhaps it should also have examined what the ACCC might have mistakenly approved?

The concept of active enforcement was crucial for Fels. Business, he says, always has recourse to the courts or political lobbying if dissatisfied with ACCC decisions. But the public has no such protection against weak or sleepy law enforcers. 'The public has no safeguards if regulators cave in', he says.

Fels believes the global links he has pursued for the ACCC will add impetus to Australia's competitive culture whatever the political climate. Globalisation, he believes, may bring benefits but it also facilitates new cartels. The ACCC has signed information-sharing agreements with several countries, including the US. The major animal vitamins cartel bust in Australia in 2000 came through US and European information. The ACCC is currently investigating several as yet unnamed global cartels believed to be operating in Australia.

One area where a competition culture has not spread as much as Fels would like is within the Australian judiciary. Court judgements on interpretation of the *Trade Practices Act* have been largely disappointing, as evident in the 2003 Boral case. Some legal practitioners believe Australian judges, unlike their US counterparts, have not yet grasped the economic conceptual side of competition as distinct from the letter of the law. Fels sees a possible failing of the ACCC here. Did it bowl up to the courts too many open and shut breaches of the law rather than harder test cases?

Whether or not a Felsian style is ingrained in regulators now, Fels is quietly working on assuring that it may be in the future. The new Australia and New Zealand School of Government which he will chair will try to educate a new generation of public servants not just about Fels' energetic enforcement and publicity style but also into awareness of the political reality, or 'authorising environment' in which they will work. The media, Fels believes, is crucial for public servants and regulators in building legitimacy for policies.

Fels laughs when asked if this means a whole new generation of 'little Felses' coming along, posing a threat to the Australian mania for government secrecy. Certainly the man himself, who pioneered media as an art form for regulators, has no intention of now hiding behind academic cloisters. Would he still be available?, a journalist asked at a press conference on the day he announced his departure. 'If the media calls they won't be turned away', he replied.

POSTSCRIPT: On July 17, 2003, the South Australian Government withdrew its opposition to Graeme Samuel as Chairman of the ACCC, breaking the deadlock between the states. Treasurer Peter Costello then moved to extend the Samuel appointment to a full five-year term. South Australian Treasurer Kevin Foley said SA remained concerned about Mr Samuel's ability to fill the post, but believed Samuel should be given an opportunity to dispel those fears.

Mr Costello indicated he would now begin negotiations with the states on the proposed appointment of Ms Louise Sylvan as Deputy Chairman. The post has been vacant since late 2000.

READING

Allens Arthur Robinson. Submission to the Dawson Committee review of the Trade Practices Act, July 2002.

Arbouw J. The competitive Allan Fels. Company Director, July 2002.

Argy F. Where to from here: Australia's egalitarianism under threat. Allen & Unwin, Australia, 2003.

Australian Chamber of Commerce and Industry. Submission to the Dawson review of the Trade Practices Act. July 2002.

Australian Competition and Consumer Commission.

—accc.gov.au

—Draft determination. Application for authorisation. The Royal Australasian College of Surgeons. February 2003.

—Potential consumer benefits of repealing the importation provisions of the Copyright Act 1968 as they apply to books and computer software, March 1999.

—Report to Senator Alston, Minister for Communications, Information Technology and the Arts, on emerging market structures in the communications sector, June 2003.

—Submission to the Productivity Commission review of telecommunications specific competition regulation, August 2000.

—Submission to the Trade Practices Act review, June 2002.

Australian Consumers' Association. Submission to the review of the competition provisions of the Trade Practices Act 1974. July 2002.

Australian Council of Professions. National competition policy and the professions.

Australian Financial Review Power 2002. October 2002.

Australian Industry Group. Submission to the Dawson review of the competition provisions of the Trade Practices Act. July 2002.

Australian Medical Association. Submission to the Dawson review of the competition provisions of the Trade Practices Act. September 2002.

Australian Publishers' Association. Submission to committee of inquiry into the competition provisions of the Trade Practices Act 1974.

Baker JB. Unilateral competitive effects theories in merger analysis. Antitrust, vol 11 no 2, Spring 1997.

Banks G.

—Competition regulation of infrastructure: getting the balance right. IIR Conference, Melbourne, March 2002.

—Competition: the best price regulator. CEDA, Hyatt Regency Hotel, Perth, November 2000.

—The drivers of Australia's productivity surge. Outlook 2002.

—Micro reform's productivity payoff. The Australian, 18 February 2002.

Bannerman RM.

—Development of trade practices law and administration. Australian Economic Review, 3rd Quarter 1985.

—The Trade Practices Act: reflections on its twenty-fifth anniversary. Trade Practices Law Journal, vol 8, September 2000.

Barnett D. John Howard Prime Minister. Viking, 1997.

Baxt R, Brunt M.

—A Guide to the Act. Australian Economic Review, April 1974.

—A modern trade practices act for a deregulated environment. Commercial Law Quarterly, September 2001.

—The Murphy trade practices bill: admirable objective, inadequate means. Australian Business Law Review, April 1974.

Bhojani S.

—Competition laws: the ACCC's role and public interest issues. Royal Australasian College of Surgeons conference, October 1999.

—Law enforcement cooperation in the global digital economy. OECD-APEC Global Forum, Honolulu, January 2003.

—National competition policy and regulation of medicine in Australia. Australian and New Zealand Medical Boards and Councils, November 1998.

—Principles of fairness and accountability. Australian Law Reform conference, June 2001.

Brandis G. Small Business: Predatory Pricing. Senate Hansard, 26 March 2003.

Bresnahan TF. The economics of the Microsoft case.

Brunt M.

—The Australian antitrust law and 20 years: a stocktake. Review of Industrial Organisations 9(5) October 1994.

—Legislation in search of an objective. Australian Trade Practice Readings. Nieuwenhuysen JP, ed, Cheshire, Melbourne 1970.

—'Market definition' issues in Australian and New Zealand trade practices litigation. Australian Business Law Review, April 1990.

Business Council of Australia.

—Australian and New Zealand competition law and policy. Fordham Corporate Law Institute, Hawk B, ed, 1993.

—Confidential draft of submission to the Trade Practices Act review committee. Undated.

—Supplementary submission to the review of the Trade Practices Act 1974 and its administration. 2 October 2002.

Caltex Australia Limited. Submission to the review of the competition provisions of the Trade Practices Act, July 2002.

Canberra Bulletin of Public Administration. Economics or law—the second oldest profession? Panel discussion sponsored by the Economic Society (ACT Branch) and the Law Council of Australia. 3 August 1999, No 95, March 2000.

Carmody K. Avenging angel who puts people and justice first. The Catholic Weekly, 8 April 2001.

Carroll VJ. When a regulator turns pro. The Independent Monthly, September 1995.

Clarke P, Corones S. Competition law and policy, cases and materials. Oxford University Press Australia, 1999.

Clayton Utz. Submission to the committee of inquiry into the competition provisions of the Trade Practices Act 1974 and their administration. August 2002.

Commonwealth of Australia. Can the professions survive under a national competition policy? AGPS 1997.

Corones SG. Competition law in Australia. LBC Information Services, Sydney, 1999.

Costello P.

—Farewell to Professor Allan Fels. Hyatt Hotel, Canberra, 2 June 2003.

—Press Conference, 16 April 2003.

—Release of the report on competition provisions of the Trade Practices Act, and Commonwealth response. Canberra, 16 April 2003.

—25 Years of competition law: a political perspective. Steinwall R, ed, Reed International, 2000.

Council of Small Business Organisation of Australia Ltd. Submission to the Trade Practices Act review, July 2002.

Cousins D.

—Future directions for prices surveillance in Australia. Paper at 24th Conference of Economists, Adelaide, September 1995.

—Implementing the Hilmer reforms: achieving a better balance between competition and regulation. Paper to CEDA, October 1996.

—The role of the ACCC in implementation of the New Tax System changes. 30th Annual Conference of Economists, Perth, 23-26 September 2001.

De Jonquieres G. Report counts cost of anti-dumping. Financial Times, 21 September 1995.

Durie J. School for Bureaucrats. The Australian Financial Review, 27 November 2002.

Ergas H.

—Are the ACCC's merger guidelines too strict? A critical review of the Industry Commission's information paper on merger regulation. Competition & Consumer Law Journal, vol 6 no 3, April 1999.

—The uneasy (and somewhat messy) interaction of the IP laws and the competition laws. Network Economics Consulting Group, Canberra.

Fair Trading Coalition. Submission to the review of the Trade Practices Act, July 2002.

Fels A.

—The ACCC and the Trade Practices Act: implications for the rural sector. Rural Press Club of Victoria, June 1998.

—Address to the Committee for the Economic Development of Australia. Melbourne, July 2001.

—The British prices and incomes board. Cambridge University Press, 1972.

—The change from a dominance to a substantial lessening of competition test in Australia's merger law. Fordham Corporate Law Institute Conference, October 2002.

—Competition in telecommunications. ATUG, March 2003.

—Economics or law: the second oldest profession? Panel discussion, Economics Society (ACT Branch) and the Law Council of Australia, March 2000.

—Efficiency in delivering health care: the professions, competition and the ACCC. Speech at Monash University, November 2001.

—Efficient energy markets. Inaugural conference of Energy Users' Association, 19 November 2001.

—The future of competition policy. National Press Club, October 1991.

—Globalisation and competition policy. The Sydney Institute, 23 April 2001.

—Intellectual property, competition and trade policy implications of parallel import restrictions. Rome, 23 May 2001.

—Media ownership in Australia. Communications Law Centre, 10 April 1997.

—Monopolies, mergers and media. Melbourne Press Club, July 1996.

—Occupational regulation. Apec Regulatory Forum, Kuantan, Malaysia, September 1988. Co-authors David Parker, Blair Comley and Vishal Beri, the Treasury.

—The political economy of regulation. UNSW Law Journal, vol 5, 1982.

—Regulation and the future of the Telecommunications Industry, CISCO Lecture Series. 26 March 2001.

—Regulation, competition and the professions. Industry Economics Conference, July 2001.

—The review of the Trade Practices Act and issues concerning the ACCC and the media. National Press Club, July 2002.

—Towards a modern Trade Practices Act: a regulator's perspective. NSW Press Club, September 2002.

—The Trade Practices Act after 25 years: mergers and the role of the ACCC. Shann Memorial Lecture, University of Western Australia, 1999.

—The Trade Practices Act: are we becoming a branch office economy? University of Melbourne, 4 April 2002.

—Trade Practices Act past, present and future. Paper to Trade Practices and Consumer Protection law Conference, Sydney, June 2000.

—Watchdog and the waterfront. The Age, 4 May 1998.

Fels A, Walker J. The market for books and the importation provisions of the Copyright Act 1968. Melbourne University Law Review, vol 17 no 4, December 1990.

Ferguson A. New role for old watchdog. Business Review Weekly, 15 March 1999.

Flanagan M. Fishing for the real Fels. The Age, 6 October 2001.

Friedman M. Capitalism and freedom. University of Chicago Press, Chicago, 1974.

Galbraith JK. The anatomy of power. Houghton Mifflin Company, Boston, 1983.

Garnaut R. Australia as a branch office economy. Paper to the 2002 Conference of the Australian Agricultural and Resource Economics Society (AARESA), Canberra, 13 February 2002.

Gittins R.

—A Fels swoop on the recording industry. Sydney Morning Herald, 11 September 1991.

—Allan Fels: economic rationalist hero of the decade. Sydney Morning Herald, July 2002.

Grabosky P, Braithwaite J. Of manners gentle: enforcement strategies of Australian business regulatory agencies. Oxford University Press, Melbourne, 1986.

Griffin J. Key elements of an effective antitrust policy and criminal penalties and deterrence: the American experience. ACCC seminar, Sydney, July 2002.

Griggs L, Hardy S. ACCC v Boral: the High Court awaits another Section 46 case! Trade Practices Law Journal, no 9, December 2001.

Guinness D. Fit enough to tackle the competition. Sydney Morning Herald, 20 May 2000.

High Court of Australia. Boral Besser Masonry Limited (now Boral Masonry Ltd) v. Australian competition and Cons (2003) HCA 5 (7 February 2003).

The HIH Royal Commission. The failure of HIH Insurance. (Three volumes.) Commonwealth of Australia, 2003.

Hopkins A. Crime, law and business: the sociological sources of Australian monopoly law. Australian Institute of Criminology, Canberra, 1978.

House of Representatives Standing Committee on Economics, Finance and Public Administration.

—Competing interests: is there balance? Commonwealth of Australia, 2001.

—Review of the Australian Competition and Consumer Commission, Annual reports. June 1997 and March 1998.

House of Representatives Standing Committee on Industry, Science and Technology. Finding a balance: towards fair trading in Australia. Commonwealth of Australia, 1997.

House of Representatives Standing Committee on Legal and Constitutional Affairs. Mergers, takeovers and monopolies: profiting from competition? May 1989.

Howarth D. Predatory pricing after Boral: let the games begin. Competition and Consumer Law Journal, vol 9 no 1, July 2001.

IMD World Competitiveness Yearbook 2003. IMD, Lausanne, Switzerland.

Industry Commission. The growth and revenue implications of Hilmer and related reforms. March 1995.

Jones R.

—Competition, broadcasting and pay TV. February 2003.

—Difficulties between the pro-competitive community and intellectual property. Queensland Law Society Seminar, 11 May 2001.

Karmel PH, Brunt M. The Structure of the Australian Economy. FW, Cheshire, 1966.

King S. Competition policy and regulation. Australian Encylopedia of Social Sciences, 2003.

King S, Lloyd P, eds. Economic rationalism: dead end or way forward? Allen & Unwin, 1993.

Law Council of Australia. Submission to the Senate Legal and Constitutional Committee, February 2002.

Leonard P.

—Best practice telecommunications regulation: is Australia heading in the right direction? UNSW seminar on Competition Law, 15 May 2001.

—A hostile land: competition regulation and Australian telecommunications, 1997–2000. Gilbert & Tobin, 19 September 2000.

Little J. Among the money-changers. Together interview, 26 March 2001.

Marris S. Fels in the firing line. The Australian, 15 August 2001.

Marsh I, ed. Implementing the Hilmer reforms. Committee for the Economic Development of Australia, 1996.

McAllister I, Dowrick S, Hassan R, eds. Cambridge Handbook of Social Sciences in Australia. Melbourne, Cambridge University Press.

McGirr M. The consumer watchdog. Australian Catholics, Christmas 2000.

Melbourne Business School. Henry Bosch at the NCSC. 2003.

Miller RV. Miller's annotated Trade Practices Act 1974. Lawbook Company, 23rd edn, 2002.

Minter Ellison Legal Group. Submission to Trade Practices Act review committee, June 2002.

National Association of Retail Grocers of Australia. Submission to the Dawson Committee Trade Practices Act review, July 2002.

National Competition Council.

—Assessment of governments' progress in implementing the National Competition Policy and related reforms. Volume One: Assessment, August 2002.

—Reforming the regulation of the professions. Staff discussion paper, May 2001.

—Some impacts on society and the economy. January 1999.

National Competition Policy. Report of the Independent Committee of Inquiry, August 1993. (The Hilmer review.)

Nieuwenhuysen JP, Norman NR. Australian competition and prices policy. Croom Helm Ltd, London, 1976.

O'Bryan M. Section 46: legal and economic principles and reasoning in Melway and Boral. Competition and Consumer Law Journal, vol 8 no 3, April 2001.

Parham D. Microeconomic reforms and the revival in Australia's growth in productivity and living standards. Conference of Economists, Adelaide, 1 October 2002.

Pengilley W.

—Competition regulation in Australia: a discussion of a spider web and its weaving. Competition and Consumer Law Journal, vol 8 no 3, April 2001.

—Misuse of market power: Australian Post, Melway and Boral. Competition & Consumer Law Journal, vol 9 no 3, March 2002.

—Submission to Trade Practices Act Review Committee, June 2002.

Posner RA. Antitrust law: an economic perspective. The University of Chicago Press, 1976.

Porter ME.

—Competition and antitrust: towards a productivity-based approach to evaluating mergers and joint ventures. The Antitrust Bulletin, Heritage Hills, New York, Federal Legal Publications, Winter 2001.

—The competitive advantage of nations. The Free Press, New York, 1998.

Productivity Commission.

—Distribution of the economic gains of the 1990s. Staff research paper, November 2000.

—Impact of competition policy reforms on rural and regional Australia. Draft report, May 1999.

—Microeconomic reform and productivity growth. Workshop proceedings, Australian National University, 26–27 February 1998.

—Microeconomic reforms and Australian productivity: exploring the links. Commission research paper, vol 1, Report, vol 2, Case studies, November 1999.

—Offshore investment by Australian firms: survey evidence. February 2002.

—Productivity Commission submission to the review of the Trade Practices Act 1974. July 2002.

Review of intellectual property legislation under the Competition Principles Agreement. Commonwealth of Australia, 2000.

Review of the competition provisions of the Trade Practices Act. Chaired by Sir Daryl Dawson, Department of Communications, Information Technology and Arts, Canberra 2003.

Review of the impact of Part IV of the Trade Practices Act 1974 on the recruitment and retention of medical practitioners in rural and regional Australia. Commonwealth Department of Health and Ageing, 2002.

Ross IS. The life of Adam Smith. Oxford University Press, Oxford, 1995.

Round D. An empirical analysis of price-fixing penalties in Australia from 1974 to 1999: have Australia's corporate colluders been corralled? Competition and Consumer Law Journal, vol 8 no 2, December 2000.

Samuel G. It's too late to stop now. The Australian, 22 February 2001.

Schmidt L. Fels fights on. Business Review Weekly, 13 October 2000.

Seah W. Fair competition or unfair predation: identifying the misuse of market power under Section 46. Trade Practices Law Journal, vol 9, December 2002.

Senate Economics Legislation Committee. A New Tax System. 1 May 2001.

Senate Legal and Constitutional References Committee.

—Inquiry into s46 and s50 of the Trade Practices Act 1974, May 2002.

—Inquiry into the provisions of the Copyright Amendment (Parallel Importation) Bill, May 2001.

Senate Select Committee on the Socio-Economic Consequences of the National Competition Policy. Riding the waves of change. February 2000.

Senate Standing Committee on Legal and Constitutional Affairs. Mergers, monopolies and acquisitions: adequacy of existing legislative controls. December 1991.

Shogren R. Implementing and effective competition policy: skills and synergies. Paper at 28th Trade and Development Conference, Manila, September 2002.

Spier Consulting. Submission to the Senate Legal and Constitutional Reference Committee Inquiry into Section 46. November 2001.

Spier H.

—Bannerman. Australian Trade Practices Law Journal, vol 9, June 2001.

—Baxt. Australian Trade Practices Law Journal, vol 11, June 2003.

—Commission cameos. Trade Practices Law Journal, vol 9, March 2001.

—McComas. Australian Trade Practices Law Journal, vol 10, June 2002.

Steinwall R. 25 Years of Australian competition law. Butterworths Australia, 2000.

Stewart C. Making markets add up. Weekend Australian, 8–9 June 2002.

Stretton R. A watchdog shows his teeth. The Bulletin, 5 November 1991.

Sylvan L. Muzzled ACCC only helps big business. The Australian Financial Review, 5 June 2002.

Tanner S, Richardson J. Fels family: Silesia to South Australia. E-Gee Printers, Bairnsdale, Victoria, 1996.

Telstra. Initial Submission to the Dawson Committee Review of the Trade Practices Act, July 2002.

Thomson J. Fels fights back. Business Review Weekly, 4–10 July 2002.

Trade Practices Act Review Committee. Report to the Minister for Business and Consumer Affairs. August 1976. (The Swanson report.)

Trade Practices Commission.

—Annual Report 1983–84.

—Study of the professions, final report, legal, March 1994.

Trinca H, Davies A. Waterfront, the battle that changed Australia. Doubleday, 2000.

Tyson N, Griggs L. Mergers and metaphors. Trade Practices Law Journal, vol 9, June 2001.

University of New South Wales, Faculty of Law. Competition law and regulation. Conference papers from 2000 and 2001.

University of Western Australia. Uniview Magazine, vol 20 no 1, February 2001.

Venturini, VG. Malpractice: the administration of the Murphy Trade Practices Act. Non Mollare, Sydney, 1980.

Weller P. Australia's Mandarins. Allen & Unwin, Australia, 2001.

Westfield M.

—The gatekeepers: the global media battle to control Australia's pay TV. Pluto Press, Australia, 2000.

—HIH: the inside story of Australia's biggest corporate collapse. John Wiley & Sons, 2003.

Widmer GK. Restrictive trade practices and mergers. Law Book Company, Sydney, 1977.

Wilks S. In the public interest. Manchester University Press, 1999.

Wilks S, Bartle I. The unanticipated consequences of creating independent competition agencies. West European Politics, vol 25 no 1, January 2002.

Yeung K. Is the use of informal adverse publicity a legitimate regulatory compliance technique? Paper presented to the Australian Institute of Criminology Conference, Current issues in regulation: enforcement and compliance, Melbourne, September 2002.

Zumbo F. Boral ruling calls for Section 46 review. The Australian Financial Review, 4 March 2003.

INDEX